JAYWALKING

Also by the same author
Rebel Without Applause

JAY LANDESMAN

JAYWALKING

WEIDENFELD AND NICOLSON
London

First published in Great Britain in 1992 by
George Weidenfeld & Nicolson Limited
The Orion Publishing Group
Orion House, 5 Upper St Martin's Lane,
London, WC2H 9EA

A catalogue reference is available
from the British Library

ISBN 0 297 81303 X

Typeset at The Spartan Press Ltd
Lymington, Hants
Printed in Great Britain by
Butler & Tanner Ltd
Frome and London

For Fran, who egged me on

CHAPTER ONE

In February 1964 the *St Louis Post-Dispatch* announced that the Landesmans were off to London for a year's talent tune-up. 'Their decision to leave St Louis marked the end of an era,' wrote Martin Quigley later.

> They are leaving with no boo-hoos, no bitterness, with a little sadness and a touch of puzzlement. They are not leaving for a better offer. They are leaving to get away from us and take a look around another town. What are they worth to us? What did they cost that we were not willing to pay? All of us, those who love them and those who are saying good riddance, have been enriched by them. We become a little more drab as we wave goodbye.

St Louis was a very dull city; it hadn't had anything going for it since the World's Fair of 1904. For the next fifty years it might be said that the Landesman family subtly figured in the cultural life of St Louis, beginning with my father's arrival from Berlin to decorate the German Pavilion with murals of frolicsome nymphs and Teutonic-looking cherubs. For the next twenty-five years he painted the same scenes on the walls and ceilings of the St Louis rich. During the Depression he had a part-time antique business, which he turned over to my mother when a government works project invited him to join a group of distinguished unemployed artists brightening up the local post offices and hospitals. His convivial cherubs and nymphs showed up again in murals of local historical significance.

The contribution of his four children to the cultural life of St Louis was less obvious, but equally subtle. At the age of fourteen, I opened up an art gallery in my father's garage, selling the drawings and sculpture of my school mates. Fred, the artist, won a Red Cross poster contest, but had the prize withdrawn when someone noticed 'cross' was misspelt. Gene was talked into taking violin lessons in spite of his withered bow hand. Gertrude subscribed to the *New Yorker*.

For me, a stint at Missouri University and Rice Institute in Texas followed, but I ended up without a degree in anything, joining the family antique business back in St Louis. In 1948, seeking greater glory, I founded and edited a quarterly magazine, *Neurotica*, the purpose of which was to 'shake up' the world. The first two issues earned me a reputation for *chutzpah* and enough guts to leave the family business and move to New York.

I moved into a funky brownstone flat in mid-Manhattan with ten-foot ceilings and Jackson Pollock floors. It was the perfect background for my debut into the literary world. It took seven more issues of *Neurotica* to convince me the literary life was not for me. At a Greenwich Village party to celebrate the release of Antonin Artaud from an asylum, I fell for a girl who was introduced to me as 'Peaches'. She had the complexion of one, and the rest of her was appealing. A soft pair of lips, a mouthful of beautiful teeth, a perfect gum line and eyes that were hungry for a life she had never led. She was a Jewish princess in full rebellion, looking for someone to plumb the depths of despair with. The ex-editor of a highbrow literary quarterly was her idea of the ideal partner. She was an insurance policy against boredom with a premium I could afford. After a whirlwind courtship, we married that summer and from then on we were 'Jay and Fran', one name unpronounceable without the other.

'You can't stay married and make it in New York' was the opening line in the novel I was writing at the time. Too many parties, too many pals; without a cause or a job, New York can be hard on a marriage. I suddenly panicked for security, returned to

St Louis and the family business with a very unenthusiastic wife. Fran thought St Louis was somewhere in Iowa – more a life sentence than a city. The self-proclaimed rebel she had married was turning into a businessman before her still hungry eyes. Had it not been for Fred's bright idea of opening up a bar to keep her from becoming bored and going home, I might have had a brilliant future.

'Look,' he said to us in all seriousness, 'we could use a place to hang out, attract some new faces, have a party. If Marion Davies can spend $50,000 to give a party for Johnnie Ray, we can treat ourselves to a bar. Even if it closes in a month, it won't cost much.' It was always easy to spot when Fred was being serious – his upper lip twisted in an evil smile. 'Besides, there's nowhere decent to have a drink in this town. What do you think?'

What followed was the Crystal Palace, perhaps the most beautiful little bar in America. It was decorated with the urban archaeology Fred had collected by following the demolition crews through St Louis's destruction of its past: drug store fixtures, etched glass doors, elevator cages, church pews, stained glass windows, and amusing Victorian *objets d'art*. From the moment you entered the Crystal Palace, before the first encounter with a frosted martini, you began to feel a bit better about your chances of surviving the night. There was something about the air-conditioned darkness mixed with crystal chandeliers, whiskey and the tinkling of ice and a piano that people found irresistible; if you stayed around for a while, your life would never be the same. People came regularly, the way they might have gone to church in the old days, seeking absolution and some sex. Affairs flourished, as did divorces. There was a local psychiatrist who advised his patients – as a health precaution – to take cold showers and stay away from the Crystal Palace.

Even I was worried that it was not the ideal milieu in which to groom Fran for motherhood. I might have been influenced by reading *The Decline and Fall of the Roman Empire* at the time. Visions of saturnalia and other excesses involving drink were fresh in my mind, considering there was hardly a yard of space in the Palace where you couldn't make out and that included the lavatory, the store room, outside the back door, behind the ice-cube maker, in the cloakroom and under the piano. I made Fran a part of the operation so that there was less to worry about. In the morning she would let herself into the Palace, mix a large brandy and cream cocktail for breakfast and sit down with her adding machine to do her chores. During the day I worked in the galleries; in the evening, after dinner, I would write for a couple of hours. By nine o'clock I was ready to join the party with a smartly dressed and 'speedy' wife at my side.

In the beginning the only entertainment was a resident jazz pianist, Tommy Wolf, and the folk singer Will Holt. In those days folk singers were thin on the ground, needing all the love and attention they could get. There was a rumour that Fred had opened the bar to advance young Holt's aspirations, as well as satisfying Fran's drive to be a misfit. Anyone who heard Holt doing his interpretations of Brecht and Weill knew he was destined for better things than singing *There's A Hole in My Bucket*.

We discovered Tommy Wolf playing background piano for stumbling conventioners at a local hotel. Holt drew an audience of sophisticated taste; Wolf's audiences were the jazz *aficionados* who had no taste at all, but their language was tasty. They spoke of 'pads', 'hung up' or 'hip' and few of the customers knew what they were talking about.

'If April is the cruellest month, as Eliot claimed, how would you say the same thing in hip language?' Fran asked Wolf one spring day.

Wolf didn't have a clue.

'How about: "Spring can really hang you up the most"?' She hoped he'd appreciate her little joke.

'That'd make a good title for a song,' Wolf said. 'Seriously, why don't you write a lyric?'

Two days later she slipped a piece of paper in Wolf's pocket as he sat playing the piano, almost embarrassed by what she had written. Whether it expressed the state of Fran's emotional life at the time or not, there was no doubt, when Wolf set it to music, that a new songwriting team was born. *Spring Can Really Hang You Up The Most* has become a jazz classic recorded by singers who know a great torch song when they hear one.

4

In 1957 the Crystal Palace hired the Compass Players, a group of improvisational actors from Chicago that included Mike Nichols, Elaine May, Severn Darden, Del Close, and later Nancy Ponder and Alan Arkin. The Compass Players were seasoned performers able to turn a flawed idea from the audience into an inspired sketch. After a long run, amid squabbling about artistic differences, the relationship between Mike and Elaine deteriorated. Elaine demanded that Mike be fired, claiming she would leave the show if he wasn't. I had the fun of firing Nichols, but it didn't save the show.

The Compass Players left St Louis and re-formed without Mike and Elaine to become a success in New York, as did Nichols and May, by then reconciled. The Compass director, Theodore J. Flicker, stayed behind. He had an idea that we should do a production of *Waiting For Godot* in our small bar, which seated only ninety people. Giving them a bit of Beckett with their Budweiser was considered daring. To our surprise, the audience loved *Godot*. Every night for the next eight weeks was standing room only.

Its phenomenal success started us thinking in terms of bigger productions with our own theatre company. Flicker came up with a package of ideas and figures that was both innovative and practical. We moved to the growing Gaslight Square area and built a new Crystal Palace that seated 300 people, who could drink and smoke during the show, the way civilized people used to do. For thirty-two weeks we did experimental and original theatre. The rest of the season I produced Julius Monk-style satirical revues and brought in popular star attractions which paid for the loss-making theatrical productions.

For me, the real excitement came from spotting the stars of tomorrow and bringing them to the Palace to polish their act. Most of them found it a sympathetic environment, with fringe benefits that made their engagements a home away from home. There were, however, a few like Woody Allen and Lenny Bruce whose experience there made them wish they'd never left home. Woody, in a letter to a friend, quoted in Eric Lax's recent biography, wrote:

I don't know what happened but this morning I woke up and found myself in St Louis, Missouri. With sedate aplomb I fled screaming to the airport where two dynamically juxtaposed southern bullies prevented me from boarding my flight because of a well-placed phone call from a man named Jay Landesman who seems to have an incredible amount of influence locally stemming from the fact he has me under contract. It has also been made quite apparent to me that the disobeying of a nightclub owner's orders while out of town goes under the heading of mutiny and is punishable by hanging . . . And so I pass my time prudently reticent in the confines of my luxurious no-room apartment trying to keep the mirror from steaming up the air conditioner . . . The nightclub by the way is a study in anti-matter and turns in on itself. Rococo balconies abound . . . magnificent stained glass windows give one the feeling of being in the original Crystal Palace . . . Please excuse the penmanship as I am writing this in the bath tub.

A bit of an exaggeration, but what really upset him was his fear of failure. Woody was terrified of an audience. He used to pace the dressing-room floor muttering, 'I hope they like me, I hope they like me.' They didn't. At the end of each performance he'd make a long-distance call to his psychiatrist to get him out of his desperate situation. By the end of the first week his phone bill was larger than his salary. He felt so bad about his reception that he told us to give his cheque to the musicians 'who at least earned it'. By the close of his engagement we gave him a gold watch for bravery beyond the call of duty.

Lenny Bruce was another entertainer who was confused by the Palace. On his opening night he looked at the floor-to-ceiling murals of stained glass and shook his head in disbelief. 'This place looks like a church that's gone bad. First they started with bingo, then they thought, "What the hell, let's sell a few drinks". Next month they bring in the strippers. I've never worked in a church, but I'll try not to let it inhibit me.' And it didn't. Especially when it came to flirting with Fran. 'I love you because we have identical teeth. Your canines and incisors exactly match mine. It's like looking into my own mouth.'

His engagement was a howling success. The fact that I didn't come up to his conception of a nightclub owner worried him. 'Jay's overbred, baby,' he told Fran. 'Let's you and me go on the road. We'll send him a little money now and then.'

With the Palace leading the way, Gaslight Square attracted other young entrepreneurs and, within a short time, the area was a multi-million-dollar entertainment industry. *Time* magazine saw it as an American success story. Under the heading NO SQUARES ON THE SQUARE, their team of reporters summed up what was happening:

> In the gazetteer of US nightlife, St Louis has never been placed high . . . most of St Louis spent its evening the way much of the rest of the US did: watching television or drinking beer in somebody else's living-room. But now all that is changed. St Louis finally has a place to go at night and the place is Gaslight Square, a three-block oasis of nostalgic frivolity where some fifty gaudily atmospheric taverns, cabarets, restaurants and antique shops are packed together in fine, *fin de siècle* jumble . . . it combines a sort of Disneyland quaintness with the gaiety of Copenhagen's Tivoli Gardens and the innocent naughtiness of Gay Nineties beerhalls . . . Jay Landesman has been voted unofficial mayor of the quarter. Says Landesman grandly: 'It means nothing. I'd rather be king . . .'

After that accolade, there was only place to go – down, and it didn't take long. Visitors to the square were looking for a different kind of excitement. They were no longer interested in atmosphere. Satire had gone out of style with the Vietnam war. Urban blight surrounded the Square. The Youth Culture was emerging. We had become the Establishment. What started out as a party ended up a tragedy. The first mugging in Gaslight Square took place in the 1963. The first murder took place in the winter of 1964. The first casualty was the Crystal Palace.

After twelve years of producing shows, I was creatively

exhausted. Without the Palace I didn't see any future for us in St Louis. We began to think of places to escape to. I fantasized about going somewhere exotic like a Greek island, leaving the entertainment world behind. 'I want to watch the flowers grow,' I said, hoping it would sound romantic. The idea of communing with nature gave Fran the horrors.

'If we have to leave, I want to go to a large city where they speak English,' she stated in no uncertain terms.

That left New York and London. New York was the logical place for the songwriter Fran 'Peaches' Landesman. Her career could have flourished with new collaborators in either city, but what did New York hold for me? I had used it up years ago. It would have been a disaster to try to recapture past glories and failures at the age of forty-five.

As we were only going to be away for a year, London seemed to be the logical place. Our two young boys could get a decent education; there were no medical bills to pay; there was a thriving theatre scene. The music business was very much alive with the advent of the Beatles. Perhaps I could get some of my new plays produced and my old ones revived.

We made our escape, leaving the house and all our personal possessions for Fred to sort out. His wife, Paula, said she was going to miss us. 'It's never going to be the same around here without you two.' It cheered me up. Leaving them and Fran in New York, I flew ahead to London to find us a place to live.

After two weeks, all leads still led to nowhere. Desperate, I was tempted to take a house in Hampstead's Vale of Health because of its colourful name. Instead I found a hotel near Earls Court that I could afford until we found a place.

As Fran and the children were about to board the plane in New York, over the loudspeaker came the message: 'Would Mrs Landesman come to the information desk.' The last call for passengers had been announced. Fran was in a panic. What message was awaiting her? Picking up the phone, she expected the worst. Instead she got the offer she had been waiting for all her life. On the other end of the phone a Broadway producer was asking her to do the lyrics for an upcoming musical entitled *Man of La*

Mancha. He told her W. H. Auden had been their first choice, but his lyrics weren't 'song-ee', so they had paid him off. They wanted her to cancel the trip, stay in New York and get to work. Last warning for passengers was announced again. 'Write and tell me all about it and I'll see what I can do,' she said, which was uncharacteristic. Normally, with an offer like that, she'd have said yes on the spot.

I picked up the family at the airport. The reunion was a huge success. I took along some typical English artefacts including a rolled umbrella, which made a hit. We discovered we had missed each other, but the novelty soon wore thin. Living in one room with two rambunctious children and a wife who had just given up a golden opportunity wasn't easy. In desperation I put an advertisement in *The Times*: 'American author desperately needs flat with character . . .' The response was immediate. A posh voice at the other end of the phone said: 'If it's character you're after, perhaps you should have a look . . .'

What we saw that day at the Angel in Islington was a maisonette in a Georgian terraced house filled with enough antiques to make us feel at home. A statue of a reclining lion guarded the front entrance. The rent was ten guineas a week. Since we were only going to be in London for a year, the ten-month lease wasn't a problem. We moved in next day.

The Angel turned out to have a notorious reputation: we were told it had once been called 'Murder Mile', which went over big with the boys. That night we took a walk around the new area, discovering sights we had only seen in pictures of London in the blitz. There was still the skeleton of a bombed-out church; craters dotted the landscape where rows of houses once stood. Its most glamorous feature was a canal that wound its way through the neighbourhood. We retired that night, convinced it was going to be a struggle to fit in.

We were amazed at how easily people accepted us, without knowing or even caring about our economic or social back-ground. What a relief it was not to be asked, 'And what do you do for a living?' The amount of politeness we experienced was unsettling. I couldn't go into a public toilet without getting a 'thank you' from the attendant for choosing his facilities. The indiscriminate use of the word 'please' was a novelty I soon learned to live with. Since we came from the land of central heating and mod. cons, it took considerable patience to adjust to the flat's primitive conditions. Keeping the coal-burning stoves and open fireplaces functioning for twenty-four hours required a degree in heating engineering. Even with a ridiculous number of hot water bottles in our bed, getting between the damp sheets at night was a masochistic experience. There were times when, upon waking in the morning, we could see our breath in the living-room. Fran compared the ordeal to *Nanook of the North*. And it was only March! We had seen nothing but rain since we arrived. Fran was crossing off the days till she could return to civilization.

Shopping in Chapel Market required some skills we had yet to acquire. Going from stall to stall for individual items seemed like a waste of time. Queueing to make purchases was irritating. Asking for a pound of hamburger was an ordeal. 'Mince' was a word I associated with homosexuals, not something to eat. Asking for black pepper was almost an obscene act. 'That's a continental item. We don't do that,' they would say, baring their rotten teeth. Still, the market had its charms. The variety and beauty of the vegetables on display was dazzling. A cauliflower as big as my head cost 3d. There was a modest thrill in finding the shop that specialized in broken biscuits at a discount. Once we'd learned the dos and don'ts ('Don't touch the merchandise, lady,') our shopping trips became the best part of our day, which seemed to consist of nothing but household chores.

Fran, who had never lifted a finger in St Louis, was confronted with a whole new way of life she resented and resisted. I found a daily, which temporarily eased matters. She would have been perfect if she hadn't had a problem with the bottle. By the end of her two hours she had managed to get pissed, but accomplished little else. Consequently, I took over some of the chores, and all of the laundry and ironing.

The council's Merlin Street Baths was an ancient institution catering to the community's needs. In the laundry room, its collection of worn-out mums, burnt-out pensioners and flighty young brides was a piece of theatre I fell in love with. Everyone looked as if they had been sent from Central Casting to appear in some cycle of mystery plays. The women congregated in front of the machines, with cigarettes hanging from lips that had spilled out a torrent of abuse from birth. They would put their laundry in the washers, close the door (amen!) and rejoin the congregation for a session of local gossip. I would depart to the park opposite, to read the obituary column in *Variety*.

From the time I left the house, no matter on what mission, the most important thing to do was establish a daily rapport with the denizens of the area, beginning with the milkman and ending with the street cleaner. In between there was the grumpy newsagent, who had to be cheered up, the baker's wife to be winked at, the tobacconist to discuss local issues with. A visit to the crippled philosophical cobbler offered choice tidbits on how to mend a soul. But, by far, my favourite was the 'Demon Sweeper'. It wasn't just his cultivated spit-curl carefully pasted to the middle of his forehead that attracted me; it was his ferocious relationship with litter. He was a one-man crusade before it was chic to say, 'Keep Britain Tidy'. He swept with the tenacity of a Jehovah's Witness, but had the humour of a Groucho Marx. We developed a minor street drama between us which drew 'ohs' and 'aws' from a startled audience. I would pretend to catch him resting on the job and demand to know why he was shirking his responsibilities.

'Wasting time again?' I'd ask in an authoritative voice.

'I'm sorry, sir,' he would plead, bowing and scraping like a demented Uriah Heep. 'I've just put down my broom for a minute, sir,' looking around for some sympathy from the crowd. 'Please don't report me again, sir.'

That was the cue to threaten him with immediate dismissal. I retreated, leaving him to deal with an agitated group of witnesses. 'Who is that awful man?' they'd ask. He'd tell them I was the head of the council refuse department. 'What a mean man,' they'd say collectively. Then the Demon Sweeper and I would meet at the Angel Café to discuss, over a nice cup of tea, the finer points of our recent performance. With various plot and venue changes, our show was destined to run for years.

At the local library we were told we'd have to wait a couple of weeks before we could obtain a card, 'but you can take books home today.' I chose a book on Guy Burgess. Fran took Simone de Beauvoir's *Marquis de Sade*. Miles picked Rumer Godden's *The Mouse House*, and macho Cosmo picked *Gloves, Glory and God* by Henry Armstrong. I wondered what a psychiatrist would have made of our choice of books.

CHAPTER TWO

The only things we brought with us from the States were all the wrong clothes, a trunk full of manuscripts, and Peter Cook's phone number, given to us by poet Adrian Mitchell, the only Englishman we knew. The Cooks took us under their wing. They did everything within the bounds of decency to make us feel comfortable, but it was hard to function at their parties filled with famous overachievers of the Sixties. I must have met Kenneth Tynan half a dozen times in Peter's living-room without exchanging a compound sentence. Fran congratulated me on my restraint in not giving him a good thrashing for his devastating review in the *New Yorker* of our 1959 Broadway musical *The Nervous Set*, a satire on the Beat Generation which he took seriously.

I did manage to exchange phone numbers with Malcolm Muggeridge, but only because we lived next to his daughter, whom he visited occasionally. What could I have contributed to the discussion between Michael Foot and Bernard Levin on Shakespeare's hidden motives in *Two Gentlemen of Verona*? Lord knows, I couldn't swap *bons mots* with Willie Rushton at a *Private Eye* luncheon to which Peter once invited me to contribute some ideas. I did mention that a nude picture of one of the Beatles on the cover might sell a few copies, but that didn't go down well with Richard Ingrams. When they finally did a nude cover, it was of the wrong Beatle.

Fran did well with Annie Ross, who threatened to sing one of her songs some day. She did even better with Dudley Moore, who began to set some of her lyrics. It was only at the Cooks' more intimate dinners that I occasionally held the restless audience with tales of our spectacular failures in show business. These had a certain nostalgic quality that went down well with actors over brandy and coffee.

Peter was at the height of his popularity, enjoying it with a modesty and good humour that would have been unheard of in America. Having watched the disastrous effect success had had on so many of our friends in the same situation, I warned him of the perils which lay ahead. 'Why should success change me?' Peter asked. 'I'll have the same wife and friends that I have now.' We wanted to believe him, but as his career moved from strength to international recognition, we watched the tiny cracks form in their once idyllic marriage. I told them the reason we were still married was because neither of us had ever had a success that lasted more than fifteen seconds. When Wendy told Fran how lucky she was to be married to such a funny man, we suspected the marriage was really in trouble. Fran couldn't believe there could be anyone funnier than Peter Cook. By then, neither could he.

From almost the first day we arrived, we were introduced to a touch of English eccentricity as represented by Claire and her sister Sandy. Claire lived in a historic house in Southwark, across from St Paul's. Sir Christopher Wren had lived there while rebuilding the cathedral – the view from her kitchen window was awesome. The house was owned by a young millionaire whose hobby was collecting historic houses and finding interesting people to live in them. They took us around a London far removed from the world of the Cooks, apologizing for any signs of progress we might have seen. We soon discovered that the sombre grey and bowler-hatted image of London was changing dramatically. Claire spoke of the change as something she had to put up with, but loathed. She longed for the good old days she had read about in the novels of Ford Madox Ford and Jerome K. Jerome.

The sisters introduced us to their friends – a collection of obscure poets who read their poems in pubs to bewildered audiences, ancient instrument players from quartets, toe-dancers from off-beat dance companies, and graduates of the Royal School of Needlework. All of them had their charms, but were a little short on laughs.

The kindness of Claire and Sandy in those early days was memorable, but literally short lived. Sandy died suddenly of a mysterious illness. Claire was heartbroken, retiring into a strange kind of mourning: she refused to accept the tragedy. As she was being driven to the airport for a trip to New York, a friend noticed she was furiously knitting and asked what she was making. 'I'm knitting a pair of socks for Sandy,' she said. How typical of Claire, her friend thought, to want to remember her beloved sister in such a way. When we heard that the plane had crashed in the Atlantic, we weren't her only friends who believed that Sandy would get her socks. Claire was the kind of woman who never let anybody down.

Within a few months we had established a wide circle of friends and contacts that threatened to engulf us in a steady round of social activity. Meeting Jeremy and Eleanor Brooks was a turning point. They were the first couple we had met in London who didn't have matching silverware. Coming from America, where it was a crime not to have place mats and matching plates even at breakfast, it was a great relief to Fran to watch Eleanor serve dinner directly from the pot.

Jeremy was a novelist, playwright and Literary Manager of the Royal Shakespeare Company. Eleanor was an artist with a sense of humour and compassion. (Her daily help had become so awful at the job, she paid her not to even try. Unable to fire her, she used her as a model for a *tour de force* exhibit, *A Portrait of Mrs Spinks*.) As a couple, they presented a picture of impoverished, upper-class solidity. That we should have anything in common except a passion for vintage Bentleys and a love of the theatre seemed improbable, but we soon discovered we both had marriages which went beyond the conventional boundaries.

I asked Jeremy to give me an opinion of a play I had finished before I left the States. I had given it to Anne Bancroft, when she was in London for the première of *The Pumpkin Eater*. Columbia Pictures called to tell me she liked it well enough to take it back to

New York. I sent another copy around to Judy Garland's agent, when she was in a London nursing home after one of her 'accidents'. It would have been perfect for her, but her agent said she was 'too much trouble' to bother with and that he no longer represented her. I gave the manuscript to Georgia Brown, Annie Ross and Fenella Fielding, all actresses whose age and singing ability would be appropriate for the role. To a woman they said they were much too young for a comeback role. I think the play's title, *Nobody Knows the Trouble I've Been*, might have put them off.

Brooks returned my play with a note: 'I expected something more outrageous from you.' After years of being told my work was often too ahead of its time, it was a shock to the nervous system to hear now that it was dated. When Fran and I went to the première of *The Persecution and Assassination of Marat as Performed by the Inmates of the Asylum of Charenton Under the Direction of the Marquis de Sade*, I understood what Jeremy meant. I even understood Peter Cook's comment that night: 'It's your all fun show.'

When the children's school broke for the summer holidays, we took them to Brighton for what I had heard was the last of pier-type entertainment. Our kids had never seen anything like it, nor had we. The West Pier's attractions consisted of a collection of ancient 'What the Butler Saw' photo-machines, penny one-arm bandits, mechanical tableaux and corny live shows we thought had disappeared years ago. Cosmo developed a Dostoievskian gambling fever: he claimed to have some kind of system for beating the fruit machines when he ended up with what he started with. I wondered at the time if he had hit upon the secret of life: 'To break even, is to win.' Miles was fiendishly enjoying a mechanical scene of a head being cut off in slow motion. He demanded to know how they got the heads back on; so did I.

It was the first time either of them had ever seen the sea, so they didn't know what to do with it. They wandered up and down the beach looking for sand, which they had heard went with a large body of water, but found nothing but shingle. The afternoon ended with my bringing to the beach a Metropole Hotel tea-tray with a mound of tiny sandwiches, which made a big hit. I was well on the way to becoming civilized.

16

A tour of the Royal Pavilion was convincing, but it was the museum next door that was choice. Great old Victorian paintings of mad-faced royalty, suspicious mistresses, and scenes of contented cows in pastures mouldy green: England at its most eccentric. One room was full of stuffed animals of every species looking as though they knew their moment of truth had come. I never saw such a collection of sad eyes, even if they were only glass. The Art Deco wing was ahead of its time, unappreciated, but surely it must have ranked as one of the most outstanding collections in the UK. By the end of the tour, I was grateful for the rooms where there was practically nothing on display.

When everyone went to bed, happy and tired, I prowled around Brighton looking for something human. I tried a brief conversation with some tired 'forty-something' women loitering outside a pub, who I discovered were tourists like myself. I asked them why they came to Brighton. 'Oh, we couldn't tell you that,' they said, flashing a smile that was meant to be as mysterious as a dirty weekend. I sheepishly entered a casino at the top of one of the big hotels, not knowing what danger awaited. In atmosphere and decor it resembled a well appointed mortuary, but the stick-men who ran the roulette table spoke in French, which I took to be a serious attempt at being 'Continental'.

Walking along the deserted waterfront, I struck up a conversation with a German 'Rocker', who said he heard there was to be an 'orgy' under the 'Vest' Pier that night. When we got there, everyone was in sleeping bags, being serenaded by an inept guitarist singing *Good Night Irene* and it was only eleven o'clock. I was half expecting a mob of Mods to materialize on their mopeds and descend on the sleeping Rockers. But no such luck. I made my way back to the hotel, wondering what Graham Greene ever saw in the place.

That summer I wrote a piece on the changing scene in London for the *St Louis Post-Dispatch*. They liked it so much that I was made their 'Special Correspondent' in London. It looked good on the cards I had printed – these gave us entry to every theatre and opening we cared to attend. My features on 'The Biba Birds',

'London Throws a Jolly Good Party', 'Arts Brought to People in England', and 'Fun and Games Are Big in London' kept the wires hot between London and St Louis. By the end of the summer, if I had no future in the theatre, I certainly could have one in journalism.

Only a few months were left on our lease and we couldn't find anything decent. Once again I put an advertisement in *The Times*. 'Shabby-chic lodgings required by American family for short term lease . . .' Again a posh voice on the phone answered. 'My name is Tom Driberg. I have a little country place you might be interested in seeing . . .' We had no specific plans for country life, but he made the place sound so exciting we arranged to meet him for a drink on the House of Commons terrace. The first of many surprises we experienced in his company was his showing up for the trip to the country with a handsome young French boy, whom he introduced as his au pair.

Bradwell Lodge, he told us, had once been the summer studio of Thomas Gainsborough. What might have been perfect for Gainsborough in the eighteenth century was too much for the Landesmans in the twentieth. For a start, its glass-domed observatory at the top of the house overlooked a nuclear power station. The ceiling of one its many rooms had been painted by Angelica Kauffmann; the Adam brothers' handiwork was everywhere. With two frisky children and no help, keeping such a treasure trove from disintegrating would have been too big a responsibility for Fran. Reluctantly we turned it down. On the way home Miles got carsick, throwing up over Driberg. Far from being put off by the incident, he invited us the next week to join him on a pub crawl on the Isle of Dogs.

He took us to a pub whose entire clientèle comprised of lesbians, transvestites, young Danish sailors, ageing pederasts and an assortment of amputees. Fran and I felt like the odd couple in such a scene. I mentioned how much Tennessee Williams would have liked the place. Fran said she had been reading *The Roman Spring of Mrs Stone*. Driberg raised an eyebrow and asked why. Fran said, rather dramatically, 'It's my future.' He looked surprised at her for a few seconds and delivered the saddest line of the night. 'It's my present, dear.' Then he smiled. 'This kind of place keeps me in touch with my constituents. I'm Labour, you know.' He was the only Labour MP who sounded like Noël Coward and knew René Clair and Elsa Schiaparelli. We saw him only occasionally after that, but he did enliven one of our parties by showing up with a new Italian *au pair* even better looking than the last one.

The first batch of mail we received after a protracted postal strike was mainly from the States. It was reassuring to know we had made the right move by leaving. The hot summer of race riots, the Barry Goldwater presidential bid and the personal hang-ups of those we had left behind were too depressing to think about. 'I'm headed for an old age of terrible misanthropy and total withdrawal . . . Oh well, back to my cucumber mousse . . .' Virginia Robinson wrote. Another letter was from Carole Mann, who was living in a New York commune founded by Timothy Leary and Richard Alper on an estate in Millbrook, given to them by the Hitchcock family. She confessed that, even with unlimited LSD, one could get depressed in paradise. Another correspondent spelt it out: 'Whatever you do, don't come back to America.'

There was a letter from Cutie, my mother, which was pure pain and pleasure. The pain was that at her age she had to find a new place to live. The pleasure was that she thought we were leading, for once, a 'normal life'. Knowing Cutie, that meant any day I'd be returning to St Louis and the antique business. A card from Martin Quigley, the PR who had written our 'obituary' read: 'There isn't a decent place to get a drink in this town since you left.' That same day, on the BBC, an American critic, called Reyner Banham announced in a speech before the American Institute of Architects that St Louis was 'officially dead'.

At a party in Guy de Roche's antique shop in Camden Passage we met his friend Tony Flavell. It turned out Tony owned an empty house in Duncan Terrace, three doors away from where we were living. We must have passed it hundreds of times. A former industrial workshop, it was in such a distressed state that even gypsies would have turned it down. We were desperate, however, and took it when he said the rent would be £30 a month. Even though we had to fix it up at our own expense, knowing there was going to be a roof over her head was enough to allay Fran's anxiety about being homeless.

With the help of the children and their mates, we set about making the place habitable without any major remodelling. The boys chopped all the rotting plaster from the walls, exposing beautiful red bricks, and we left it that way. Stripping the walls also exposed fragments of the original William Morris wallpaper, which we left. An electrician only charged us £40 plus materials to rewire the house. I was just beginning to run out of money when I had the idea of putting another ad. in *The Times*. 'Unsuccessful American writer in love with London has empty Georgian house. Anything you'd like carted away? Has flamboyant taste, but will compromise . . .' I began to feel that *The Times* Personal column might become a way of life.

A reporter from the *Daily Herald* was the first respondent. He seemed to doubt that there was such a thing as an 'unsuccessful' American in England. I told him it meant I didn't have a swimming pool. He laughed. The second and last call was from a woman who said she'd give me a houseful of furniture, linen, dishes, glasses – everything, if I'd only pay the storage bill of £50 a case. I had to turn it down when she told me she had a hundred cases! The discovery of an antique shop in Highbury called Chaos Corner, which sold round, Victorian, rosewood dining tables for £12 and a set of chairs to match for £3 each, restored my faith in capitalism. I went back to Camden Passage for some pub mirrors I had had my eye on. Engraved on one of them were the words, 'Take Courage'; it was the one I bought.

Fran pitched in with some neat curtain-making and cushion-covering. Her most creative contribution to the house consisted of sewing orange-coloured gum balls on to the branches of an almost leafless tree in the living-room. People thought the gum balls were tiny oranges; it was the one touch that people liked most about the house. She said she derived more pleasure out of sewing than she got out of her last two royalty cheques. My pleasure came from finishing a job I never thought I was capable of starting. I found a standing giant Klieg light in a skip. It proved the crowning touch for the living-room of two show-business refugees.

We realized we had fallen in love with London by only scratching its surface. Cosmo had benefited from wearing a uniform to school and becoming a connoisseur of fish fingers. Miles showed initiative in making a few bob on Guy Fawkes' Day. Neither of them had broken anything more serious than a few childish promises. I had learned to say 'please' and 'thank you', but neither Fran nor I had accomplished anything from a career viewpoint. With a solid base to operate from, it was time to think about our future. So many of the people we had known and worked with in the past had gone on to successful careers. Nichols and May were the hottest things on Broadway. Flicker, ex-director of the Compass, was in Hollywood directing his first feature film. The singer Will Holt was appearing in the West End with Martha Schlamme in *An Evening of Kurt Weill*. Woody Allen had become a stand-up comic role model. We began to wonder if we had any talent left to tune up.

Fran's first chance came with Ned Sherrin's invitation to come round to his office to discuss doing some topical lyrics for his *Not So Much a Programme, More A Way Of Life* – the most talked-of television show since *That Was The Week That Was*. Fran had no doubts she could do the job, but finding his office was a major problem. The address turned out to be in a mansion flat in Shepherd's Bush. Without a guide, she walked down endless halls, looking in each room for some sign of life. The only thing she found was a man in a string vest frying up an English breakfast. It was hardly the setting for the producer of the show all London was watching.

When she finally found his office, his friendly, 'Hello, I'm Ned Sherrin and I'm thrilled you found the place,' did much to soothe her nerves. He turned out to be a secret fan, having heard her *Ballad of the Sad Young Men* in an H. M. Tennent West End revue *On The Avenue* some years previously. He had seen the show with Noël Coward, who had insisted on going backstage to congratulate the singer on 'doing justice to such a wonderful song'. Fran promised to rent a television set to watch his show. 'I hope you do,'

21

he said. 'We're doing one of your songs from *The Nervous Set* this week.' Once told what was expected of her, she left his office with that old feeling of 'This is it!'

We began to think seriously about acquiring an agent. We asked around for the best, which led us to Peter Cook's agent, Peter Rawley. 'I'm a terrific lover,' he told Fran over drinks, 'but a lousy agent.' 'Oh, what a shame,' she said. 'I have a lousy lover, what I need is a terrific agent.' We compromised. Rawley became my agent, and Fran was lucky enough to get Peggy Ramsey.

We realized we weren't the only Americans over here trying to get their act together when we invited Lionel Stander to dinner. He is best remembered as the gravel-voiced character in 1930s' films that included *The Scoundrel*, *Mr Deeds Goes to Town* and *A Star is Born*. Now he is best known as the lovable rogue in the successful television series *Hart to Hart*. His career in Hollywood ended when he was blacklisted by the Communist witchhunts of the 1950s. He became a successful stockbroker on Wall Street, leading the rich, self-indulgent life until he decided to go back into show business. He'd been in London almost the same amount of time as we had, and was having about as much career luck as we were. He received rave reviews for his role in Brecht's *St Joan of the Stockyards* in London, but the show closed quickly and he'd done nothing since. His style of living was much higher than ours, but his depression was at about the same level. He was going back to the States if nothing broke for him. Desperate, he asked me to ghost his autobiography as a means of obtaining some ready cash to enable him to stay. Even though he had led an amazing life, my chance of getting an advance on someone not in the public eye was too slim to count on.

I didn't see him again till the latter part of 1965, when he returned to London to do *Cul de Sac* with Roman Polanski. He rented our old flat, which was something of a come-down for him, yet he managed to entertain as if he were at the Ritz. Complaining that his busy schedule left him no time for certain personal details, he hired Cosmo, who was only eleven at the time, to be his personal valet. Cosmo doubted he could fill the position convincingly, but I told him to take it anyway. 'It'll look good on your CV.'

Through Stander's lavish entertaining, we met a constant stream of people who were amusing for a night or two. One day, though, he lured two girls back to his flat with the prospect of meeting 'a crazy American' who lived next door. One was the Jamaican jazz singer Billie Lane, who had returned to London to discover her lover no longer liked jazz or her. 'Dat's cool,' she said, 'I never liked his wife either.' The other girl, Hanya Kochansky, looked like she'd just stepped out of the pages of *Vogue*. After listening to Stander's political, economic and sociological analysis of the state of the world, I invited the girls to come next door for tea. Hanya took one look around, positioned herself in front of the Klieg light and announced to the world, 'I'm home!'

When we received the news that Fran's parents were coming for Christmas, we were prepared for the worst, but we needn't have been. Their Christmas present to us was an offer to finance the 'talent tune up' for another year with the proviso that, if we didn't make it by then, we had to return to the States. We spent Christmas wrapping gifts and decorating the tree. On New Year's Eve we drank Israeli 'champagne', ate smoked salmon and felt like a family for the first time since we left America. After everyone else retired, Fran and I changed into formal dress and arrived on the stroke of midnight at the best New Year's Eve party in London, feeling 1965 was going to be our year.

CHAPTER THREE

'Stick to one thing; stay home; good news,' read my horoscope at the beginning of January 1965. Not that I believed in astrology, but nothing else was happening. I followed instructions; things began to happen. Charles Kasher, who was co-producing the film of *The Ipcress File*, put composer John Barry and Fran together to write its title song. West End producer Michael Codron asked to see my play *Nobody Knows The Trouble I've Been*. I received a commission from the *St Louis Post-Dispatch* to write a one-act play for their bicentennial issue for a £400 fee. Hunter Davies wrote a *Sunday Times* feature on an American 'Salinger-type' family that had invaded London that spring ('How to hang you up the most'). Wolf Mankowitz expressed an interest in *Dearest Dracula*, a horror musical I was trying to get produced. Fran was now a regular contributor to *Not So Much A Programme . . .* Music publishers E. B. Morriss set up Fran with Tom Springfield, the hot-pop composer, promising her meetings with other hit songwriters. The editor of *Vogue* asked me to do a sample column on Americans in London. Peter Cook wanted me to replace him in a five-minute television spot he was tired of doing on someone else's show. With so many marvellous things happening, I thought we were in Camelot instead of Islington.

The atmosphere around the house was electric. Even Cosmo and Miles were caught up in it. On Sundays they set up a sidewalk stall in Brick Lane, selling their American comic books and the games, toys and clothes they'd outgrown. To attract an older crowd, I gathered up a collection of artifacts that included all the disappointing Christmas and birthday presents Fran and I had given each other, many in their original wrappings. Cosmo and I would spend our time in the local bagel shop, while Miles, looking like Oliver Twist, stood shivering in front of his pitch, praying people would take pity on him and buy something. At the end of the day, the boys always managed to spend as much they took in, but that was part of Cosmo's philosophy of 'winning by breaking even'.

I wrote the column for *Vogue*. 'Too hip for our audience,' the editor wrote back. I showed the letter to Fran, who took one look and let it drop to the floor. 'Where have we heard that one before?' she asked. On April Fools' Day, we heard that the Springfield/Landesman song was being recorded by a new group to rival The Seekers. (Word went around that it could go either way.)

I finished the commissioned play, but not without a struggle; Fran thought it was the best thing I had ever done. I should have known replacing Peter Cook even for five minutes was hopeless, but it gave me a chance to introduce the 'mystery comic' act I used to do at the Crystal Palace before a bewildered audience. After a couple of minutes I thought I was back at the Palace; Peter masterfully withheld any signs of laughter. 'This is subliminal humour, Peter. My act is designed to take the laughter out of comedy.' It was a concept even an absurdist like Peter found difficult to assimilate.

The migration of Americans to London was charging the scene with a lot of energy. Many of them, mostly in show business, could be found playing baseball in Hyde Park on any Sunday morning. Whenever an American puts on a uniform, even if it's only a baseball cap, he tends to take himself seriously. This was especially true when the players were Tony Curtis, John Cassavetes, Larry Gelbart, Marlon Brando and Charles Bronson, and the umpire was Phil Silvers. Once, when Silvers was called away, I was asked to replace him; it was a hard act to follow. Within ten minutes I made so many wrong calls and bad jokes I was asked to leave before I emptied Hyde Park.

Norman Mailer was in town promoting a new book. We went

back to the days in the mid-1950s when he first became interested in hipsters and Beats, a piece of research that led to his famous essay on the White Hipster. Told that I was one of the originals on the Beat scene, he was extremely accessible when we got together. In London we met up at his publisher's party. Andre Deutsch had rounded up the usual suspects: critics, columnists, PRs, Sonia Orwell and Jonathan Miller. Surrounded by a crowd of sycophants, Mailer looked so self-satisfied in his three-piece Savile Row suit I felt it was my duty to dirty him up a little bit. Unable to get anywhere near him, I slipped the joint that would do the deed to Deutsch instead. 'For Norman,' I whispered, 'he'll probably need it about now.' Instead of thanking me, Deutsch grew quite upset. 'He doesn't do that any more,' he hissed. If so, he could have at least given me back the joint.

At dinner at our house, and later in his speech at the Mayfair Theatre, Mailer's view of America confirmed that we'd left just in time. 'Fucking has become a matter of status in America,' he told a contentious audience. 'The civil rights movement will never solve anything. As long as people see themselves as a minority, there is no hope for them. The matter will be decided by an increase in violence . . . Modern man is becoming schizophrenic, caught in a double bind, between the dream that the culture tries to sell him and the realities of life.' His views were not what a predominantly leftish British audience expected from the spokesman of liberal culture. Was Mailer making a Right turn? With Malcolm Muggeridge giving him glowing credentials in his introduction, there was reason to believe Mailer had arrived at a crossroads. But at our party, he seemed to have cheered up; many of the guests saw him as just a famous writer who was a 'nice guy'.

To neighbour and artist Michael Andrews, Mailer was someone very special. It was his novel *The Deer Park* which inspired one of Andrews's most famous paintings, *The Deer Park*, which now hangs in the Tate Gallery. For Mailer it was a treat to meet someone as modest as Andrews. Mailer had a nice word for everyone at the party, including me. For some inexplicable reason he saw me that night as a kind of Jewish 'saint' ensuring that everyone was having a good time. It was only when I became a publisher, years later, that he decided I was a devil. Yet, when I asked him for a cover blurb for *Rebel Without Applause*, he came through with a dandy: 'Jay and Fran Landesman could be accused of starting it all. By God, were they there at the beginning.'

Around the same time, Timothy Leary, another figure from our past, dropped in at Duncan Terrace. He was repaying a visit we had made to his Millbrook commune when we were looking for places to escape to from St Louis. We had met him and Richard Alpert there while they were on one of their speaking tours spreading the gospel of LSD. While at Millbrook, I took my first trip in their 'nose cone', a room in the tower of their great Victorian house especially equipped for space travelling. The music, the food, the lighting, and the ground crew created the ideal setting for the journey; LSD was a serious business with them. After hours of waiting for lift off, Leary could not account for my still being grounded. While he and Alpert debated whether to give me a booster shot of DMT, I told them I would settle for a couple of hits of Columbia Gold. Leary claimed I was too 'transcendental' for LSD. Certainly the rest of the house wasn't transcendental, but it was extraordinary for a commune of acid-heads. There was a cellar with a bowling alley; a billard room and a trophy room with mounted elk heads on the walls. There was a frozen lake with people skating hand in hand in the moonlight. From the outside, it was reminiscent of a *Saturday Evening Post* cover by Norman Rockwell.

In spite of its corny aspects, we thought Millbrook might be the answer for us until we attended a committee meeting where Leary and Alpert laid down the rules of conduct required for a 'liberated' community. Fran decided it was too much like the rules her parents had laid down when she was a child. This was confirmed when our friend, actress Carole Mann, who had been living there for six months – she was fed up – asked us what the theatre scene was like in London.

Had I had the foresight to book Leary and Alpert to break in their act at the Crystal Palace, I'd have earned my footnote in history for discovering that the two heroes of a generation were really a couple of stand-up comics with great punch lines like 'Tune in, turn on, drop out.'

Leary was in town to touch base with R. D. Laing. 'He's very important,' he said, 'you should meet him.' Of course I had heard of him, but not all of it was good. Arrangements were made to meet him at Kingsley Hall in the East End. At lunch with Laing's extended family of schizophrenics and staff, it was difficult for me to distinguish the one group from the other. It was when we saw the 'hopeless' cases lying uncommunicative in rooms of indescribable squalor that I realized why Leary was anxious to meet Laing. Leary thought LSD might be useful in Laing's treatment of such hopeless cases.

While I couldn't help but admire Laing's dedication, there was another side to him I got to know and learned to love: Laing at home, in front of a piano, with a glass of Scotch and a joint, playing Cole Porter, Rodgers and Hart, and the George and Ira Gershwin songbook. If he hadn't become a doctor, he could have always made a living as a jazz pianist. His appreciation of jazz and the men who played it was often this side of envy. When we took him to hear jazz pianist Bob Dorough, he was so moved that he rose from his seat, unsteady, and began to howl as if he were a pack of starving wolves. It completely drowned out Dorough's performance. Casey Salkin, who was notorious for running a tight ship for the artists performing in his room, took me aside. 'Get that nutcase out of here.' I tried to explain that it was the famous R. D. Laing, who was only expressing his appreciation. 'I don't give a fuck who he is. He's howling off key!'

Once, at a small party that included Zen writer Alan Watts, his wife, and novelists Jakov Lind and Iris Owens, the talk was so stratospheric, I was reduced to silence. Nobody was tripping, but we were on different planets. Laing, noticing my unusual silence, asked me why. I told him I thought it was going to be a party, not a seminar. 'I'm wearing my dancing shoes, but nobody's dancing.' Laing held out his arms in a gesture of solidarity. 'Well, Jay, let's dance.' And we did, and he let me lead!

Of the divided Laing, I preferred the frivolous half. He always seemed so unhappy when he was being serious. The last time I saw Ronnie, I asked him if he had enjoyed his fame. 'It's been a great consolation,' he said, but I didn't believe him. A short time later,

28

his drinking increased, his behaviour deteriorated and his marriage fell apart. It's worth recalling that during his last few years, when his fame was tarnished and he was no longer practising, he acquired a new wife and new baby, gave up drink and pot, and went to live in a new country, enjoying his anonymity.

An interesting postscript of our relationship occurred during a tarot reading I was subjected to by Hanya Kochansky, who was a greater friend of Ronnie Laing's than I. She was very disturbed when the death card turned up. 'It's not your card. Something strange is happening here,' she said. Five minutes later the phone rang. It was his ex-wife, Jutta Laing, with the news that Ronnie had just died on a tennis court in France.

By the end of May, all our projects were either stalled, on hold, or rejected. Fran's collaboration with Springfield went the 'other way'. My play for the newspaper was rejected by the editor, who claimed he 'couldn't see the point of it'. Michael Codron turned down the other play. Any thoughts of Fran's getting another title song like *Goldfinger* out of the collaboration with John Barry sank without a word.

As the rejections poured in, however, so did more invitations to dinners and parties. Charlie Kasher, who made millions out of pitching a hair-oil cure for baldness although bald as a cue ball, was determined to 'sell' us. When he set up an evening with Harry Saltzman, his co-producer on *The Ipcress File*, he said he just 'wanted to see if we mixed'. Saltzman was the kind of American whose wheeling and dealing with entertainment moguls left scant energy to waste on Charlie Kasher's fringe friends. We didn't mix.

Saltzman walked Fran and me to the lift. 'I think I saw you two recently. Do you drive around in a convertible Monza?' If he had shown signs of being that observant earlier in the evening, we might have been able to mix.

Kasher's dinner with Michael Caine was more amusing, especially when Fran offered him a hit on the joint that was going around. 'Oh, no,' he cried out. 'I'm an actor. I can't touch the stuff.

I have to remember lines. That stuff ruins your memory.' Fran tried to tell him that was an old wives' tale. Twenty-five years later, Fran's memory was shot and Caine's was good enough to remember me, although we'd met only twice in the Sixties. One meeting was at the première of *The Ipcress File*. He looked worried. I told him there was nothing to worry about, 'It's a good film.' He smiled, still worried. 'Thanks, Jay, but will my mother like it?' A few years later I saw a Cockney-looking villain type loading up a car with paintings outside my house. I was about to go back in and call the police when he called me by name. 'What the hell are you doing?' I asked, recognizing him. He had just purchased a triptych from Michael Andrews, who lived a few doors from us. Even then he looked worried about whether he had made the right move spending £10,000. 'Do you think Andrews is a good hedge against inflation?' he asked, as I gave him a hand with the paintings.

The first time we met Fenella Fielding at a party, she stood out like a gem; it was instant love. On our first double date with the American actor Weston Gavin, the four of us laughed so much that we agreed we could never meet again. 'Well, gang, we've used up all our best material and there's nothing left for an encore,' Weston said. Fenella knew everyone in show business worth knowing; what made her so endearing was her cynical attitude to it all. Her unmistakable voice-overs for television commercials were so successful, it had me wondering why she didn't appear more on telly. 'I don't like to do that, darling. It's just too awful to think of those window cleaners sitting in the pub in front of the telly nudging their mates in the ribs. "See her, matey? I've 'ad her."' She quickly added, coyly, 'It could give a girl such a naughty reputation, whether it was true or not, darling.'

Waiting for Fenella to turn up, I always experienced a pleasant feeling of excitement. People expected her to be exotic if she just went to the corner news-stand. What exaggerated version of Fenella would I be confronted with? Would her hairpiece be as outrageous as her last one? What would she be wearing? Did she have an arrangement with the *Carry On* wardrobe mistress? Stories of her life with father and mother were tales of classic rejection. Once, as a star-struck young actress, she came down to the family dinner on the Sabbath dressed as Noël Coward, complete with cigarette holder. Instead of a laugh, she got a slap. Her love affairs were seldom as traumatic, but there is a piece of gossip that once a slightly-the-worse-for-drink partner fell asleep. If it were true, I'm sure Fenella wouldn't have thrown him out without first giving him some notes on his performance.

At parties Fenella would be surrounded by young men. They'd confess that not only had they been in love with her since puberty, but their mother had been too. 'How sweet,' she'd say. But her eyes said, 'Fuck off.' I once fixed her up with the Beat poet Gregory Corso. He was in London performing at Westminster Abbey as part of Michael Horovitz's Poetry Olympics. I wasn't surprised when he used the F-word in that sacred temple, but when he asked Fenella – five minutes after they met – for a blow job, I knew it wasn't the way to a girl's heart. Tapping me on the shoulder, she said, 'Darling, I think you better let me off at the corner. I just remembered I left the house on fire.'

When agents don't return your calls and your glamorous friends invite you to dinner where the biggest name is their accountant, you know it's time to find another circle. We started to see a lot of Hanya and her husband Hugh, a couple who couldn't possibly help our careers, but who knew where the action was. The Pickwick Club in Great Newport Street, off Charing Cross Road, was the first port of call. It offered a civilized menu, live music, attractive people and lively conversation. I was shocked when I heard writer Sandy Fawkes use the word 'cunt' at the bar and even more shocked to hear actress Katie Fitzroy using it as a term of endearment. In America, any combination of dirty words could be used except that one. Even Lenny Bruce put 'cunt' on hold.

It was inevitable that a club named after Mr Pickwick should be the scene of unrestricted recreation, harmless pleasure and, on some nights, mischievous behaviour. On such an evening, I was entertaining the American agent Irwin Arthur, while Princess Margaret and Lord Snowdon were having dinner at a table near the bar. Arthur, like most Americans, was impressed with being in the same room as royalty. Suddenly there was a commotion around His Lordship's table. The next thing we saw was actor John Bey being escorted out the door by Angelo, the *maître d'* and several waiters. I thought that to get physically bounced out of the Pickwick required nothing less than an act of indecent exposure. He had evidently unknowingly invaded their privacy. The sad, confused look on Bey's face as he was hustled past our view was a cry for help which could have won him a part in any Samuel Beckett play.

I mentioned to the gang at my table that Lord Snowdon looked bored. 'We've been treating the royals shabbily.' I threatened to go over to his table to cheer him up. 'I know just how to do it. Leave it to me, I'll have His Lordship eating out of my hand within minutes.'

Hanya and Hugh begged me to reconsider. Their, 'It's not done, Jay,' only made me want to do it more. Poor Fran ducked into the toilet immediately to avoid the kind of embarrassment she claimed I had subjected her to all her married life. The agent didn't make a move. 'This is one act I don't want to miss,' he said.

I weaved my way over to the bar, next to His Lordship's table, ordered a drink, looked over at him, caught his eye and said, 'I liked your aviary,' in a voice loud enough for Princess Margaret to hear. At the time his structure in Regent's Park was a controversial post-modern design with few defenders. Lord Snowdon seemed quite pleased. After I got my drink, he invited me to join their table. For the next ten minutes I talked 'aviary aesthetics' with him with an expertise I'd never suspected I had. Words like 'organic', 'revolutionary', 'environmental compatibility', 'spatial configurations' cascaded from my lips. When I realized I was in danger of running out of architecture-babble, I thanked him for the interesting exchange, expressing the hope we could meet again some day and continue the discussion. I returned to the table where my guests were eager to hear what had happened.

I wasn't there ten minutes before Angelo came over with a look that seemed to threaten me with the John Bey treatment. 'His Lordship would like you to return to his table,' he announced instead, his eyes lifting heavenward.

There was a deathly silence. 'Don't go, Jay,' Hanya said again. 'Quit winners, Jay boy,' added Fran. Irwin Arthur stood up and offered a toast. 'Jeeze, Jay, I knew you were a big shot back in St Louis, but this is ridiculous.'

The return engagement lacked the spontaneity of the initial meeting. His Lordship's interest waned as I tried to tell him the story of my life, even though it was the *Reader's Digest* version. Mr Pickwick would have recognized that the game was up and so did I. I weaved my way back to my table, wondering why he hadn't introduced me to his wife. The next day I received a telephone call from his office inviting me to dinner. I knew it was a hoax call from someone who had witnessed the scene, but I took down all the details just in case.

One night we met Mel Brooks at the Pickwick and hit it off through the Woody Allen connection. He was so friendly and outrageous, Fran and Hanya asked him if he wanted to join them in the ladies' room for a smoke. When they got there, Fran dropped the piece of hash she was preparing. Brooks, ever the gentleman, dropped to his hands and knees to look for it. Just before they left the toilet, they were intrigued by a piece of graffiti that had been written in lipstick: 'Terry Cooper is a lousy fuck'. Underneath it was a postscript – 'Now you tell me'. When they returned to the bar, sitting there was actor Terry Cooper, looking hopeful as usual. Fran could not resist introducing him. 'Mel, this is Terry Cooper, whom you've read so much about.'

Next door to the Pickwick was the Kismet, an afternoon drinking club which was host to a collection of Soho writers, artists, punters, drunks, and brain-damaged ex-Rank starlets, whose past was their only recommendation. There is a story Jeffrey Bernard tells of a stranger entering the bowels of the Kismet for the first time and asking, 'What is that smell?' Without looking up from his glass, John Bey shouted, 'Failure.' Eddi McPherson, the bartender, was a strapping, goodlooking, big-bosomed, tough young woman who filled the drinker's need for a basement madonna. But not everybody at the Kismet was a loser. On a good day there would be such characters as comedian Marty Feldman, actors Peter Finch, Alan Lake, Sean Lynch, writers Frank Norman, James Deakin,

33

Dan Farson, Jeffrey Bernard, artist Francis Bacon, dancer Sue Bardolph, voice-over king Bill Mitchell, Rank starlet Susan Shaw, and Christine Keeler. Most of the Kismet's regulars I had only heard of, but once I showed promise as a potential 'loser', it was easy to make friends with the High and the Lonely.

At the Kismet I met the kind of people who, although younger than I by a generation, were steeped in the life-style of the Fifties. They still liked their jazz pure, their women not so pure. The women liked men with a past more than those with a future. They were less inclined to do anything about changing the Sixties.

It was at the Kismet that Hugh Bebb introduced me to Christine Keeler. She was still attractive and vivacious, but suspicious of people, particularly 'curiosity seekers' whose stupid questions about her past she parried with the skill of a seasoned street fighter. She became a friend whose presence lent a certain *soupçon* of mystery, if not of glamour, to our parties. As we came to know one another, she relaxed enough to see that Fran and I wanted nothing from her. In fact, she asked Fran to give her a list of books she might read to improve her mind. When she was in our kitchen one night helping Fran get dinner together, she asked her, 'Who are Rosemary and Basil and why are their names on those canisters?' Fran gave her a copy of *Catcher in the Rye* and hoped for the best.

John Clellon Holmes met her at our house, playing the Truth Game. He wrote about it in his book *Displaced Person* (1987):

CHRISTINE TO LORRAINE: 'When are you going to make it with me?'
CHRISTINE TO ME: 'Are you going to fuck your wife tonight?'
JAY TO CHRISTINE: 'John said today that maybe I was bucking for saint because I don't do anything any more, except things like this. Have you ever thought of that as an alternative?'
ME TO CHRISTINE: 'Why don't you just decide to love your-self?' . . . It can be said that that night the Truth Game, which I had seen shrivel egos and pulverise relationships in the past, brought certain honesties out into that room everyone there having drunk enough to lay it down, or smoked enough, lost enough, whatever it was, the way it seemed to them. . . . Still

Christine, when she left, had re-achieved the sardonic, offhand mask without which, perhaps, her London might have become Blake's London, and when I took her small, rather soft little hand, she glanced at me, and said indifferently: 'Anyway, it doesn't matter much, any of it does it? . . . Have you had a good stay in England?'

In his final analysis, John described her as 'a stubborn girl, canny rather than bright; a girl who mistook airs for manners'. I saw her as a lot of fun when she wasn't conscious of being Christine Keeler. She may have liked the Kismet, but she'd seen Cliveden and that could spoil a girl more sensitive than Miss Keeler.

CHAPTER FOUR

J ust as I was beginning to enjoy my indulgent lifestyle, the Dublin Theatre Festival decided that they wanted to do *Dearest Dracula*. We had almost forgotten they had the manuscript. They offered $10,000 towards its production. As the producer, I was required to raise the rest of the money. A letter to fifty close friends and former business associates in St Louis to invest in our talent brought thirty-nine cheques within two weeks. Everything went smoothly over the summer and the show, which had been conceived above a garage in St Louis and rehearsed above a pub in Islington, duly arrived at Dublin's Olympia Theatre, thanks to the Irish sense of humour.

The theatre was in the same state of decay as I imagined Dracula's castle to be. We found the stage hands charming and often helpful, but we were a little nervous about their stories of musicians who went out for a drink during intermission and never returned. On opening night, the musical received a seven-minute ovation. The Irish critics were enthusiastic – one local critic went over the top with superlatives: 'A production which, for visual attack, stagecraft and all-round excellence of singing, acting and dancing surpasses anything I have seen in Dublin in the field of musical comedy.'

A reputation for pulling off the impossible was about to be revived. A review written by an independent critic especially for the *St Louis Post-Dispatch* was splashed across its entertainment page: 'They love *Dearest Dracula* in London! Musical Produced by St Louisian Jay Landesman, with Lyrics by Wife Fran, Is a Hit at Festival.' Cosmo, who was eleven at the time, struck about the right note: 'It was fine, apart from all that love stuff.' The St Louis backers were ecstatic. A few transatlantic calls came through with nothing but superlatives for our achievement. I was becoming very nervous. The English critics were yet to be heard from.

Watching a singing, romantic Dracula prancing around the stage of the Olympia Theatre touched a nerve in the English critics *en masse*. 'Where are the gore and Gothic horror of the old Dracula?' they asked. Harold Hobson of the *Sunday Times* called it the most inept production he had ever seen. The humiliation continued with a précis of all the bad reviews published in St Louis's other paper under the caption 'Landesman's Show a Flop'. Feeling that the investors needed some explanation, I sent them a favourable review by *Variety*, but in my heart I knew the English critics had nailed Dracula through the heart with a stake.

If Busby Berkeley hadn't come to London to give a talk at the opening of a season of his films, Dracula would have remained that way. Berkeley had been one of the heroes of my youth; I knew his career well enough to answer *Mastermind* questions on the subject. The affair was held at the National Film Society and was chaired by film historian Philip Jenkinson. Only clips of the production numbers were shown that night, with Jenkinson giving his unique interpretations of the action. He introduced the guest of honour as 'Busby *Barkley*', which raised a laugh or two. There were complicated questions from the duffle-coat brigade of film buffs, which Berkeley fielded with unexpected simplicity. 'All I wanted to do was to use those beautiful girls looking beautiful,' he said, slightly annoyed that anyone should think there was some other motive. After the questioning, he introduced Ruby Keeler, who came out breathlessly, holding up her hands to the audience: 'It's ok. It's ok. I'm not going to sing.' Like Berkeley, she was bewildered by the attention. 'When my son came home and said, "Why, Mom, do you know that you're the Queen of Camp?" I didn't know what he was talking about.'

I immediately made arrangements to interview Berkeley for

another of my hot dispatches to the home front. He turned out to be a very uncomplex person; I could see that all the attention was making him restless. Suddenly it occurred to me that he might like to work again. I told him about the romantic, dancing Irish Dracula fiasco and his eyes lit up like the light around his memorable neon violin production number. Seeing his reaction, I sensed he might be the director Dracula had been waiting for all his life. All the time I was thinking what a great idea it was to bring Berkeley back to Broadway with a dancing chorus of vampires and a tango-mad Dracula.

The next day I had some second thoughts. He hadn't worked in years. Even though camp was 'in', there was still a long way to go before Berkeley would be bankable. Crazy as the idea was, I felt I owed it to the investors to keep the project alive. I had contacted Vincent Price, when he was filming in London the previous summer. He thought it was a great idea and asked to see the script. He said he'd be coming back in October and we'd talk about it again. He thought it sounded like 'great fun'. I wrote to Berkeley asking him if he would work with me on the revisions, adding, 'How would you like to stage and direct the show?' I received his reply almost immediately:

> . . . So far, I think your suggestions well taken. I like the therapy idea – the mad doctor and the mad patient. It also might be well to lose the romance between Seward and Lucy . . . You state that in asking me to work with you on the rewrite you are asking a lot of me without any 'front money' – but if I accept your offer and my name is associated with the project from the beginning you will be able to raise the front money and it will be a big help in raising the balance . . . I like you personally, Jay, and I instinctively believe you have a potential property that can be developed into a most unusual and exciting hit! My services would not only require work on the rewrite but would also include imaginative and creative production thinking with reference to the musical aspect as well. The right preparation is nine tenths of the battle in doing a musical – take it from one who knows! . . . I firmly believe you have the capabilities, courage and determination to launch a most unusual and exciting show –

and it would be a pleasure working with you, Jay. Warm personal regards, as always, Buzz.

There was no doubt Buzz was serious, especially about 'front money', which I did not have, nor could I raise it without a commitment from Vincent Price or interest from a legitimate Broadway producer. I sent the script to Ed Padula, the only producer I knew, letting him know Price was interested. Meanwhile, Berkeley was sitting it out in Palm Desert waiting for a word from me. Another letter from him: 'I have read *Dearest Dracula* again, a couple of times . . . As I told you, I think it has terrific possibilities, with a little fixing . . . a horror musical to begin with is exciting and back this up with some extremely imaginative and creative stagecraft, you have one hell of a show.'

Padula was interested. I made plans to go to New York and have Buzz meet us there for an initial conference. Everything was on go. It wasn't difficult to convince my original backers that *Dracula* lived.

Then came a letter from Padula's office telling us he had been involved in a serious auto accident. Price called saying he would love to do it, but his schedule was already fixed for the next two years. I stalled Buzz as long as possible, hoping something would turn up. I finally had to level with him – the project was dead. I didn't have the heart to tell him that maybe the whole idea was crazy to begin with. When George Hamilton played a prancing Dracula in the hit film *Love at First Bite*, I thought of how close I had come to fulfilling two of my favourite fantasies – pumping life into something that was already dead and working with Busby Berkeley.

The beginning of 1966 started out with an invitation from the Cooks to dinner with Paul McCartney. Fran and I couldn't understand why the Cooks would ever do a thing like that. Former pop-singer turned actor, Paul Jones gave us the answer: 'You two are closer to being "niggers" than anyone they know in London'. The invitation caused a flutter around the house. Even Cosmo, who kept a close watch on our descent into folly, was impressed. Miles was speechless. Fran's problem of what to wear was nothing compared to mine – how to avoid talking about myself!

Before dinner, to show Paul we weren't your ordinary, middle-aged Beatniks, Wendy showed him the original cast album of *The Nervous Set*. The temptation to explain its plot was overwhelming. As Paul studied Jules Feiffer's caricature of a Beatnik on the album cover, I remained silent, giving him the opportunity to read the sleeve notes and reflect on my contribution to American folklore. 'That's — ' Paul stumbled for words while my heart skipped a beat. 'That's, ah,' he began again, 'a nice drawing,' handing it back to Wendy. I was reminded of Akim Tamiroff's line when being tortured in *For Whom the Bell Tolls*: 'I will not provoke!'

We moved down to the kitchen. Word had evidently got around Hampstead that a Beatle had been caught. Before we finished the first course, the local fans had caused an obstruction. The scene was reminiscent of pre-French Revolution days when the hungry masses beat on the windows of the rich, demanding food. The only difference was that this mob was demanding autographs. Fran told the embarrassing story of my experiences with autograph hounds in St Louis. 'Frankly, I wondered why he signed so many until a friend told me Jay's secret. He used to say to the innocent passer-by who happened to make eye contact, "I suppose you want my autograph too?"'

When we moved on to a disco in St James's Place, it was a surprise to realize his presence attracted so little attention. Nobody came over to the table for his autograph, Peter Cook's or even mine. A tall, rather sad figure came over to Paul, and stood there silent and motionless as if paying some kind of Buddhist homage. Paul greeted him by name. When the stranger left, Paul told us what a good musician Long John Baldry was. 'If we hadn't come along, Baldry would have probably been the next big star.'

When Wendy and I were on the dance floor, and Peter was involved elsewhere, Paul and Fran began to build a pyramid of glasses while talking about the songwriting game. He confided to her that he and John Lennon wanted to write the kind of songs Bob

Dylan wrote, but that their record company was being difficult. The pyramid grew to Olympian heights. He whispered the lines of a song he was working on about a girl named Eleanor Rigby. As he got to end of the lyric, the pyramid came crashing to the ground. A waiter rushed over to the table, took a look at the wreckage, bowed and said, 'That's quite all right, Mr McCartney. Would you like another drink?'

At closing time, we all moved out to our cars. It's hard to believe that a Beatle could be lonesome, but what other reason was there for Paul to ask, 'Where to now, Jay?' When I said, 'I don't know about you, but I'm going home,' Fran gave me a kick that could have seriously damaged my manhood if it had connected. She told the boys about it the next morning. I don't think my family ever forgave me for trying to get some much-needed sleep that night. But Paul did. At a Soho restaurant, where I was entertaining Fran's brother, Sam Deitsch, Paul stopped by the table to say hello. Sam, impressed, thought I had set the whole thing up for his benefit. It reminded him of the old joke about the guy who hounds Sinatra to come by his table and ask to meet his wife; when he does, he tells Sinatra to 'fuck off'. The temptation was great, but I'm glad I didn't, because years later, when I sent Paul an advance copy of Fran's verse *Is It Overcrowded In Heaven* for a blurb, he sent the shortest one in Christendom: 'Great!' We have not seen him again, which is a shame; we could have told him that he owned the music publishing rights to *The Nervous Set*.

Next time, when John and Cynthia Lennon were the guests, Wendy didn't supply a background for us, which must have left Lennon with the impression that we were a straight middle-aged couple who happened to be the Cooks' house guests and therefore had to be invited. The dinner was not a relaxed affair. He was uptight about Wendy's insistence that he sample her *salade Niçoise*, a dish he was highly suspicious of and couldn't pronounce. Christopher Logue irritated him even more by demanding to know why the Beatles wouldn't play a *Private Eye* benefit to raise money for a libel action they had lost. 'I'd rather give you the money than play a benefit,' was Lennon's reply. There was no way I could get to know him, but my heart went out to his wife Cynthia. 'Look,' she said, excited as a child, 'isn't it wonderful how John and Peter are communicating!'

Later, at the same disco, I thought there was nothing I could do to get John's interest until I began to dance with Cynthia. We danced in such an abandoned manner, we managed to catch Fran's attention. 'He's not a bad dancer for an old man,' she said to John, who obviously caught my act, and replied: 'He's not bad even for a young one. I couldn't do that in a million years.' We never saw John again, but having dinner with two Beatles was certainly rich enough for anyone's fruit cake of memories.

My career was going slowly down the drain, but Fran's was bubbling. When Steve Lawrence's single of *The Ballad of the Sad Young Men* hit *Billboard's* Easy Listening chart, her New York publishers wrote asking what they could do to help her career. 'Give me a contract and $200 a month advance against future royalties, fix me up with some new collaborators and I'm yours,' she wrote back. They agreed to everything and even promised more. 'When I think of how your career was mishandled, it brings tears to my eyes,' publisher Larry Coleman told her. It was a relief that somebody in the family was finally bringing in money on a regular basis, other than Miles's income from a paper round and my occasional cheque for newspaper articles.

I was still feeling the scars of the *Dracula* experience, but I decided they were the last scars I was going to get. 'Making it' had become less important to me than it was to Fran. Success was something I only wanted a taste of, not the whole cake. We used to have insane arguments about it back in the States. 'Don't knock it unless you had some,' she used to snap when I belittled success. It wasn't meant to hurt, but it always did. Her attitude had mellowed since coming to London. 'Yeah, it's too bad we can't just enjoy ourselves without it, but let's give it another try. Once we've had it, we can put it down with authority.' My only consolation was that London was the right place to be a failure in.

Fran spent her mornings asleep in her womblike room, but by the afternoon she would begin her writing chores, which occupied her until dinner. I kept busy watching the prize-winning dahlias grow in our park and making friendly gestures to the old age pensioners' dogs. Once in a while I'd chat with the meths drinkers, but I never drank any of their cider lest the neighbours suspect I had finally joined their ranks. Instead, I did the next best thing – I joined the newly opened Playboy Club. (Membership fee was only £15.) The first person I took to lunch there was my bank manager, a jazz enthusiast who kept a close watch on our careers. The fact that I knew Annie Ross kept our relationship alive. He and his wife came to one of our New Year's Day parties with an open mind and an Irish thirst. I took great pleasure introducing him to Annie Ross, who later told me he was a very interesting guy. Both of them told me how much they enjoyed the evening and what a treat it was to meet so many interesting people. We stayed friends as he moved to the higher levels of the Royal Bank of Scotland. He made it to the top and, when the offices moved to London, the first thing he did was to invite me to lunch with him in the directors' room. Neither of us had changed a bit.

We were in for a big change when, in April 1966, Fran's father died. For the first time since we left the States we were financially secure, temporarily. I continued to write the occasional article of 'lasting insignificance' for my paper; the fire of the original copy had died down by now.

When the Art Destructionists invaded London for three days, your reporter was on the scene covering the 'relationship existing between aggression and destruction in society and the destruction in Art'. After three days of watching them blowing up empty buildings, throwing acid on canvases, burning towers of books, pulverizing typewriters, crushing automobiles, setting fire to a huge pin-up of Robert Mitchum ('I feel cleansed,' screamed a pretty girl as Mitchum went up in smoke), I was beginning to get into the swing of things. I watched the Viennese artist Muench skin a dead lamb; I can't say it was an edifying experience. Neither did the police, who charged Otto Metzger, one of the organizers of the event, with 'offences against society'. I felt like volunteering to be a witness for the prosecution, but I ended up a witness for the defence, out of loyalty to Art.

'Destruction has no place in society – it belongs to our dreams; it belongs to art,' was American artist Ralph Ortiz's excuse. He asked me during a lull in activities, 'Like, man, do you have a piano around the house I could wreck?' We did have the piano on which the music to *Dearest Dracula* had been written; I wouldn't mind the sacrifice. His mouth watered at the sight of the old scarred upright. 'Let's have a party and invite a couple of curators around from the Tate. They'll appreciate an historic art event.' With the help of Miles's mates, we got the piano stuck halfway down the steps to the basement, where we had planned to stage the event. It wouldn't budge. We had to carry on with it wedged where it was.

Two gay curators arrived, slightly apprehensive at what they might find. Never did they expect to see a six-foot-four, handsome Puerto Rican American greeting them at the door with an extended axe, an infectious smile, and a short printed statement on the New Aesthetic:

I have been destroying things for six years and find that it is truly the essential break with tradition. Art has always been the business of making something, whether of this world or nether worlds. Very few artists today are inspired to acts of naughti-ness. Many naughty images have been created, but very few artists employ daemonic acts as a means to their art. To destroy is the only act civilization abhors. It is the only process of which civilization is in awe. Think of all the ritual, religion and sport that spring from and have at their core the act of destruction. Here in the United States we have a destruction stock car derby. Cars crash into each other until all but one are demolished, the surviving car wins. It's an unbelievable sight. Buddhist immola-tions in Vietnam are the most religious destructions to have occurred in recent history. I feel that underlying Destructivist Art there is the aesthetic of both the destruction derby and the immolation. RALPH ORTIZ.

Ortiz has the event wired up for sound, with Miles at the controls. Drinks are passed around. Ortiz checks his weaponry: a Boy Scout hatchet, a heavy-headed sledgehammer and a regula-tion fireman's axe. He strips to the waist; he begins his descent into 'benevolent violence'. The striking of the axe against the wood, wires and metal produces a frightful cacophony. One of Miles's mates, who came late, thinks it must be a new rock group, rehearsing. 'Isn't it beautiful,' one of the curators exclaims, and I know he's not referring to the music. 'Yes, and what a magnificent stroke,' says the other. As pieces of wood and metal fly around the stairway, Ortiz keeps up a running commentary on his struggle 'to give a moral parable to destruction.'

'Each axe swing unmakes this made thing called a piano. Each destruction unmakes my made relationships to it. It is no longer for playing; it is no longer beautifully designed or ugly . . .'

As he hacks away on the ivory keys, the men from the Tate are caught up in Ortiz's personal 'voyage toward individual salvation'. I seem to be undergoing a personal exorcism of any bourgeois tendencies I might still be harbouring. When it is over, people file past the remains as if at a funeral, viewing the deceased for the last time. 'The piano never looked so good,' I said to Ortiz, who returned a wicked wink. Ortiz called his 'masterpiece' *Piano Destruction Concert, Number 8* and left his phone number with the awed Tate curators.

The next day, for an encore, he disembowelled a large mattress. It ended up looking like a monstrous horse-hair vagina. 'Big Alice' hung over the hearth without incident until Victor Lownes, on seeing the biggest 'cunt' in the art world, sent his art expert Barry Miller for a serious aesthetic appraisal. Negotiations for possession began. The price was fixed at £500. I balked at letting him try it out on approval but said that in his case, if he gave me a £50 administration fee and drayage, I'd make an exception. Although I hated to see it go, the idea of 'Big Alice' being a part of the Playboy collection of erotic artifacts appealed to my sense of history.

Word came through Barry Miller that the Bunnies couldn't stand the competition and had asked Victor to 'shift it'. Charlie Kasher wanted to buy it, if the Tate would accept it for their collection. He was told it was rejected on the grounds that it might become a health hazard. I found a place for 'Big Alice' in the garden, where she remains, deteriorating somewhat from lack of attention, a problem I was not unfamiliar with at the time.

CHAPTER FIVE

By 1967 Swinging London was turning into Raving London. In King's Road on a Saturday afternoon it seemed that everybody was in some kind of uniform left over from the Hertfordshire Regiment, auditioning for a part in *The Chocolate Soldier*. 'I Was Lord Kitchener's Valet' and 'Granny Takes a Trip' were favourite haunts of these rich, beautiful people. I wondered about the psychology behind Britain's new kinky army. Was it a nostalgia for Britain's days of imperial glory or were they trying it on for *sighs*? In Parlia- ment, Lord Ailwyn delivered a fiery speech in defence of tattooing. 'Don't let us become too sissy,' he begged his fellow Lords.

UFO was a basement club in Tottenham Court Road which gave a new dimension to the word 'Underground'. Once a week from 10.30 pm to 6 am there was the new, shattering sound of Pink Floyd, Soft Machine and the Sadie-May antics of Mick Farren's Social Deviants. Liquid light shows were projected on the walls and the half-naked bodies of the blissed-out dancers threatened to become a new art form.

Anthony Lewis, London-based reporter for the *New York Times*, claimed London was on the road to perdition. Billy Graham, preaching to record crowds in Britain, agreed. A correspondent from *Izvestia* defended England. 'What is decadence?' he asked. 'It is when a young boy meets a young girl and, instead of kissing her, begins to discuss the weakening of the pound.' He liked Britain's new look, even if it made the other critics anxious. The *Observer* correspondent John Crosby was an exception. He blasted the *New York Times* for its puritanical stand. 'It's very thorough at wars, famines, pestilence, but it has always reported on the amenities of good living with a lack of charm and, one might say, a complete absence of conviction.' The British press and television were obsessed with the subject. New books, lightweight and serious ones, poured forth weekly, dissecting the Anatomy of Britain to the last knuckle.

Once again your now ageing reporter was at the scene. Interviewing a cherub-faced teeny-bopper who must have been pushing sixteen and who was wearing a 1930s silver fox stole, I was taken aback by her directness. 'Listen, mate, I may not know what I'm looking for, but ever since I've been fourteen I felt there was something more to life than what I was getting in the convent.' I asked what was bugging her. 'Old folks. I'm under tension from old folks.' It was right after this interview that this 'mate' bought his first pair of plastic leather trousers (made in Singapore). I knew I had made the right decision when I wore them to meet BBC producer Julian Holland at El Vino in Fleet Street and was refused service. I was forty-seven years old, but slipping back to childhood fast.

Our house was declared an open living-room. Friends from America, friends passing through to Europe, friends of friends, friends met the night before, friends we'd forgotten we'd had gave the house the atmosphere of a Feydeau farce. The children never knew what to expect when they came down in the morning, and sometimes neither did we. Unidentifiable bodies that had crashed out on the mattress-sofas the night before had to be sorted out by noon. People who made us laugh, who brought their own dope or who were capable of changing our lives were welcome to stick around. Others were asked, 'What are your plans?'

Cosmo's terror at our descent into hippydom became obvious. We were proving to be an embarrassment. So sensitive was he to our behaviour that, when asked about his parents, he'd say they 'died in a plane crash'. Years later he wrote about our decline and fall in the *Literary Review*:

All well and good. A bout of youthful Bohemianism and experimentation is to be expected. Getting married, having children was their one attempt to live conventionally. It did not last. They soon abandoned the straight and narrow for the crooked and the carefree. By the time Flower Power came around, they were in the twilight world of middle-age. Their hair became longer, their dress became wilder, the drugs got stronger and marriage became more experimental. Children are by nature conservative; they want to have parents like other parents. I tried to get them to stay at home more instead of rushing round to the pop festivals, and I warned them about the friends they ran around with. The thing that upset me the most was their dress and appearance. I can remember when I first thought of having them committed to the Institute for the Criminally Dressed. It was Parents' Day at school. They arrived looking like two hippies who had failed the audition for the musical *Hair*. Mother wore a purple-dyed Afghan coat that from a distance looked like a seasick piece of mutton. She was wearing enough bits of glass beads and jewellery to resemble Brighton beach after a bank holiday rumble. Dad came with his long hair, mirror-lens sun glasses: the *pièce de resistance* of this visual cacophony was not the orange rudiments of a shirt, but the black plastic trousers. In those days the only people who wore them were industrial workers and the insane. My classmates stared in disbelief as I shrivelled in horror. Now that the embarrassment has abated, some twenty years later, I can laugh at it all.

Miles felt differently about us; he didn't mind our getting down to his age-level. When he brought one of his mates home to find Fran in a bikini getting some sun, his friend told him, 'Your Mum doesn't look like a Mum. She looks like a gorgeous bird.'

The link between Pop Art and pop music was going to the Tate Gallery to see the latest 'destructions' in the day and ending up watching The Who destroy themselves at the Marquee that night. But nobody back in 1959 would have dreamed there was any connection between Pop Art and Pop Tailoring. In that year, back in St Louis, *The Nervous Set* was heading for Broadway. Pop artist E. T. Trova suggested that I should have something special to wear to the première. He wanted to combine the look of the Hollywood gangster with the archetypical Englishman, Trevor Howard. It took twenty fittings, two virtual nervous breakdowns, one master tailor and three assistants, eight yards of pin-striped cloth, thirty buttons – including those on the fly – and blood, sweat and tears to make the suit. The show and the suit were both ahead of their time, but the suit was more successful than the show, which closed after twenty-eight days. I brought the suit to England, hoping to leave it to the nation some day.

I mentioned all this to Pop anarchists Roger Law and David King, editors on the *Sunday Times* magazine. They were known as the 'bad boys' on the magazine, but their work was so highly respected that they could get away with anything. When they talked of doing a feature on the suit, I thought they were really pushing their luck, but I was wrong. Fashion editor Meriel McCooey thought it would be 'great fun' and hired the fashionable photographer Duffy for the photos. It *was* great fun sending up the fashion world with a serious display of 'Tailoring of the Absurd'. To commemorate the occasion, Roger, who was to continue sending up the nation with his *Spitting Image* puppets, presented me with a three-dimensional collage of a photo of me wearing the suit and his painting of Trova, looking very self- satisfied.

Other days were spent roving London on my 50cc Suzuki in search of material for future articles. I had used up Swinging London and was looking for something with a little human interest. One morning, in Covent Garden, I noticed a young girl begging for food from the stall-holders. I discovered it wasn't for her, but for an organization she worked for called The Simon Community, a mission for misfits. She turned out to have one hell of a story. She was a twenty-one-year-old American, who worked up to sixteen hours a day to help keep the shelter open. She earned £2 a week, plus a tobacco allowance. Once a week, late at night, she operated a soup kitchen for homeless men whose permanent address was Waterloo Bridge. Another night she gave out clothing to helpless meths drinkers in deserted houses. In between, she ran the office and tried to bring some kind of order to the community project that was down, but not out.

I tagged along with her to see for myself if there was such a thing as an American saint in London. Mary Ruddy introduced me to the founder of the Community, Anton Wallich-Clifford, a former parole officer. 'The best way to help drop-outs is to get down to their level of existence,' he said. 'One must suffer the agonies and humiliations they have to suffer. Only by so doing will you ever gain a misfit's trust.' A tour through the house proved his point: old men in soiled clothing, living out their lives in quiet resignation; a schizoid young artist, rejected by clinics and society; a teenage drug addict mysteriously arrived and departed. Nobody asked questions. There was even gallows humour. An aging thief, who had spent all his adult life in jails, now stole only from the inhabitants of the house. 'Harry, have you seen my good sweater?' asked Mary. 'Oh, yes, dear. You'll find it under my bed.' Harry was pleased to have been caught.

Mary talked of the problem she had with her visiting parents, who took one look at her skid-row environment and begged her to come home. 'There's a lot of work to do in America too,' they said. Mary had an answer for me, but I don't think it would have satisfied her mother. 'Sure, I could get my degree and a legitimate job, but there are a lot of people in the States who are willing to do just that. Nobody wants to help these people. You don't get any credits for this course.' When we parted, she asked me if anybody out there was listening. I left her with the promise that I'd write her story. I didn't have the heart to tell her that I didn't think anyone was listening.

I read recently that The Simon Community was still going stronger than ever and still had a 'Mary Ruddy' who was now getting £12 a week and no tobacco allowance.

There was a different kind of American girl in London at that same time, who also worked with 'misfits'. Nineteen-year-old Suzy Creamcheese had come from California to turn on London to Happenings. She was a graduate of the Frank Zappa Mothers of Invention Charm School and a genius at public relations. In

London, her performances were well attended by fans, television cameras and the press, and occasionally by the police. At her Piccadilly Circus Happening, three Susy Creamcheesettes, chained to lamp-posts with toilet paper, unfurled posters declaring POT IS FUN and LEGALISE SUZY CREAMCHEESE. The police stood around asking if the Happenings had happened yet. Only when Suzy started to hand out apples did the police take an interest. As the first apple-core was tossed into the fountain, the police stepped in and staged their own Happening. 'Right,' they said, 'we've seen enough,' as they chased Suzy and her 'ettes' up Shaftesbury Avenue.

The twenty-four-hour Technicolor Dream was happening at the Alexandra Palace. There was the *International Times* (*IT*) to keep the Underground informed of past events and current abuses. Indica's bookshop wrapping-paper was designed by Paul McCartney. Better Books on Charing Cross Road was burning stacks of books in the fight against 'verbal pollution'. Yoko Ono hosted a thirteen-day do-it-yourself Dance Festival. 'Send £1. If you don't have £1, send £1's worth of flowers and thirteen stamps,' she wrote on her flyer. *Macbeth* was at the Theatre Royal, Haymarket, 'Joseph Goebbels couldn't have done better,' wrote Herbert Kretzmer. (I thought it was brilliant, but that's only because I'd never seen *Macbeth*.) People began to take hair-stylists seriously. A Magic Theatre opened in Camden Passage. Oxford held its first 'legalize pot' rally. Mickey Mouse watches were selling at a premium. Elizabeth Smart threw a party at the Roundhouse for the paperback publication of *By Grand Central Station I Sat Down and Wept*.

One opening at the Robert Fraser Gallery was as star-studded as a West End first night. Marlon Brando was there looking intently at the paintings. For years I'd heard Fran recall having found herself sitting next to him at a Greenwich Village party when they were both young and being so stunned by his 'beauty' that she was unable to utter a word. I introduced them and once again she was dumbfounded. She couldn't even acknowledge the introduction. I quickly covered the gap. 'What do you think of the paintings?' I asked Brando. He was silent for what seemed like ages. 'The elephant is slow to mate,' he finally mumbled. Neither Fran nor I recognized the quote from D. H. Lawrence's animal poems, but we realized he was 'undecided'. Fran's obsession lasted until Hollywood director Paul Mazursky told her, 'I saw Brando the other day. He's gotten as fat as Orson Welles.' It was good news to Fran. 'I don't have to worry about that any more,' she wrote in a poem about him that night.

Being without a project, I was open to suggestions. An American stockbroker in the City who had heard of my entrepreneurial past contacted me. He was starting a disco in Covent Garden based on the Underground formula of mixed media, 'only this one is going to be for grown ups,' he said, proudly. I immediately recognized him as an American casualty of Swinging London. He already had the mistress, the E-type Jag, the wife, the children, and the money. All he needed was some 'youth cred' to complete his mid-life crisis. He also wanted an Artistic Director to save his project, which was a terrific idea if you were in love with failure.

The Electric Garden was in the last stage of construction. A quick estimate of what it must have cost staggered the imagination; I could see it was already dated before it was finished. As he poured out his troubles, I began to feel sorry for him. He didn't have a clue what to do about the place once it was finished. He had hired some straight people who had experience in running discos to manage the place, but he wasn't crazy about the kind of entertainment they were planning. I told him his only salvation was to go for something that nobody else was offering, not even the legitimate Underground. Talking to many of the artists who had taken part in the Art Destructionists symposium, I discovered they were real hams whose need to perform was their motivating force. Why not take their act out of the galleries and the streets into this new kind of environment? That it was a mixed-media disco only added to the challenge of performing for hundreds of people a night. It would be innovative, daring and publicity-friendly. Both the artists and the stockbroker agreed. 'I can get you the kind of performers that know how to freak an audience out, but in the name of ART. That's what people want today,' I assured him. He bought the idea hook, line and sucker. The idea even appealed to me. The pay – £200 a week for the Artistic Director – was also attractive.

The club's name lent itself to promotional possibilities. I furnished the copy: 'Plug in to the Electric Garden. Projections, immodest patterns, tricky extensions, hard-edge ravishings, nourishments, belly timber – refreshing the inner YOU. Elevations, swellings, events, non-events, vital fixes. All thirst problems lovingly solved.'

As chief switcher-on, I charged forward with annihilating press releases:

The Electric Garden announces a series of summer environmental entertainments on Sunday nights . . . Warp-In-Rites will probe areas of contemporary tensions . . . Rope (a study in bondage); Coloured Tape (interlocking envy problems) . . . Drag-It-On-Home-Baby (a psychedelic drag show); Books (a physical fitness programme for diary devotees) and Concert (visual trickery incorporating non-musical instruments).

On Sunday 16 July, nine artists will present 'Fused', an evening of shattering experiences. 'Fused' will include a Neon ballet, spontaneous harangues (four speakers from Hyde Park Corner), visual dialogues based on recently discovered medieval texts, electronic confessions, surprise sound and machines, and hate-waves based on audience paranoia . . .

'Night Life Sensation', 'Pop Underground Surfaces in West End', 'Covent Garden Goes Electric' were just some of the headlines we made before the place even opened. Opening night lived up to them. Tom Mangold and a television crew for the BBC made a big impression recording the historic event. By the end of the night, there was a lot of talk about life, liberation, art and love as people drove off in Ferraris and E-types.

The opening week's programme included art destructionists John Latham, Mark Boyle and Jeffrey Shaw. For drama, there was *The Crazy World of Arthur Brown*, Sam Gopal, and The Pineapple Truck, the group from Cambridge 'with the highest IQ in Pop'. When the real Underground came in the next night, attempting to sell their mouthpiece, the *International Times*, they were told by the professional bouncers hired without my approval to, 'Get out, we don't want that bloody newspaper in here.' I had invited them to set up a stand and sell their paper, and offered them dual membership, being convinced that you couldn't bar the real Underground from the pseudo-Underground without courting disaster. I was overruled. 'We don't need them,' the owner said. I told him that was his second mistake; hiring me was the first. I insisted that the bouncers go, but he liked the idea of a well-run place.

As predicted, an article appeared in the next issue of their paper with an attack on the club, but it was nothing compared to the attack on Yoko Ono's debut at the Electric Garden. Everything was going smoothly. Yoko sat on a platform, bound in surgical gauze, and invited people to cut little pieces off in an attempt at 'mass communication'. It was very quiet, with a few people from the audience responding to the challenge. Under the impression that she was 'communicating' love vibes, Yoko made love noises for about five minutes and then screamed for another five. Most of the audience were fascinated, but some weren't. When they began to hurl abuse her way, the managers lost their cool – they demanded I stop Yoko's act. I refused. She continued to scream as the guests took sides, creating a scene out of *Metropolis*.

The electrician killed her microphone. The DJ cut in with loud music. I encouraged Yoko to continue screaming. 'Good background music. You've got the place jumping at last,' I said enthusiastically. Her husband, Tony Cox, rushed to the tape deck to cut the blasting music. He was grabbed by the manager and bouncers, dragged to a corner and thrown on the floor, and was about to be pummelled when I arrived. I told Cox to announce to the audience what had happened. 'This club is run by gangsters,' he hollered into the mike. 'Will somebody call the fuzz?'

The audience lapped it up, thinking it was all part of the show. Yoko was still screaming, helpless in her bondage. Order was restored when she stopped. She and Tony were bewildered at the turn of events. At midnight the police arrived. Tony and the manager were having a shouting match not unlike Yoko's performance, 'life imitates art'. I tried to cool the scene. Yoko's and Tony's demands for payment were refused. They left. When I confronted the owner and manager, I was fired. By 2 am, after a serious discussion about the future of the club, I was reinstated with complete control over artistic matters.

I called Tony and Yoko the next morning to tell them the people responsible for the attack had been fired. I promised to drop by with some grass to soothe their hurt nerves.

In the next issue of *International Times* there was an attack by Judy Gems:

> What the fuck is happening on the scene? Where do the real threats emerge from? No, baby, that was yesterday's naivety . . . there are bad, evil, vibrations with the scene, which, if not blocked, may just blow the whole thing apart . . . the explosion at the Electric Garden exposed a group of hard cash-gangsters whose sole intention is to cash in to exploit known artists on the scene, and yourself, the audience. How did this come about? Who scored? Wake up, Jay Landesman, you're the connection.

Yoko Ono wrote her version of the story, incorporating a defence of her appearance there:

> People said I should have known that it was a bad scene. Listen, baby, to me, any scene can be a bad scene or a good one. I don't have any preconception as to what scene is in or out. All I know is that I had a thirst for a beautiful scene. People long for things like that and it's never enough . . . there is talk that my art was defamed, and I should make a court case out of it . . . as far as I'm concerned those were not the most regrettable things that happened that night and later. Let's not throw bad vibrations at each other. Let's all be beautiful together. Let's.

The lights went out at the Electric Garden soon after. Reconnected as Middle-Earth, without the art and without the stockbroker, but with a new Artistic Director, it became the new headquarters of the Underground and a big success. So far my record was one hundred percent *projectus interruptus*.

CHAPTER SIX

'You've come just in time,' I told John Clellon Holmes on his first visit to the Angel. 'I'm going through a very social phase.'

He had just come from a tour of Yeats territory, and was ready for some partying. Fuelled by a martini lunch, I pored over my address book. Christine Keeler was out. William Burroughs couldn't come till next Tuesday. Director Tom O'Horgan, who once played ancient instruments at the Crystal Palace, was involved in rehearsals for *Futz*. Annie Ross was singing in a jazz club in Manchester. The Cooks, Alan and Nancy Brien, and Yoko Ono were tied up, but not together. Michael Andrews, Jeremy and Eleanor Brooks were the only friends available – not counting the notorious foul-talking parrot, George, who came in on the shoulder of Heather Smyth and an American girl I didn't know who was worried about the evil of the 'Giant Universal Computer'. By this time the wine bottles were lined up like dead soldiers and the room was as foggy with smoke as the street outside.

Irwin and his Magic Theatre troupe showed up with his wife and three tripping acid-heads dressed in Edwardian gear. Their heads moved back and forth trying to follow the conversational ball; they looked like stoned anthropologists watching a tennis match. Irwin broke silence by declaring he was going to Ischia as soon as he finished his joint. His wife was more upset with her sagging hose than his news. Peter Cook called back to say he still couldn't come.

Weston Gavin arrived with the news that singer Mama Cass had been busted in Southampton with her boyfriend. I spent the next hour trying to get in touch with them. Cass could always be counted on to liven things up.

Two days later she arrived in a chauffeur-driven Daimler limousine, which gave us some reverse street cred. We knew Cass long before she was a member of the Mamas and Papas; she'd auditioned for the Crystal Palace years ago. I thought she was a very hip chick then, more ambitious than Fran, and twice as hungry. 'I'm going to be big,' she told us at the time. I had no doubt she would be. With her talent, plain looks and gross figure, she had a glamour that was attractive to men who dig distortion. Now she was sitting at our table, eating Fran's famous chopped chicken liver and peeling a tangerine, while getting a foot massage from her aspiring rock star boyfriend. I couldn't help but grab the camera to record the cosy scene. 'You can't take a picture of me in this setting. I'm a teenage idol. What will my fans think?' I snapped the picture as she did her 'glamorous' pose for her fans.

Filling us in on the story of her break-up with the group, she revealed an unexpected side of her character. 'We got on each other's nerves. John [Phillips] kept mouthing groovy tidbits like, "Cass, you're not listening to the Distant Trumpets any more".' I often wondered why she had listened to them in the first place; now a solo success, it was obvious she had only rented her talent to the rock scene on a record-to-record basis. She became quite philosophical. 'Well, shit, man, we had a symbiotic relationship, trying to become a real group, to think alike, but our emotional lives got all mixed up with one another.' Fran said that sounded like fun, which Cass did not appreciate. 'It's uncool, it's messy, it's *decadent*.'

Fran took exception. 'You mean you're hung up on monogamy? God, it's all *that* crap that's decadent to me. Because people of our age always assumed that people of your age live by a new and saner morality, a morality that we tried to pioneer, and now – ' she looked disappointedly at Cass – 'that's weird.'

Cass looked crestfallen; she saw us as her show-business parents who could do no wrong. The next time we saw her she was headlining her own show at the Palladium. Her views on sexual behaviour had radically changed. She confessed to Fran that she'd had several affairs since we saw her last. This time Fran was not amused. 'Here I am dieting like mad trying to look glamorous and she gets all the action.' We were all great friends again.

We were Cass's guests at Crockfords for an evening of old-fashioned decadence – gambling and eating. She heard it was my birthday. Ten minutes later, a cake with 'Happy Birthday, Jay' written on it arrived at our table. Even at the exclusive Crockfords, she got the star treatment. I told her how much I liked her style. Fran said how much she admired her show. 'You did enough tap dancing to kill a horse,' she said. Cass laughed and said she had some tickets for Miles.

After the show, Miles went back stage. Cass told him she was going to sing all his mother's songs on her next album. Two days later she was dead. Fran and I felt we had lost a good friend before we'd even known her.

Determined to show Holmes a slice of our London life, we took him to what I hoped would be a wild party at Irwin's 'magic lantern' flat, the top floor of a dilapidated mansion block. Our host, a vision in a black velvet jacket and a silver lamé shirt, took us on a quick tour of the four rooms, which rocked with people dancing, rolling joints and talking gibberish. Holmes decided our host looked like a well-dressed Dormouse at the Mad Hatter's tea party as he pointed out people in various states of frantic imbecility. His wife was still having a problem with her stockings, which were now sagging at the knees. He led us to a special room to see his collection of Beardsley illustrations for *Lysistrata*. He was like a young kid showing off his naughtiness. The place began to fill up with people who had only *heard* about the party; someone was having a bad trip in the bathroom. Holmes gave me one of the incredulous looks I knew so well. 'What is this, Jay, pseudo-hippydom revisited?'

We settled for a small room where someone was demonstrating the magic of his lantern. Drops of oil and water created images of swollen phalluses swimming in a coloured field of sperm. When the lantern lens stuck, the focusing and unfocusing accidentally centred on a magenta dot creating an image of a contracting anus. Like Phil Silvers, it was a hard act to follow.

Even when the movie projector broke down, our host was determined not to let anything spoil the party's spontaneity. His fixed smile did not alter when the fuse blew or someone was sick over the dancers. While we waited for the miracle that would restore sanity, someone fixed the projector. The film turned out to be a ten-minute 1930s French porno classic; it would have seemed almost childish, if it hadn't been so ridiculously French. It opened with grainy frames of a girl masturbating – disjointed cuts of thrashing thighs, begging lips, and then an art deco fucking machine, which the girl was desperately trying to mount. Who should turn up to join her on the ride but a wet-lipped Father Christmas. By this time, Holmes and I were hooked on watching the guests watching each other watching the Father Christmas having his way with the girl.

There were a lot of coughs as the lights went up. A blonde girl wanted to know why porno films never showed blonde pubic hair. A voice from the rear: 'But the details always fascinate me. I mean, the decor was right out of a Max Ophuls room.' I couldn't resist telling them about the porn movie I always wanted to make: 'There's a part for everyone. A young couple are trapped in Madame Tussaud's overnight. The eerie atmosphere arouses their appetite for new sexual experiences. The famous waxwork figures, excited at seeing the couple discharge so much sexual energy, come alive. The orgy begins.'

I suggested various combinations, being very explicit about the action between them. The audience began to respond. 'How about Marie Antoinette being sodomized by General De Gaulle?' A purist in the audience felt that, for historical accuracy, it should be Robespierre. A fat boy, obviously identifying with Khrushchev's figure, suggested Eisenhower do 'naughty things to him for perpetuating the Cold War'. Our host stepped in: 'Leave politics out of this.' His contribution – Jack the Ripper and the Brontë sisters – was too much for some of the guests. Holmes leapt in:

'How about a movie about people planning to make a dirty movie. That's the *real* film. You might even get art-house distribution.'

I confessed that I only wanted to see if a real orgy might come out of the fanciful one. Holmes reminded me that an orgy is only an orgy when it isn't held nightly everywhere by everyone. Our host looked confused. His wife was trying to get her eyebrows unknitted.

The next day I took Holmes to meet somebody sensible – the hair stylist Gary Craze. I'd always had a barber shop thing, having spent a lifetime searching out the perfect one, always ending with the one who had the best conversation. 'Gary's got a line on the whole thing – split ends, teasing, replacing lost body – and is the hippest man in any room.'

After submitting to a sensitive trim, we had artichoke hearts and Frascati at the San Frediana. A promenade down King's Road gave Holmes a peek at London's version of Flower Power. Disappointed, he thought London hippies were less convincing, less original, than the American ones.

'What about their hippy gear? You have to admit it's original,' I said.

Now he was serious. 'If dressing up in hip gear, and sucking the wet end of a badly rolled bomber, and groping the boy or girl next to you could blow a mind, what kind of mind was it?' he asked. He told us Flower Power was on the way out in America, citing the plague of hepatitis in San Francisco.

We went for an afternoon drink at the Queen's Elm, where Holmes had a reunion drink with actor Ben Carruthers, who had once appeared in an experimental play of his in the Village. We had another drink with Eddi at the Kismet. He thought it was a bar for unemployed actors and 'counterfeit Brendan Behans'.

On the back of my Suzuki, I whizzed him off to Jim Haynes's Arts Lab, then under construction. I explained what Haynes had in mind: a theatre, a film room, an art gallery, a disco, and a restaurant all under one roof. Holmes thought it was another of those 'fashionable ideas predicated on the assumption that something might become clear if everyone pooled their separate muddles'.

The Crazy World of Arthur Brown was playing at the Roundhouse. How could he not appreciate a piece of showmanship that began with Brown making his entrance on a high-flying crane and ending his act by setting fire to his hair? He wasn't impressed.

Off to Kentish Town to meet Sally Ducksbury, whose painting I had fallen in love with too. Holmes was impressed by her wallpaper of stark images of sex, war, irony and death; the black mirrors surrounding her bed made him a little uncomfortable. We went on to the Playboy Club, where everything was so air-conditioned and sanitized, including the Bunnies, that we thought we were back in America. Victor Lownes was giving a party for Cy Coleman and Dorothy Fields, whose musical *Sweet Charity* had just opened in the West End. I was wearing a four-inch wide, hand-painted psychedelic tie; Fran, in a fur-trimmed 1920s coat, looked like Zelda Fitzgerald. She introduced herself to fellow lyricist Dorothy Fields, whom she had admired for years. Miss Fields didn't know any of Fran's songs, but Fran saw no reason to revise her opinion; she still considered Fields one of the greats. She retreated to sit out the rest of the party sneaking glances at the 'beautiful' actor Terence Stamp.

Holmes, used to Bunnies with harsh American accents, was momentarily disoriented at hearing so many Liverpool and Manchester ones coming out of the mouths of the same plastic Bunnies. He was also having difficulty balancing canapés and his Jack Daniels in the company of film star Farley Granger, dancer Juliet Prowse, Rolling Stone Brian Jones, a Guinness heiress and people he had no interest in getting to know better. Lownes, the perfect host, introduced Holmes as one of Playboy's 'distinguished writers', and me as the owner of the 'biggest cunt in town', hastening to add, 'Not his wife but a destroyed mattress that looks like one.'

He pointed out a couple who ran orgies in the Temple Bar area. For the next ten minutes we watched them proposition the Token Black, the Ingénue, the Drunken Reporter and assorted Biba Birds, who were being monopolized by the Foot Fetishist. (It looked as if we weren't going to be invited to the 'A' party.) 'God,' said Holmes, well lubricated by the constant flow of Jack Daniels, 'doesn't it seem to you we've spent years in rooms like this? You can taste the salt of boredom in its *hors-d'oeuvres*.'

Holmes had a few more days in London. I had the impression that I had failed him in some way. Everything seemed to be one big *déja vu* experience for him. In the old days he would have laughed at it all. It remained a mystery to me for years until I read his travel essays. Holmes was homesick – for the old ways and the old country. He resented a 'rotting America' in- truding on his pleasures and dreams. I tried a last-ditch effort to make his visit memorable – I took him to the new Yoko Ono exhibition.

The large gallery was much too small for Yoko's enigmatic Zen concepts. One room was filled with 'half things': half a chair, half a shoe, half a bed. Holmes was quite moved by it all, seeing it as the work of a calm mind. In another room, we had to take off our shoes, sit on the floor and watch lights circle for two minutes. Just as we were about to leave, Yoko made an appearance. It had been raining. She looked so helpless and wistful dripping on the floor that half of me wanted to say something and the other half wanted to remain silent. I told her I thought her show compared favourably with her recent attempt to cover the lions of Nelson's column to commemorate 200 years of British indifference. She agreed. Before we left, Holmes was overcome with a feeling of compassion for Yoko. He leaned over and kissed her hand. 'You're a princess who got out of the tower,' he told her. She gave him one of her famous half smiles. I didn't know what it meant until I heard that the night before she had met John Lennon for the first time.

A wave of depression followed Holmes' departure. He made me feel the life I was leading was a complete waste. For years Holmes had done everything possible to keep the Landesman legend alive in the many articles he wrote about the Fifties and the Beats. With the publication of his *Nothing More To Declare*, his portraits of what he called 'representative men' of his generation – Allen Ginsberg, Jack Kerouac, G. Legman, and Jay Landesman – restored my self-confidence. In fact, I said to Fran, 'I would have liked to have met that guy. Too bad he's dead.' The portrait of me was a brave attempt on Holmes's part to explain 'Landesmania':

Whenever I met Jay Landesman in a bar in the old days, I always seemed to arrive first. I waited around, and far from being piqued, I discovered that I was experiencing a pleasant little ping-ping-ping of anticipation. What I was anticipating was laughter . . . There wasn't a proper epigram in him. Nor one of those living-room Berles, machine-gunning everyone with gags. It was that he saw everything on the bias. It was that everything he did had an air of elaborate burlesque about it . . . You laughed at all this. You said, 'Good old Jay, what the hell kind of wild stunt will he pull off next?' You always looked forward to seeing him, and what he pulled off next was always more outlandish than you had anticipated. A million laughs all right. A hip, sardonic mind behind it. No doubt of that. 'Landesmania', his friends called it. A life-style that was a wacky amalgam of Hellzappopin', Theatre of the Absurd, and Pop Art. But serious? You must be kidding . . . and yet there was that damn underlayer to all of it . . . His personal preoccupations had the maddening habit of becoming cultural tendencies ten years later. You never took him seriously at the time, and you were never sure that he did either, and then all of a sudden everywhere you went in New York during the Sixties there was a sort of public version of Landesmania . . . He has been variously described as a 'puppet-master with an aggressive lack of talent; the Mike Todd of dying cities' and 'a genie with a certain sense of merchandising'. There is a bit of truth in all these estimates, but the whole truth is not there . . . I would say that Landesman possessed, years before it was either chic or marketable, what would now be called the Pop Imagination . . . For any and all evidences of a unique and unconventional point of view interested him, and he looked for those evidences in junk shops, movie houses, and news-stands, as well as in bookstores, art galleries and theatres . . . When enlightened people sat in their Eames chairs, under their Calders, talking about T. S. Eliot, Landesman was already living in a thicket of Victorian bric-à-brac, and publishing Allen Ginsberg. He had an omnivorous interest in popular culture, and long before it was High Camp to collect back issues of *Batman* and idolise the horror movies of Tod

Browning, he was publishing articles that anatomized the one, and scouring the most dismal reaches of Brooklyn for screenings of the other . . . Like many of us in the late Forties, he felt that the fine arts were so tyranized by one or another version of the New Criticism that they had become little more than lifeless appendages of it, but, unlike a lot of people in later years, he shifted his attention to the popular arts without sacrificing his sense of culture as a whole . . . Soon he grew bored with hunting the culture's various psychic Snarks; he was not imprisoned by a single perception, and world- changing was not his wine. The trait that had distinguished everything that Landesman had done surfaced in him rapidly, until it became clear that what drove him was an overiding theatrical sense – a sense of how to put a point of view on display, how to isolate a falsehood so that it could be seen, how to reveal a subtle truth through sheer exaggeration . . . To me, Landesman repre-sented a side of my generation, and its experiences, that I have come to fully appreciate as we have all gotten older and less amusing: the game-playing, style-enamoured, pomposity-puncturing side. The side that practiced its 'futility rites' with so much energy, and wit, and unconscious courage. The funny, hip, mordant, nosy, meaningful side. Not the deepest side perhaps, too impatient and too facile, too continually aware of everything to pause for the probe to ultimate causes. But a side that lived intensely up to its times, nevertheless.

A few weeks later, I was still basking in the glow of Holmes' piece when Fran had to go to New York. It was the first time we were to be apart since arriving in London. Neither of us looked forward to the separation, especially since she didn't know how long she'd have to be with her ill mother.

To our surprise, being apart gave us the opportunity to say things in letters we couldn't possibly say in person: 'OK. Let's get down to those letters of yours. My god, I feel almost like one of your lovers instead of your husband,' I wrote. She had only been away about a week. 'I'm so homesick I can't bear it. Jay-sick really, you lovely person. Please let's try to meet each other when I'm home. It's the only real thing, at least you are for me. All the rest is just goofy movie dreams and vanity, vanity, vanity! I love you, I really do.' I couldn't remember the last time she ever told me anything that approximated this feeling. 'When you say, "we've got a lot of talk coming," I almost came. I do love you, you marvellous girl.' She probably couldn't remember the last time I'd told her 'I love you' either.

Her last letter: 'Write me all the news and please tell me you're having a little fun. I don't want to think of you being lonesome. I'd like to think you were getting some writing done and making some new friends so London will be a little more stimulating when I return. I do love you. There's no one here in your league.'

When she returned, we took advantage of the Summer of Love. Picnics at Kenwood on Hampstead Heath, swimming in the Serpentine, flying kites on Primrose Hill with Yoko Ono and her sad-faced little girl. Everybody was singing *All You Need Is Love*. A powerful piece of graffiti, 'Make love not war', made its appearance to everyone's approval. (My old editor at *Neurotica*, G. Legman, was the source of that particular piece of advice which he subsequently regretted.) 'A family that gets high together stays together' was just a joke, but a family that went to pop concerts together had a good time. From the free concert in Hyde Park to three-day festivals on Salisbury Plain, we travelled around in a customized Mini-Cooper that had once belonged to the Rolling Stones' manager, Andrew Oldham. When they saw its POP 69 registration plate, people anticipated that somebody important had arrived. When a middle-aged couple emerged, the cheers from disappointed bystanders turned almost nasty.

While the children were at the concerts at night, Fran and I remained behind, amusing ourselves with impromptu light shows against our tent and trying to make sense out of readings from the Tibetan *Book of the Dead*. These idyllic times came to an abrupt halt after a weekend of torrential rain that seeped into our tent. 'I am now old enough never to have to go to another fucking outdoor pop concert,' Fran declared vehemently.

CHAPTER SEVEN

Often in a volatile marriage, when one partner is up, the other is down. With little on my horizon, I had nothing to be up about. Fran had. Her collaboration with Georgie Fame resulted in *Try My World*, a single record that got the full treatment – *Top of the Pops* and *Juke Box Jury*, where it was given the thumbs up by all the judges – always a bad sign. I liked the record, but thought the music was too soft for the hard-rock marketplace; it sank without trace. Despite the disappointment, the collaboration survived to rise again another day.

A deep feeling of frustration pervaded me. A letter from my brother Fred brought some relief. 'I do still think that all you need to have everything fall into place with deeply satisfying results is for you to write your story.' I'd threatened to do it for years. All my friends from the old days had written their sagas, which gave them recognition and sometimes money. It didn't seem to help them come to terms with real life. They either ended up bored to death teaching at universities like Holmes, or drinking themselves to death like Kerouac. If they were deeply cynical, they worked for *Time* or *Look* like Chandler Brossard and Anatole Broyard. Despite all the options open to them after their initial success, they never seemed to choose one that would improve the quality of their lives. I was still labouring under the romantic notion that living an unstructured creative life was more rewarding than fictionalizing one. Fran said at the time that I was filled with envy, 'suffering those lack-of-recognition blues'. She was right, of course. I didn't think going back into the antique business was the remedy, but at least it was something I could handle.

The antique trade was invented for people who, like myself, had nothing better to do. As a business, it was a safe investment – a hedge against inflation – and, as overheads were low, few dealers ever went broke. Camden Passage was a community of eccentric personalities who lived in the cloister-like atmosphere of a modern Carcassonne. All their desires, passions, frustrations and 'closet' inclinations could be fulfilled within its confines and without social disapproval. To me, the relationships between the dealers were fascinating. After the shops closed, the main business of the day began. In addition to the talk of deals made and of which dealers were in town, the main preoccupation was who was having it off with whom. The local pub was the hot centre for sorting out these romantic entanglements, which gave me the opportunity to assume the role of an Agony Uncle, one which I relished.

I was a familiar figure in Camden Passage, having practically furnished our house from there in the days when bargains were still to be had. The logical next step was to get involved. There was a couple from Norfolk whose shop was only open on market days and Saturdays. Their taste was impeccable, their business methods slightly mysterious, but I didn't care. So what if they weren't the Marquis and Marquise they claimed to be? They were fun to be with; a rich mixture of trade gossip and social striving enlivened their anecdotes. Before I invested money in their enterprise, I did mention it to another dealer in the Passage. 'They're crooks,' she said. 'You'd be better off if you gave the money directly to Bangladesh.' By now I was so determined to get back to my antique roots that I didn't even look at the books or ask for a profit and loss statement. It was enough to see their invoice book filled with Bloomingdale's and Neiman-Marcus purchases.

The arrangement seemed ideal. I would run the shop during the week, draw a small salary and share in the profits. Business was so good, I guaranteed an overdraft for the shop at my bank to cover our increased activity. I doubled the retail trade, confirming that I was still the super-salesman I had been back in St Louis. There were some who thought I was the owner. When I started to do a little buying for the shop, the Marquis began to think so too. To my astonishment, he claimed I was lowering the shop's 'tone' and asked me to leave the buying to them. Even my purchase of a rare nineteenth-century book-binding press annoyed them. When I told them I had sold it at a massive profit within forty-eight hours, they insisted I 'stop the "stock pollution" whatever the cost'. It somewhat dampened my enthusiasm as well as my respect for their business acumen.

Getting out of the partnership proved to be complicated. When threatened with an injunction, they simply moved all the stock to an undisclosed location. When I brought the bailiff to their house to claim their personal property, they became the down-at-heel aristocrats and denied that they had any personal possessions left, the family having lost everything in the French Revolution. Awed by this display of class, the bailiff retreated, apologizing for having disturbed them. I left empty handed, but filled with admiration for the class system in action. The experience did not enhance Fran's opinion of my business methods. 'Face it, Jay,' she said, 'you're a disgrace to your heritage. Whoever heard of a dumb Jewish businessman?'

In my next letter to my mother, I wrote that I was through with the antique business once and for all. 'You'll be happy to know that I'm thinking of going back to school to take up dentistry.'

An invitation to dinner from Cambridge lecturer and fellow American Nathan Silver was my introduction to Cambridge academic life. Silver was the author of Fran's favourite book, *Lost New York*, a photographic essay of the New York she loved and lost. I expected a roomful of musty dons drinking sherry, but it was a small affair, with only George Steiner and poet John Hollander, their wives and us. I knew Hollander from my days in New York, but why Silver would have the esteemed philosopher George Steiner at the same table with us was a mystery. I was apprehensive at meeting Steiner, whose books I had bought for years in an attempt to lend some class to my bookshelves; I even read some of them. 'Ah, Landesman,' Steiner said when we were introduced. 'The editor of *Neurotica*. I remember your magazine well.' Our controversial musings on the decline of the West convinced Silver that we were fellow conspirators, riding on different trains, but towards the same destination.

In checking that particular evening with Silver recently, he confessed there was an element of provocation, if not outright nastiness, in the invitation. 'I had been discussing with a friend about "dramatic contrasts" between people on a social level. The idea of you in a room with George Steiner would prove my point that nothing good could come out of it except a confrontation between two totally different types.' He was a shade disappointed that Steiner and I had foiled his plan.

At another of Silver's invitations I met someone as provocative as Steiner, with a line of intellectual one-liners that clearly marked her for a brilliant future as an academic stand-up comic. Germaine Greer arrived late, drenched from the rain, and then proceeded to strip off her wet blouse – she had obviously burned her bra. Even the women present recognized that quality of uninhibited *chutzpah* she was later to make her trademark. She was beautiful, she was funny, she was smart, and she knew it. After *The Female Eunuch*, the rest of the world knew it too.

We were completely taken by her. When she moved to London, we met occasionally, often in the oddest places. One night, in the Speakeasy, I watched her challenge Jimi Hendrix to an arm-wrestling match, and win. Another time, at a lunch at the Roundhouse, I introduced her to Norman Mailer, who lived to regret the occasion – she later thrashed him in a debate that set a new record for viciousness. She was the champ, or so we thought, until we received a mayday call from her. 'May I spend the night at your place?' she asked in her direct way. 'I'm fed up with my lover. Never want to see him again.' After dinner she became restless, explaining that she was worried about his state of mind, since he'd been tripping when she left him. Would it be all right if she called him? Once connected, the Boadicea of the woman's movement turned into a coy, baby-voiced little girl, offering to return if he was unwell. When she left, it was the first indication that the 'movement' was one thing and needing a man was something else.

Another invitation arrived from Silver. He had been commissioned by Mark Boxer of the *Sunday Times* magazine to do a special on the theory and practice of contemporary party-giving, and wanted my opinions. 'Parties are too serious a matter to be left to the host and hostess. Accordingly, we have summoned experts to guide the amateur through the hazards of the season' was the caption. Silver wrote on the logistics of Partymanship. In collaboration with my friend Jeremy Brooks, I wrote an article on the basic human requirements for a successful party:

Parties come in three forms: small parties, large parties and orgies. The purpose of a large party should be to generate a little more life. The purpose of an orgy is to have an orgy. Excluded are parties for the wrong reasons; celebrations of birthdays, publication days, first nights; the raising of funds or the host's social status; for returning travellers; for departing brains joining the drain; for births, marriages and deaths. No genuine party, large or small, ever survives being dominated by an event to which people may have emotional responses. Non-events, or imaginary events, may be used to provide the excuse for a party, but ideally no excuse should be needed. We all need a little more love, a little more life.

Small parties, which need to sustain a high ecstasy count, must consist largely of intimate friends; yet some little element of extraneous excitement should be introduced. The introduction of a new lover or the unloading of an old one could fill the bill. It could be a proving-ground where there is careful testing of the qualifications of a potential new member by the basic unit's members. Small parties are essentially opportunities for the reassessment of long-standing relationships. At the end of the evening an even richer pattern should emerge from the ruins of the familiar one, without actually being reduced to wrangling about front door keys.

Since the purpose of a large party is to generate more life, it is essential to create a situation in which things can grow. (One of the things that can grow is your reputation as a giver of good parties.) Nothing will ever grow out of a party which consists of all the people you really like plus all your pay-backs. Everyone's address book has a different value on the open market, but for our purpose we must assume one which embraces every possibility; it is, of course, purely symbolic. One man's local councillor is another man's Peter O'Toole. The programming of a guest list requires infinite care, and few marriages can survive it. So here's a guest list that could save your marriage and give you one hell of a party:

Minimum of three potential celebrities; at least one real celebrity (any field); a foolish couple; a serious couple (straight feed for comics); an engineer, or non-speaking Czech (to point out); somebody who moves well (male or female); one beautiful Fascist (to confuse people); six swinging teenagers (girls); a bitchy girl who can generate masochism in men; a gym instructress who drinks too much; an older woman who sits and smiles (who is she?); a ruined beauty (who was she?); Christine Keeler; no fat people, unless Robert Morley, or Peter Ustinov; nobody jet or Court Circular; no dogs; no Peter Hall, Jonathan Miller, David Frost (or equivalents); no crew cuts; a swinging accountant; a buff (a jazz-hair or gambling-buff); two attractive lesbians (to get wrong); one international drug trafficker (to point out); a beautiful flawed couple; a gay MP; one coloured TV personality (if in town); Tariq Ali (not Christopher Logue); an Irish show-business GP; a titled person (to show you're not snobbish); no artists' agents, editors or publishers; no children or head-shrinkers (except R. D. Laing); an eccentric lawyer or priest (no respecters of confessionals); an articulate tradesman (electrician, cabinetmaker, house painter, bank manager); a forgotten culture hero; a reliable loudmouth who'll come early and leave early; the ex-wife of a world celebrity; a pop singer no one recognizes; a girl with buck teeth, a corrective shoe, or both; a girl in a twin-set and pearls (to sneer at); an established figure who decides that night to drop out . . .

Working a room is an essential technique of both party-giving and party-going. As a guest, the timing of your entrance must be judged with precision; never come so early that you blow your best material nor so late that all the good roles have been taken. In breaking down the barriers between people, a creative approach is one that gives rather than asks for help. 'Let me get you a drink,' is better than nothing; but how much further the new relationship is carried with, 'I've seen your haunted face all over town. I think I can help you.' Everyone needs help at a party. Even the dedicated bore needs release from his own obsessions. People trapped in negative roles can be released to a new freedom by a good opening first line. Since you're not necessarily out to form lifetime relationships, learn to lie a lot. 'I need your advice – I've just inherited a fortune and can't cope with the guilt problem. Can you help me?' Never try to move in on a working unit; find one that is dying and make it work, and be willing to die like a dog in the attempt. Sometimes it's even necessary to work a room, or part of a room, past embarrassment through to humiliation; new creative highs have been achieved by someone's willingness to offer himself for public humiliation . . .

It seemed that Fran and I were doing what everybody was doing by the end of the decade – non-stop partying. For me, the best ones had a genuine celebrity to confront, win over or relieve of their deep sense of boredom. They required a party line original in concept, never fawning, modest in approach, and knowledgeable. I was put to the test at a party given by librettist and playright Julian More. The celebrity was Marlene Dietrich, so beloved by us we named our cat after her. I had read somewhere that polishing furniture was one of her favourite pastimes. When introduced to her as 'an American playwright', I quickly confided to her that I knew more about furniture polish than I did about playwriting, a revelation that resulted in a spirited conversation on the comparative quality of brand name polishes. She was momentarily impressed; I held fast to the opinion that Johnson & Johnson was the only polish, in spite of her unwavering defense of an obscure beeswax from Munich. To die sticking to your guns was more heroic than winning prosaically, I told myself, as her interest in me faded.

Victor Lownes's parties were legendary; they aroused great expectations, but seldom lived up to them. They were a perfect vindication of Fran's theory that parties are good in an inverse ratio to the amount of money spent on amenities and entertainment. I remember one 4 July party where vintage planes staged realistic dogfights in the air. As if that wasn't enough, Victor brought over cabaret artist Bobby Short and his trio direct from the Carlyle Hotel in New York. Beloved by America's cabaret world, Short, playing in a tent, was less enthusiastically welcomed by the English Playboy set. Lownes was so upset he was forced to apologize for his guests' rudeness and gave a brief speech about showing some 'respect for an artist'.

However, giving a party with few amenities does not ensure success. It often ends with a clash of personalities. Duke Moscowitz, who was the Diaper King of St Louis – his slogan was 'Rock-a-Dry-Baby' – gave a party in his suite at the Dorchester Hotel over a Bank Holiday weekend and asked me to invite some of my friends. Almost everybody I knew was out of town or unavailable. When I discovered Woody Allen was in London that weekend, I felt an invitation might help him overcome his natural feeling of being abandoned. I knew him well enough to risk a rejection. Duke was on speaking terms with Marcel Marceau, who was also in London, being very quiet. When he and Woody met, only one of them talked – Marceau. Woody sat in a corner wondering what he had done in a previous life that deserved his being held in a garishly decorated suite at the Dorchester Hotel with the Diaper King and a former nightclub owner whom he had once worked for, but had little affinity with.

Perhaps the best party we went to had no amenities at all. It was held in the warehouse of Harmony Foods on a New Year's Eve. Guests were told 'any item of clothing not identifiable as a costume must be checked at the door'.

Our parties were mostly impromptu, but, when friends from America were in town, special rituals had to be observed. When Barbra Streisand and Tommy Smothers of the Smothers Brothers were in London at the same time, we saw a golden opportunity to score a few points in the celebrity sweepstakes. As young unknowns, Barbra and Tommy played the Crystal Palace on the same bill. We used to hang out together in the local drug store, or have hot chili at the Rex Café after the show and talk about our futures. Tommy said he and Dickie couldn't believe they were going to be stars. Barbra had no doubt she was going to be one. My mother wrote on the back of the programme: 'This show got a wonderful reception. The singer is as good as Gypsy Rose Lee. The house just vibrated with laughter and applause. I didn't like it.' During the hot summer days, Fran and Barbra used to catch the Olive Street trolley and go shopping in the air-conditioned department stores downtown to get away from the tropical heat. Like excited schoolgirls, they would try on everything, but buy nothing. Both of them were dressed by Goodwill and Salvation Army charity stores; *Second Hand Rose* might have been written about them.

Now Barbra had arrived in London to repeat her Broadway success in *Funny Girl*. Backstage she told us she wasn't going to do the show that night, as she was feeling too ill from her pregnancy. She didn't want to let us down – she accepted the invitation to our party, but laid down one condition. 'You've got to feed me,' she cried. 'Will there be any food left by the time I get there?' At dinner, Fran cautioned the guests to go easy on the food, explaining Barbra's food anxiety. What worried me more was how all of us would react to a reunion after so many years. Last time together, we had been the big shots and they the struggling artists.

We needn't have worried; the four of us picked up right where we'd left off in St Louis. Barbra arrived in a Daimler limousine with her hairdresser and a ferocious appetite. Fran set stacks of food on the table and watched over her like a Jewish mother as she ate. Barbra couldn't be expected to notice Weston Gavin's late entrance, but she heard his opening line: 'OK, who's the Batmobile waiting for? Speak up, don't be bashful. We're just little people here.' Barbra looked up from her food mountain. 'Who the fuck do you think it's waiting for?'

Later, I asked Tommy whether he thought she had changed much. Did she remember the old days when he was the big local attraction and she used to follow him around everywhere. 'I thought she'd forgotten our little scene,' he said, 'but when I saw her alone, she brought a list of questions about things I had completely forgotten about. I couldn't believe it. It was scary.'

The *kamikaze* party was based on the theory of 'party for the sake of a party'. It didn't matter who gave it, where it was held or who was going to be there, and sometimes it wasn't a party at all, just a few friends looking for a party. Once I fell off a skateboard, broke both wrists, went to the hospital, had them set in plaster and went directly to a party I had heard was just starting. 'Party or die' was the *kamikaze* cry. They were often terrible affairs, but, when reputations were on the line, to miss one was letting the team down and serious *kamikaze aficionados* would rather die than not show.

Breaking the habits of a lifetime was difficult, but, with the help of the law of diminishing returns, I managed to cold-turkey party-going temporarily. Waiting for the phone to ring was no longer a problem. Instead I looked around for more natural foils to divert me. I found myself on a bus to Stonehenge with a group of people who were celebrating the summer solstice. At the time it seemed like the logical thing to do – ring out the old and welcome the new. On the bus were a few familiar faces, but one stood out from the rest – Jordon Reynolds. I had known him from the Underground days, when he was a bouncer at UFO.

Reynolds's act was original, but confined to a one-man guerilla war against the Western diet. 'You are what you eat,' read his T-shirt, and who dared challenge the six-foot-four tower of military menace? He saw himself as a member of the Brigade of the Betrayed, an organization devoted to lost causes. 'After all the worthwhile wars are lost, you either become a religious nut or a nutritional expert. In my diet, you get to be both,' he claimed.

It was the first time I heard the word 'macrobiotic'. On the bus Jordon had a steady spiel of dietary information that he passed on like a guide on the Green Line tour. 'The average person consumes ten times more protein than his body requires . . . food manufacturers know the poor are suckers for their processed, heavily chemicalized, carcinogenic, highly sweetened food . . . they are engaged in genocidal devastation . . .' What all this had to do with 'communing with the stones' escaped me at the time. Stonehenge turned out to be a frame of mind that was difficult enough for me to deal with.

Jordon and I got high at the sight of Stonehenge. Those were the days when sitting among the stones instead of looking at them from a distance, as is required now, gave a sense of 'being at one with the universe'. Jordon and I joined the Druid ceremony to welcome the new season by walking around in a giant circle, holding hands, waiting for the emergence of what the Master Druid called 'The Great White Light'. When it was rather slow in coming, he asked us all to go into reverse, an idea that struck us as hilarious.

I saw a lot of Jordon after our Stonehenge experience. A few pamphlets carefully placed around 'Rice House', as his squat was called, were lethal weapons in his nutritional armoury. Take the one on tobacco: 'Smoking isn't the only cure for cancer'. Another on milk warned of its dangers unless, of course, you were a calf. The founder of macrobiotics, I was told, was a middle-class Japanese, who spent a lifetime experimenting with a variety of oriental herbs to find a drink as satisfying as Scotch whisky. Jordon made light of the fact that he died of heart disease 'caused by extreme frustration and too much alcohol'. If anyone had predicted that I would give up everything I held sacred for a diet, I would have advised them to change psychics. I came from St Louis, a city that won the Quasimodo award for having the highest strontium 90 count in its milk, and the hottest chili this side of Mexico. Neither the city nor I was famous for cuisine. This all changed dramatically under the influence of Jordon Reynolds.

CHAPTER EIGHT

A fter almost six years in London, by 1970 the old pattern of 'too many parties, too many pals' experienced in New York re-emerged, only now there was no going home to mother. All the news from America was bad again. Race riots, urban decay, economic stagnation and Vietnam. How to fill the vacuum left by the demise of the hippy culture? When Fran saw me pacing the floor, she said, 'Why don't you call up Jordon and score some of that food he's always pushing. We'll try it out.' A few days later at a smart meat-eater lunch at Alvaros, I stared at my steak tartare: it looked like it was daring me to make a move. The raw meat on the plate had metamorphosed into a fragment of a Hieronymus Bosch triptych – the part that can't be looked at without killing your appetite for the human race. I couldn't wait to get home to break the news that I had seen the 'white light' of Jordon's 'ultimate truth'.

Resigned to dramatic changes over our years together, Fran watched the new convert throw away everything in the kitchen except the sink. Within twenty-four hours, restocked with traditional oriental and natural foods, stainless steel saucepans, chopsticks and a wok, our kitchen looked like a corner of a budding sushi bar. Fran was prepared for change, but the children were not. They had been dragged across an ocean against their will, and sent to the neighbourhood school against everyone's advice, and now they saw their Coca-Cola, white bread and sweets disappear. They became sullen.

If the Orientals are right about everything changing into its opposite, I was heading for sainthood before the year was out. The children worried. Little did they suspect what their lunch box would contain that fateful spring. I insisted on preparing their lunches according to the new diet: a thermos of hot *miso* soup, two lovingly hand-wrapped seaweed rice balls, tahini brown bread sandwiches with white pickled raddish and chop-sticks wrapped in a damp napkin. Stories drifted back after the first few days: horror stories of brown rice balls being tossed around the Holloway school lunch room by junk-food louts. The *tahini-miso* spread sandwiches proved to be deadly weapons when rolled up into small balls and indiscriminately catapulted through the air. Cosmo accused me of culinary sadism. Adding modest nutritional delights each day reinforced the belief that I was building their character through nutrition.

A whole new life began: it revolved around food. I did all the shopping and some of the cooking. Carried away with my new philosophy, I became a cog in a miniature macrobiotic empire started by the teenage entrepreneurs Gregory and Craig Sams, fellow Americans. They started with a macrobiotic restaurant, progressed to a natural food store, and eventually ran a wholesale distribution company. Natural foods were almost unheard of in those days; even health food stores didn't know about them. I started out as a waiter in their restaurant, rising to salesman and public relations expert, writing features on the glories of brown rice and the joys of seaweed. I felt a deep sense of accomplishment when I sold a cover story to *Fiesta* on the sexual advantages of the diet.

After a hard day at the 'tempura bar' – what we called the office – my social life consisted of sitting around swapping recipes with fellow workers. There were other, less frenzied rewards. I became a consultant to a television company that was creating a series about a health-conscious private eye called 'Mike Macro', who solved his cases through dietary analysis. In health food circles I was known as 'Stan Stunning, the Johnny Apple-seed of the natural foods movement'. A memorable event of the period was having a picture taken in a jacket made of old rice sacks (with the *yin-yang* symbol on the back), showing a package of *kombu* seaweed to the ageless and irrepressible queen of romantic novels, Barbara Cartland, whose interest in health foods was well established.

After a lifetime of struggling for recognition in various fields of endeavour, how easy it was for us to become stars in the natural food world. Fran's apple strudel won the coveted trophy of rosewood crossed chopsticks in the first International Macrobiotic Bake-Off contest. Thereafter she was known as 'Ma Landesman of Apple Strudel fame'. A pitch to the sympathetic John Pilger resulted in a full-page analysis of the event in the *Daily Mirror*. With his tongue firmly in his cheek, the ace foreign correspondent wrote: 'For those unsure of what a macrobiotic bake-off is I can only explain that it is somewhere between a gastronomical revivalist meeting and a miniature of the Denby Dale Giant-Pie Eating Affair . . . The bake-off had drawn ten entries, including a cake resembling a stack of brightly painted motor tyres and a quivering, lurching pyramid of sodden grain, like unmixed concrete, which was said to be so *yang* it was frightening . . .'

By now, a master of public relations, I invited Lesley Garner of the *Sunday Times* to a dinner which resulted in a feature on the Landesmans' new role as the 'ideal macro family'. 'It's very marriage building,' Fran told her. 'No more of Jay's twenty-four hour lunch conferences . . . We spend peaceful evenings at home reading gems from macrobiotic literature . . . Life has become simple and loving . . . Even the children have benefited . . . our son Miles's ear operation was called off. My lifelong sinus problems cleared up. Cosmo's *sanpaku* – a sign of emotional unbalance – disappeared.' The accompanying photo of the smiling children at dinner, being watched over by doting parents as they attacked their roasted buckwheat cutlets with chopsticks was photo-journalism at its most creative.

As we climbed the nutritional ladder, our former friends viewed the ascent as idiocy incarnate. Those brave enough to accept an invitation to dinner stayed for the *miso* soup, but left before the lectures. By the end of the evening, some threw books, some hid the chopsticks, others gave up on us entirely. By now, I didn't give a damn. The Swinging Sixties had come to an end and what did I have to show for it? All my abortive projects had left me feeling I had to find God, or a good substitute. That it should have turned out to be a diet was a lucky break. Finding God would have finished me off; a diet I could handle. As I became more obsessed, there were many who said I would have been better off with God. My sister was one of them. She sent me an article from the *Ladies Home Journal* on macrobiotics with the caption 'This Diet Can Kill'. It was written by an MD who was chairman of the Department of Nutrition at Harvard. To the average American, this meant it was the same as the voice from on high. To us knowing and dedicated macros, who had always been suspicious of His mysterious ways, it was nothing more than a blatant piece of propaganda circulated by the research departments who were subsidized by the food industry.

At Fran's insistence, we went to our GP to tell him of the diet. Jerry Slattery was our kind of doctor, with a no-nonsense, simple explanation for whatever the complaint: 'Nerves. A simple case of nerves. Don't worry about it,' was his usual response. Serious complaints he referred to other doctors. But I was serious about getting his opinion. After I explained the diet in detail, he said, 'It sounds all right to me.'

'But, Jerry,' Fran pleaded, 'there's no milk, no orange juice, none of those building blocks of health a family needs to build with. They even think the diet will cure cancer.'

Jerry thought a moment. 'Well, maybe it can – we certainly can't.' It was enough to convince us we were safe.

I wrote a piece for *OZ* magazine to refute the charges. I explained that macrobiotics was more than a diet: it was a way of life that had great benefits for ex-bad boys and girls. Its disciplines were refreshing after the Sixties' years of joyless 'liberation'. 'Attention control freaks,' I concluded, 'you're so busy controlling all those other people, you're unable to control what goes into your own mouth. The real revolution begins right under your nose – open your mouth and chew!' Philosophic ideas are meaningless unless their purpose is to help us towards health and happiness. A commitment to an ideology that doesn't bring joy is a bummer, and only leads to anxiety and loneliness, I read somewhere, and couldn't agree more.

In the middle of this obsession, the opportunity to buy our house came up. The asking price gave our bank manager a chance to share his opinion of the Angel's future: it was not promising. 'For £10,000 you could do better elsewhere,' he insisted.

Refused a mortgage, Fran, ever fearful of being made homeless, appealed to her mother for help. She was as unenthusiastic as the bank manager. 'The living-room is much too small to entertain in,' was her excuse, but she relented under pressure and came to our aid. And not a minute too soon. The orange gum-balls on our tree in the living-room were looking moth-eaten. The Pithers stove ceased functioning. The time had come for the industrial frosted glass windows and frames that once ensured privacy to be replaced with period-friendly Georgian ones. The living-room ceiling was slipping into a rakish angle. Into this chaos came Clive the builder. I had heard that experiences with English builders often ended in tragedy; with Clive, we opened with comedy and closed with Chekhov.

Guyanese by birth, Clive was British by choice. I had seen him around the neighbourhood working on neighbours' houses. They all said he was reliable and reasonable. What they didn't tell me was that he came to work in a classic Rover 3.5 coupé, clutching a copy of the *Daily Telegraph* and a tightly rolled umbrella. Clive's voice was abnormally high for a builder. 'Mis-dress, Mis-dress,' he would shout on arrival. 'Where is the tea?' Seeing Clive sitting in our vintage dentist's chair reading his newspaper, drinking tea with his pinkie finger extended – on my time – made a return to flogging seem attractive.

I think it was the detail of his estimates that first appealed to me: 'LIVING-ROOM: Extend iron girder two feet; build brick column to take pressure of top floors, incorporating recessed bookshelf . . .' It was written in a style I called 'Late Flourish'. Our morning conferences revolved around the current position of the Tory Party on Rhodesia, and his lament for the demise of the British working class. Being a builder was only a consolation prize in view of Clive's other talents. There was Clive the arbiter of taste: 'What is a dentist's chair doing in a living-room?' Clive the gossip: 'Have you heard that the vicar votes Labour?' Clive the expert on child behaviour: 'Your children take liberties.' Unless drastic steps were taken, he would soon become Clive the permanent guest.

As unoffical Boswell to the Landesmans, he would re-enact dramatic scenes witnessed as their official builder. He was a constant source of unbridled amusement to the neighbourhood. His party piece was a re-enactment of Fran standing in the doorway shouting at me as I fled from an argument: 'Jay Landesman, you come back here,' he would shout, laughing hysterically. Clive was married to a white woman, who was to me only a voice at the other end of the phone. On special occasions Clive and she were always invited, but it was only Clive who showed. I took pleasure in introducing him as 'Clive, the lost member of the Landesman tribe' or 'Clive, the constructive Landesman'. His demeanour at these times would alternate between that of a cricket umpire and head boy at Eton. In the beginning he didn't approve of any of our friends, especially those he suspected of having a low moral threshold. Our table fare appalled him. 'Only the poor and the sick eat brown rice,' he'd say. 'I know, because that's all I ate in my country when I was a lad.' His status as a member of the Landesman family was enhanced when he began to appreciate the fried brown rice dishes Fran whipped up for his lunches. When he began to ask for recipes, there was cautious approval. When he stopped teasing the boys about their shoulder-length hair, his membership was firmly established. That was the beginning of his downfall.

The rebel streak in Clive made our life-style too appealing for his own good. Soon he was asking the kind of metaphysical questions he'd heard make the round of our living-room – 'What does it all mean?' He discovered it gained him entry into any conversation going. He adopted it as his personal passport to social mobility. When he began to read Fran's poetry, I knew he was in deep trouble. Signs that he was to become a casualty first manifested itself in the quality of his work, and then in the quantity. Having a vested interest in Clive's work ethic, I sat him down for a talk in the hopes of restoring his good common sense; it was futile. He had tasted the wellsprings of 'liberation' and there was no going back to the conservative values of yesteryear.

When he started taking up with the local black nurse I feared the worst. He began to enjoy his intrigues, often bringing her around for a cup of tea and a little romancing to the music of Bob Marley. When he didn't show up for several weeks, I called his wife and received the news that he had run off with the nurse, deserting all the principles he once held sacred. It was symptomatic of what lay ahead for many people.

By now I had become a Born Again Nutritional Fundamentalist; the diet ruled our life. When we decided to take a holiday in the Dordogne, I loaded the boot of our big vintage Mercedes with all the basic macrobiotic food and utensils, plus a camp stove, determined to be faithful to our diet under any conditions. For the first leg of our journey, we put the car on a Swedish boat to San Sebastian in northern Spain. It was quite a coup to get the ship's chef to cook our brown rice, which we then supplemented with our provisions. We were not a family to be invited to the captain's table, but during the meal I regaled fellow diners with the macrobiotic philosophy, which did not go down well with my embarrassed family. By the time we landed I was not particularly popular with the other passengers or with the family.

Our first destination was to visit my old adversary, G. Legman, who lived on the other side of France, above Nice. We had written that we were coming, but, on our arrival, he showed no sign that he had received the letter. Although we'd had our differences, we had a non-aggression pact for over twenty years after we ceased working together on *Neurotica*. We found him sitting on the grass in his olive grove in the middle of an incredible view of the Alps and the Mediterranean. A previous visit in 1960 had established that his anarchic approach to gracious living included a house that had no electricity, gas, running water or inside or outside toilet. 'Where do you shit?' I had asked him on that visit. He'd grinned, indicating his satisfaction at my discomfort. 'Anywhere,' he screamed. 'Isn't it wonderful?'

Legman was the world's leading erotic folklorist, whose books included a seminal work on *cunnilingus*, a collection of dirty limericks and a history of the Knights Templar which had caused his publisher, Tom Maschler of Jonathan Cape, to make an unprecedented apology for the 'opinions expressed by the author'. His masterwork, *The Rationale of the Dirty Joke*, was a volume of over 2,000 dirty jokes, 'a collection based on thirty-five years of international collecting and research'. Some were about homosexuality, prostitution, scatology, castration and disease, and others were generally disgusting. His description of the jokes ensured that nobody got a laugh out of them. It was an international best-seller among collectors of erotica and antiquarian booksellers. The proceeds from this extraordinary body of work enabled him to build a studio to house his thousands of rare books, his files and his voluminous correspondence. The only concession to convenience was an inside toilet, which I was told was off limits to guests.

He still hadn't forgiven me for 'maligning' him in *The Nervous Set*. 'Did you have to make me look like a fag?' he growled. When I said we were macrobiotic, he turned nasty. 'I know all about that diet. It's a crock of shit,' he hollered and refused to let me use his stove. I cooked the rice on our camp stove, and brought it proudly to the table in spite of his protests.

After dinner, poisoned with his bad vibes, I mentioned I hadn't received a copy of the 'big joke book', for which I had sent him a cheque some time before. His explanation that the British customs probably confiscated it was marginally acceptable. Would he take a cheque for another copy? When he refused, I thought it was some kind of joke, but he insisted on being paid in cash.

The next morning I told Fran to round up the children; we were leaving. 'What a shame that a one-time giant could become so small,' I said. We packed up the tent and headed for the open road, without saying goodbye. The last thing we saw was a furious Legman running after the car, shaking his fist, shouting, 'Landesman, you can't run away like this. You haven't washed the dishes!'

When we got to our destination in the Dordogne, Fran's experience with the French stove was the first in a series of disasters; everything we cooked was covered in soot. We couldn't understand why the French shopkeepers insisted on speaking

French. She knew they spoke English when she wasn't being served. The house had no garden for the kids to run in, and no place for her to sunbathe. A cornfield was the best view we had of French village life. When we wanted to buy some corn from the farmer who owned it, he told us that the corn was for the animals, not humans. When he left, we nicked some beautiful fresh corn and for the first time I deviated from the diet.

I felt I was being punished when a tyre blew on the car. Getting it fixed proved to be a major undertaking for the man in the bicycle shop whom we appealed to for help; he had never fixed a tyre that big, but, with French determination, he struggled for hours with a collection of tools that belonged in a museum.

We decided to cut our losses and move on. Carcassonne's walled city offered some temporary relief. As we walked among the tourist sights, Fran bought a choc-ice, which was a 'no no' in the diet. A sense of betrayal swept over me. I thought the very foundation of our marriage was at stake. Fran couldn't believe anyone was silly enough to name a choc-ice as a co-respondent in a divorce, which I mentioned was a possibility now that she no longer loved me. 'Yes, I do love you, but, God, this choc-ice tastes good.' Her light-hearted attitude to my 'macro-psychotic' reaction had a therapeutic effect, making the trip home the best part of the journey.

A visit from the 'Paul Revere of ecology', Barry Commoner, convinced me I was on the right track. His book *The Closing Circle* was the most important statement yet made on the nature, cause and possible solution of the impending environmental disaster. As a scientist he was remarkably open to new ideas and he listened patiently to my unscientific explanation of the role food could play in ecology. During a mammoth jam session, I laid out all the reasons why food should be included in his thinking. I learned later from his wife Gloria that Barry thought I was 'very revolutionary with this food thing' and had gotten through to him. 'You have opened him up to what may be the missing link in his programme. You are an inspiration to Barry, as he is to you,' she wrote.

As Stan Stunning, I wrote for *Seed*, a magazine started by Gregory Sams in the hope of capturing more converts to natural eating. It led to my most successful convert, Paul Jones. The first time we had met at the Cooks, years before, he didn't impress me enough to offer him a ride home. But, after seeing his performance in *Privilege*, a bitter satire on the rock world he had just left, I was impressed. It wasn't until he moved into Duncan Terrace that I came to know him. The years as a rock idol had left a bitter taste which made him ripe for something like macrobiotics. After a few dinners at our house, a few pamphlets and some good talk, he became a convert. He wasn't your empty-headed pop star, but an intelligent Oxford *alumnus*, whose interests were wide and varied. We discovered our families had a lot in common. His wife was the novelist Sheila MacLeod, whose brilliant but depressing prose matched Fran's wry, depressing lyrics. Their two children, like Cosmo and Miles, were 'victims' of having 'notorious' parents. Paul and I had a healthy interest in jazz, good wine and good company. He was such a strict convert that he used to go across town to eat at Green Genes, the latest macrobiotic restaurant in Notting Hill. On his first solo album he paid us the honour of immortalizing us in a song titled *Stan Stunning and the Noodle Queen* – a 'thank you' note for having turned him on.

With the arrival of the militant wing of the Boston Macros, London became a battleground for ideological differences, the beginning of the Great Macro Wars. They accused the Sams brothers and London's macros of 'dietary revisionism', a crime worse than the Western diet. Determined to undermine the Sams' influence, they used every trick in the trade, including sexual entrapment. They brought with them a supremely organized chef, a woman whose main talent was renowned throughout Boston – she knew the secret of getting to the heart of the Macro Man through her superb rice balls.

Her first target was Gregory Sams, who owned the restaurant they secretly wanted to take over. We watched horror-stricken as she cooked delicious meals that went straight to his heart. They fell in love; for an engagement present he gave her the restaurant. The funky atmosphere that had made the place so popular disappeared on opening night. We were there with R. D. Laing and his friend Sean Connery. Bond's struggle through his brown rice cutlet with a straight face was a remarkable achievement even for a man who was up against some of the most difficult assignments of the Cold War.

Another blow came when the cultural commissars tried to impose their pronunciation of *yin* and *yang*. (the *yin* was to be feminized, while the *yang* was to be hardened.) The 'Third Rice Fascists' had won the war, but they were on the point of losing the Landesmans, their most dedicated soldiers.

CHAPTER NINE

Coming down from such a rigid diet, but not totally abandoning it, released a certain amount of pent-up resentment, directed mainly at me. The problems of our adolescent children magnified with the return to bad eating habits. Candy wrappers were found in the lavatory, Coke bottles in the dustbin. Rumours were going around macrobiotic society that there were 'binges' at the Landesman household. We soon found ourselves ostracized, stranded between vegetarians and Japanese pickle fanciers. Old meat-eating friends set temptation before us. The thought of ever tasting meat again made Fran sick until Annie Ross put a piece of steak in her mouth. Fran had to force herself to swallow, but, by the time she finished, she was ashamed to admit that she'd enjoyed it. 'I never knew steak could taste so delicious,' she said. Some time later author Dave Pierce caught me tucking into a steak at Jerry's Club. 'My, what unusual things they're doing with brown rice these days,' he said.

Although we still adhered to a wholefood diet, the idea that we could deviate without becoming steakoholics loosened us up in other areas. Our basement flat was constantly filled with guests, friends and occasional lovers. American composer Gary MacFarland, over here recording, began a songwriting collaboration with Fran. As the collaboration heated up, he moved out of his expensive hotel and into our basement, where, it was rumoured, he did the work he liked best.

Our friends from America Jackie Caine and Roy Kral, and their teenage daughter Dana, moved in during their gig at Ronnie Scott's. Jackie and Roy had been the first to record Landesman/ Wolf songs in the early Fifties. Their version of *Spring Can Really Hang You Up The Most* still stands as a classic among jazz purists. They were without doubt Fran's most loyal boosters and they proved it again one night at Ronnie's when they introduced Michel Legrand, a devoted fan of theirs, to Fran. If Legrand ever wanted a new lyricist, Fran Landesman's attributes, as described by Roy, would qualify her ideally. Poor Roy, he did everything short of giving Legrand Fran's social security number.

Their daughter Dana, as beautiful as her mother, intrigued everyone with her friendship with actor Derek Branch, who was then a waiter at Ronnie Scott's. Branch, a handsome Anglo-Indian, swore he would follow her to the ends of the earth unless she married him on his next night off. She asked for a rain check.

It was she who introduced us to Jason Holliday, a New York black, middle-aged homosexual who was here for the showing of Shirley Clarke's film about him, *Portrait of Jason*. His colourful, self-mocking account of the life he led was as engrossing as any film we'd seen in years. Clarke's film had given him a cult status in New York, and about fifteen minutes' attention in London. We sat up for hours, night after night, entertained by his tales. I decided that the King's Head Theatre Club needed a 'Sunday Night with Jason Holliday'. What Jason needed was to show the world what he could do on his own and it was my pleasure to present him in a two-hour, one-man show which accomplished just that. Nobody wanted the evening to end, especially me; I invited the whole audience back to our house for a party. Most of them showed, including some pub regulars who hadn't seen the show, but had heard that there would be free drinks.

Jason played the room like the star he was, graciously accepting all the embraces of his fans with typical show-business elan. As the evening progressed, he grew carelessly affectionate and slipped his hand over the ass of one of the pub crowd, a gesture that turned the man hostile. Jason, ever streetwise, fled trembling to the basement for sanctuary as the victim and his buddies went on about the 'fooking fag'. *Time Out* writer Jerome Bryne tried to lower the temperature. 'In these days, young man, may I suggest to you that a hand on one's ass is not the most awful thing that can happen.' The Irishman thought otherwise. His punch sent Jerome's granny glasses flying. Within seconds the house looked like a scene from a John Wayne bar-room fight. One of the enemy was about to strike me. 'Hey, you can't hit me, I'm the host,' I said, holding up my hand like a traffic cop. To my surprise, he respected my explanation and flattened the guy who had come to my rescue.

Jason's exit from London could have been conceived by film director Preston Sturges. All his fans, including children and babies, escorted him to the train to bid him farewell. As he stood on the train's steps waving goodbye, he began to sing the opening line of the hit song from his show: 'I'm the most happy fellow on the road of Portobello'. The train didn't move. Another take was called for. He kept singing and waving as the crowd cheered him on. The platform guard signalled again. He broke into song again. The crowd surged around him. The train didn't move. By now the crowd had been swelled by strangers eager to see what was going on. The signal came once again and the train slowly moved out of the station, the crowd running alongside shouting goodbyes and promises to write.

Whether it was the boys' diet or just an adolescent phase, their behaviour became a cause for concern. Miles became an expert at bunking off from school. One of his teachers, who liked him, told us he used the school as if it were his club, 'dropping in occasionally to see if anything was happening'. Cosmo began to read Dostoyevski, Beckett and Kafka, and to associate with Kentish Town toffs; his future as a Romantic Depressive was assured. Miles chose his friends from the council flats of Islington, which guaranteed him a future in minor crime. It didn't take a genius to realize we were a family heading for trouble.

I made an appointment with the local child guidance clinic to stop the rot. After two sessions with us as a family, they declared that Miles and Cosmo were ok, but that they'd like to see more of us. 'I love to talk about myself, but I thought this was a child guidance clinic,' Fran said. 'It was,' Robin Skynner said, 'until we met you two! We're thinking of changing it to the family guidance centre.' He obviously had a sense of humour even before he started his collaboration with John Cleese on their book *Families and How To Survive Them*.

We saw Skynner and his associate once a week. What must have gone through their minds as they watched us roar up on our Suzuki in second-hand motorcycle gear was nothing compared to what they must have suffered as they listened to tales of the rise and fall of an American post-industrial man and his success-obsessed wife. Perhaps trying to shock them became one of the reasons for continuing our sessions, but they proved to be unshockable. Our days of whines and poses were coming to an end. We savoured their final words. 'You're Hansel and Gretel walking into the woods, holding hands like children. You refuse to grow up.' It was the best news we'd had in ages. Fran was forty-two and I was only fifty-one.

After the therapy, we sank back into our hedonistic ways. I received an invitation from Jim Haynes to join a 'distinguished' group of people as a juror at the Wet Dream Festival in Amsterdam. As far as I know, it was the only festival in the world that demanded a nude photograph of each jury member. Nevertheless, getting a nude photograph taken was not easy until Jeremy Brooks volunteered, on the condition that I behaved myself. The jurors' pictures were reprinted in Jim Haynes' splendid and revealing autobiography, *Thanks For Coming*. Some smart-ass said that if it had come with a magnifying glass Jim would have had a best-seller.

The Wet Dream Festival was meant to be a mind-blowing event. It featured hard and soft core films, performing artists, parties, workshops, seminars and orgies, all in the hope that it would prove to be another of those 'liberating experiences' of the Sexual Revolution. Three days of watching practically everything porno-graphic that had been put on film really turned Fran and me off sex, but judging the winner was full of drama. Germaine Greer, one of the judges, attempted to railroad through Jean Genet's masturba-tion obsessed film, a subject on which she seemed to be an expert. Professor Greer decided that its 'literary connotations' made it worthy of a prize. I rallied the other jurors to my side and a compromise selection was made. It was a film directed by a Japanese of a Swedish farm girl's love for her German shepherd dog whose picture she wore in her locket. I don't think the Professor ever forgave me for thwarting her.

The climax of the festival occurred on its last night, when Otto Muhl's commune of sexual revolutionaries took over the stage. Their frenzied naked dancing and lewd gestures to the excruciatingly loud music of the Rolling Stones set the tone for what was to come. Muhl sat in a corner of the stage stroking a goose. Two women on their hands and knees were centre stage, each with one end of a rolling-pin up her anus. The shit hit the fan when Muhl decided to kill the goose. Heathcote Williams rushed to the stage, grabbed the goose from Muhl, and tossed it to writer Anthony Haden-Guest, who fled the hall holding the goose above his head like the cup in a football ceremony. The audience cheered; Muhl and his comrades had a tantrum. They shook their fists at the audience. Finally, to show their dedication to art, they crapped on the stage and exited.

'Yah. Sucks. Boo to the bully, Otto,' Germaine wrote. 'The under-dog goose is alive and well and living on a barge. It was bloody good fun, and we cheered like workers at a melodrama. Come his last truly great performance, he will gut himself and fuck his own liver.' She called him a Nazi; Muhl's defenders called him an 'energy release'. Neither was the whole story. Muhl was an established artist before he turned his wrath on society; he endured public contempt, physical abuse, and numerous jail sentences for what he believed was a legitimate assault on a society whose lives were being controlled by 'the omnipotent State'. Fran and others were shocked at my defense of Muhl. I explained that I didn't think killing a goose was the worst act ever committed in the name of Art. (It is one of the few views I have since regretted.)

Jim Haynes' London Arts Lab, a multi-media gallery, restaurant, bookshop and theatre, had developed into a small-scale version of the Wet Dream Festival. (I'm sure Jim wouldn't mind if I said he started it to get laid.) There was a peculiarly sexy quality to the place, encouraged by Jim's basic philosophy – 'Hello, I love you.' There were always young girls to flirt with; occasionally a pretty one showed up. The Lab attracted a miscellaneous group of cultural riff-raff from Lady Antonia Fraser to the Hell's Angels. Jim's policy of never saying no to anyone gave the place its hit and miss reputation for 'experimentation', but no one can deny that Jim's offering of Jane Arden's play *Vagina Rex and the Gas Ovens* was the act of a brave man.

No matter what play was on in the theatre, it was always a full house, thanks to Jim's ingenious idea, for a while, of not putting seats in the theatre – you bought a ticket and carried in an empty beer crate for your seat. The restaurant served decent food, but the chef looked like Morticia of the Addams Family. The floor of the cinema was covered in foam mattresses, a genuine advance in cinema- going. If the soft porn film got boring, there was always the odd couple around to provide a live show. 'The only thing I remember about the Arts Lab cinema was the smell of dirty feet,' said one disgruntled patron.

We were there one night when Jim invited us to his private quarters, a platform approached by a rope ladder – it was said that some of his conquests found climbing it a 'substitute for foreplay'. 'I have someone very special I want you to meet,' Jim said. On his bed was Ken Kesey, reading a comic book. We had never met him, but we had a lot of friends in common. To paraphrase Fran, 'we'd read a lot about and by him', but doubted if he knew anything about us. 'Landesman . . . early Beats . . . *Neurotica* . . . New York . . . Fifties,' Kesey said, extending a warm hand of recognition. We had instant rapport. I mentioned that novelist Robert Stone, who was once a passenger on Kesey's famous bus, was living in London. 'Stone's an A-number-one good guy. Do you have his phone number?'

His lack of shame of being unashamed to be an American was the first thing that struck me about Kesey and I grew to admire the way he flaunted it – he wore a removable front tooth enamelled with the Stars and Stripes. He was serious, but underneath it all was a wicked sense of play. I never heard him once put his country down, in fact he never put anything down. Coming out of a film that all of us disliked, Kesey found something good to say: 'You have to admit the costumes were sensational.'

Kesey was in London to promote *The Electric Kool-Aid Acid Test*. We went to the book launch, where I started the rumour that Kesey had laced the punch with LSD. Looking around at Kesey's friends, the Hell's Angels and their women, anybody might have thought he had. Patsy Wilson, Kesey's PR-minder, thought it was very funny and just what the launch needed. 'Would you like some punch, Jay,' she asked giving me a wicked smile. Patsy laid on a couple of buses for the guests to go on a mystery tour. We ended up dancing in an open field in Essex, which lacked the spontaneity of the original Pranksters tours.

Kesey's practice of experimenting with drugs was no secret (read *One Flew Over the Cuckoo's Nest*). The lack of them reduced him to desperate attempts to find a substitute. He would grind up some of Fran's diet pills for a fix. If that didn't work, he'd go on to shoot up Robert Stone's gout medicine. A final assault with aspirins was as low as he went. His saving grace was that he laughed at his foolish antics.

One day he decided to score some laughing gas (nitrous oxide). He planned his campaign like a four-star general. The two of us set out for the headquarters of British Oxygen, the primary source. He was dressed as a rich American farmer, in cowboy boots, a tartan windbreaker and a Stetson; he was looking good. I wore a double-breasted suit, open neck shirt, co-respondent shoes, and a simple red bandana around my neck to show I was a richer farmer. We actually thought we presented a picture of undeniable authenticity.

Obtaining authorization to buy even a canister of the gas turned out to be as difficult as buying a trigger for a nuclear warhead; it did not phase Kesey. When asked what he wanted it for, Kesey started doing the 'Gary Cooper shit-kicking bit', which was supposed to lower the tension. 'I run this herd of 400 cows down in Surrey,' he began. I watched the salesman's head snap back as if he had been hit by a professional boxer. 'I need this gas to see that the churns are sterilized like they should be. This business of just washing them out with detergents doesn't set well with me. I want my milk to be the safest milk in England.' The salesman had never heard of his method and, as Kesey tried to explain its operation, began to laugh. Kesey felt offended. He tried various other approaches, all to no avail, and we left empty handed. Once outside, he said he was so mad at the salesman he could have pissed on his shoes. Then he looked over at me, pointing to my bandana. 'It must have been the way you're dressed that threw him.'

We went down to Stonehenge with Kesey to scout the scene for a documentary he wanted to make, a sort of Hell's Angels meet the Druids. When he discovered the place was fenced in, he flipped. 'It's an outrage, man. Stonehenge is the heaviest place I know. It's a temple, man, a temple of the world.' The other cradle of civilization for Kesey was Apple; he revered the Beatles. 'Being asked by them to come to work at Apple is like a Catholic being invited to work at the Vatican. Every day I thank God for the Beatles. They wanted me to make "paperback records" of my London experiences, but Apple collapsed before I got a chance to start.' Kesey was so disappointed his project was cancelled that he liberated a professional tape recorder.

It was difficult to keep up with him. He'd phone or drop by ready for action only to find me engrossed in other activities. On these occasions Fran and he would rap for hours non-stop. He told her how much he enjoyed gossiping with her. Fran was very annoyed. 'Gossip?' she said. 'I thought we were talking about love and death – you know, major themes?' Kesey gave her his Randolph Scott smile. 'Naw, it was only gossip.' Kesey was set for an indefinite stay in London, but a telegram from home brought him the bad news that his father had died. He left with promises to return and finish his movie, and bring over his fish-tail Cadillac.

When I made my cross-country trip to America in 1971 looking for the heart of the organic movement, I called Kesey from San Francisco. 'Get your ass over here,' he bellowed. 'I'll meet you at the airport.' From the airport we went directly to a roadhouse on the highway that specialized in cocktails. I watched him down a Brandy Alexander, an Old Fashioned and a Grasshopper, as he told me he had converted to the organic way of life. Kesey lived on a big farm in Eugene, Oregon, miles from civilization, yet every nutcase-hippy managed to find him. Their invasion of his privacy had become the bane of his life – the price he paid for fame. In the middle of the farm stood the famous bus, a symbol of a life-style that had been abandoned.

He and his brother, Chuck, operated the Health Food and Pool Store. It was run with the same originality that Kesey put into fiction. The store sold natural food grown by his friends. Stock was displayed with complete disregard for order or system. No one could accuse the store of being serious with a full-size pool table on a platform in the middle of the place. 'It's for those who like a little pool with their purity,' Kesey said. In a way, the shop represented the real philosophy of the people who were into organic living. The food was cheap, the place was friendly, and they were having fun.

While in America I had stopped off in St Louis to see Cutie. She had recently recovered from being mugged by a gang of small boys, but was in hospital for other complications. Her health had deteriorated rapidly. I had always remembered Cutie as full of life and it was sad to see her lying so helpless. I don't suppose I had cried since I was a child; the boy in me welled up uncontrollably and I bawled like a baby. A passing nurse put her arm around me, and I wanted to tell her how much I loved Cutie and how much I missed her. I wanted to tell Cutie how I had settled down, as she would have liked me to do, and how happy the children and Fran were in London. She wouldn't have believed me.

Cutie rarely looked on the bright side. I brought Miles into the room to cheer her up, this being Miles' speciality, but Cutie refused to be comforted. She looked at him with a frown, then turned to me. 'His teeth need fixing,' she said bitterly.

A family decision to put her in a nursing home was a difficult one. She had always been such an independent person, never relying on anyone for anything. She never asked for favours. When she used to travel to New York, loaded down with luggage, one of us, as a joke, would tell her what streetcar connections to make to get to Union Station. She always took us seriously; she never believed any of us could be bothered to drive her.

Back in London, I could think of nothing but how I had failed

Cutie as a dutiful son. I was the youngest and felt the least loved, yet I was the one she expected the most from. All the successes I had had in St Louis, outside of the business, she had managed to see as dismal failures. The only thing she really cared about in our life together was that I should become a successful antique dealer, who knew how to run a business which made a profit. It never occurred to me that Cutie had played any part in shaping my life. Now that she was dying, I realized what an influence she had been by allowing me to do exactly what I wanted, whether in business or in pleasure. She gave me a valuable gift – the freedom to rebel against her.

This forced me to take a look at what I, as a father, was giving my children to rebel against. The fact that we lived such an unconventional life should have been sufficient. As Cosmo said, 'Children by nature are conservative', so why weren't they in rebellion? Where had I gone wrong? Anyone closely observing the way we lived in those days would have agreed with my sister's joking remark, 'The children should be put in care and the house condemned.' I was repeating the pattern of rebellion – unconsciously rebelling against my children. I couldn't bear the idea that any child of mine would end up conventional. I didn't want them to waste their lives in some dead-end job or greedy profession. I hoped they would have the good taste to invent a way of life that suited *me*.

Miles came close to fulfilling it. He put all his energy into music, but bunking into rock concerts was his real art. Cosmo saw him as a licentious nihilist who wanted something for nothing; I saw him as an unrecognized performing artist. When I heard how his spontaneous action saved him from the humiliation of being flung out of the Rolling Stones' Wembley concert, I knew he had passed the ultimate test.

Security was tight, as expected. Miles said it was like breaking out of Colditz. When he saw the guards carrying iron bars, he knew the stakes were high. He discarded the idea of a *kamikaze* dive in favour of grovelling to the guards with the excuse that the Hell's Angels had just eaten his girlfriend and that she had the tickets. Miles jumped over the wall, and found himself in the boiler room and changed into a boiler suit. With a copy of the *Daily Mirror* clutched to his breast, he strolled toward the music as though he were taking a tea break. It worked. I never worried again about Miles' ability to function under the most severe stress, even when he was caught with his hand in the till and the police called us to the station. 'He's a good lad,' they told us. Had they known that Fran was wearing a collection of clothes he had nicked from Biba's, they might have had second thoughts.

CHAPTER TEN

The first time Jeremy and Eleanor Brooks invited us to their cottage in North Wales, Fran panicked. She was a city girl, who had written many a poem in praise of concrete:

> . . . You will never catch me camping in the country
> Getting bitten in a dell or leafy thicket
> You'll fine me and my gent dancing on the cement
> Everytime I see a tree I want to kick it . . .

So it was with some reluctance that we accepted their invitation. It takes a lot to separate Fran from her bed, but the Brooks were our closest friends in London, the only ones we were really able to relax with. Their children and ours practically grew up together; we often kidded about the possibilities of any of their three beautiful daughters marrying our two boys and how we would all live happily together ever after.

I had often threatened Fran with a move to the country, but, when we got there, it was she who enjoyed its rustic charms and beautiful scenery. I took along some LSD for insurance. Their part of Wales was untouched by tourists. The house was some distance from the road, in a picturesque setting that included the proverbial babbling brook. There were enough trees for the children to climb, animals to play with, and rapids to conquer to keep them and us entertained. The amenities were minimal, which added a certain amount of tension to the visit. What added a lot more was

Eleanor's mother, who dropped in for a quick visit in the middle of our tripping.

A few hours earlier Cosmo, Fran and I had been wading in the rapids, overwhelmed by the peace we were experiencing and struck by the emerald foliage and diamond waterfalls – were we in a commercial for menthol cigarettes? We wandered around for hours, picking wild flowers, discovering the hidden delights of the landscape, feeling very close as a family coming to terms with nature, a new experience for us. Jeremy joined us to see how we were getting along. He and I wandered up the hillside to an open field, where the cows, I thought, had taken a keen interest in our conversation. Encouraged, I began to expand on the meaning of life and the 'nature of nature', believing some kind of affinity existed between the cows and me. Ten minutes later, Jeremy put his arm affectionately around my shoulder. 'Jay,' he said, 'I've seen you empty a room, but this is the first time I've seen you empty a meadow!' There wasn't a cow in sight.

A return to the cottage and Eleanor's mother should have put a damper on my exorbitant oneness with the world. It didn't. Deciding to be the perfect guest, I began to sweep the slate floor of the living room, delivering a lecture on the art of sweeping at the same time. Sweeping has been my favourite occupation since I was a child, sweeping the floor of Cutie's antique shop. My speciality was sweeping without raising dust, the only skill of any significance I remember my father passing on to me. Sweeping under ordinary circumstances is always gratifying; sweeping on acid is *satori*. I made the witch's broom fly. Nothing was safe from its progression from floor, to furniture, to ceiling. I had to resist whisking over Eleanor's mother. I received a standing ovation. The next morning, with some remorse, I tried to apologize to Eleanor. To my surprise, she said her mother had never enjoyed anything so much and thought we were a very nice family, and that I was the perfect guest.

No visit to the country is complete without its tour of the local attractions, which usually turn out to be a bird sanctuary and a pub. The visit to Portmeirion was not in that class. Clough Williams-Ellis' recreation of an Italian village became more than one man's obsession with do-it-yourself architecture; it became one of Wales' major tourist attractions after it was used as the setting for the television series *The Prisoner*. I had reservations about it until I met the man responsible. Williams-Ellis owned most of the land and cottages in the area, but, seeing him strolling briskly over the countryside, you wouldn't have thought so. He looked like any other birdwatcher on a field expedition. Meeting him briefly was enought to convince me that he was among those great eccentrics whose obsessions rule their lives.

A ride on the miniature railroad and a visit to the local pub completed the tour. The railroad was for the children, the pub was for gossip. I was briefed by Jeremy on some of the locals' contributions to the area. It was nothing more historic than building slate walls and fooling around with other people's wives. I asked one of the locals who had joined our table if Jeremy was right about all the screwing. 'What can you expect with all the terrible unemployment?' he said, holding up his empty glass for a refill. Like most people who fall in love with Wales after the first visit, Fran and I began looking in the property columns of the papers for a cottage.

We found ourselves under siege upon our return. The Islington Department of Health discovered there had been a serious accident some years previously in the plating works behind our row of houses. A poisonous chrome substance was found in samples of soil recently taken from our back garden. They descended on us like the SAS with an order for the closing down of the basement, and a demand that we decontaminate all clothing, personal possessions and fixtures therein. All pets were to be monitored, vegetable gardens destroyed, and the children cautioned not to play in the area. The chrome that permeated the walls of the basement had become carcinogenic. Strong stuff, especially for Philip Estep, our basement lodger.

He had been living there for at least a year. He was finishing a novel about a pop star's voyage to outer space 'for the ultimate trip'. Little did he suspect, he might be about to have his own. He slept all day and worked all night, which left scant time for socializing and less for taking care of his health. He attributed his yellow complexion to a lack of sun, but the Health Department took one look at him and demanded he immediately undergo a series of tests to determine the extent of his cancer.

Philip's attitude to the danger was to be loyal to us, his landlords. This was confusing to the Health Department, his new enemy. Fran implored him to comply. 'Think of the novel,' she begged. He refused to consider taking any tests without a court order, and then he would seek legal advice. 'I wasn't looking too well before I came here, so any change would be for the better,' was his final decision.

The only thing that was looking good in the area was the garden running along Duncan Terrace, which was also contaminated. The flowers, far from withering in agony, were flourishing. The park's gardener won prizes for his dahlias that summer. Philip said it reminded him of President Lincoln's line about General Grant's drinking problem: 'Whatever he's drinking, send him a case of it.' The same applied to him. 'My novel's going great. I've never been so creative. More carcinogenics!'

Springing into action, I mobilized a neighbourhood committee as liaison between the council, its health department and the tenants. Solicitors were engaged to act on our behalf in a legal action against the plating works. All was ticking away with our defensive action on schedule. When it appeared we would win our case for £1,500,000 damages, the company went into liquidation, and we went into shock. Six months later, the Department of Health told us that the contamination had moved on from our back yards into the river that flowed under the garden. The gardener came into an inheritance and moved to Jersey; no more prize-winning dahlias.

We received a visit from Chandler Brossard, a writer whose career luck had been much better than mine: he had been an art editor at *Time* magazine when he was nineteen and a *New Yorker* Talk of the Town writer at twenty-one. His visit should have been the occasion for some memorable reminiscing – we had twenty-five years of deeply shallow indulgence behind us. Why he came loaded down with a suitcase full of new problems I never suspected; it left little time for laughs. It didn't take long to realize he had become politicized. We all knew that maybe Chairman Mao might pull off the miraculous, that the Vietnam war was a disaster and that America was in big trouble, but I wasn't prepared for his new role as saviour of North Vietnam. His insistence that I give blood for the Vietnamese Committee for Medical Aid didn't strike the right note.

He had better luck with Fran, who ordinarily was sceptical of anything associated with Chandler. Even her willingness to give blood was not enough for him. He demanded that she be drug free for forty-eight hours before she became a donor. He accompanied her to the mobile van the day of the appointment to ensure she wouldn't contaminate the Vietcong. After the blood-letting, she was given a ring made out of metal from a shot-down American bomber. I did not think it was something an American could wear without cringing, but Chandler saw it as a badge of honour. (I was able to forgive the sinner, but not the sin.)

I still felt very strongly that I was an American. Even if I never returned, I wanted it to be my last resting place. I used to tell Fran to ship my body back to St Louis to be buried in the family plot. 'Are you kidding?' she'd ask. 'That sounds like a lot of work. Forget it.' How could I let down Rindskopf, the Jewish undertaker who had been sending our family beautiful Jewish calendars since I was a boy? Rindskopf was hurt that Cutie didn't use him when father died – she got a better price from his competitor. My burial plans became a joke to everyone in the family except me.

America seemed to be my main preoccupation. There were the London Vietnam protest marches; friends' letters from the States worrying about America. Like many people, my feelings about Vietnam were confused. Cosmo was of draft age by now, which was a source of despair to Fran. My flippant, 'It'll make a man of him,' did not go down well. Her answer was the same as Cutie's and that of a million other mothers: 'I didn't raise my boy to be a soldier.'

Neither of us were interested in politics, but I couldn't resist getting involved when Norman Mailer decided to run for Mayor of

New York on the battle cry of 'Vote The Rascals In'. He had many friends in London who felt the same way. A Friends of Mailer Committee was formed in London by a high-profile, eccentric hustler named Harvey Matusow, whose performance as a friendly witness for the House of Un-American Activities Committee made him a national figure, but not one that could be taken seriously. His contribution was the most bizarre testimony ever heard under oath. He reeled off a list of well-known Communists. His exposure of Shirley Temple as a Communist tool/sympathizer made headlines across the nation. As a result of his attack on this beloved figure, Matusow became possibly the most unpopular man in America. Of course, according to Matusow, he did it to embarrass the Committee, but nobody believed him. He was sent to prison for perjury, but even that had its good side. His cellmate turned out to be the psychoanalyst Wilhelm Reich, from whom he received invaluable therapy which helped reshape his life.

When I met him in London, years later, his tarnished reputation had been polished by his ventures into the *avant-garde*; he was considered a genius in promoting obscure composers and musicians. (In fact, he married one.) His concerts always attracted attention – how could a concert featuring twenty musicians in evening dress playing twenty harpsichords simultaneously fail to? Or his wife Anna Lockwood's glass concerts consisting of the sounds of broken glass? In comparison, organizing a fund-raising auction for Mailer should have been a snap.

When I saw the treasures Matusow had accumulated, I suspected that, even if he sold them all, it wouldn't pay for the rent on the hall. Among them was an intriguing collection of Yoko Ono's New York artifacts: a series of labelled bottles that might have appealed to a collector of whimsy, but would hardly pass the Trades Descriptions Act: 'Dirt from Central Park', 'Air over Greenwich Village,' 'Vial of Genuine New York Tears' and 'Jar of Captured Cloud Formations over the Bronx' were meant to evoke a sense of nostalgia among the Americans he hoped to attract.

I did my best to contribute a few items that might bring in some money, but Christine Keeler's bra was the best I could do. I obtained the services of Bill Mitchell, King of the Voice-overs, as the auctioneer. Mitchell, a former actor, maintained a sense of the absurd, contributing a metaphysical patter on the significance of the various items. The highlight of the evening was Christine's bra, which we were counting on to go for some real money. Dangling the slightly soiled bra delicately before his audience, Mitchell opened the bidding with a request for £100. There was a gasp from the audience, which included me. I knew it was going to be painful to watch him adjust the price downwards.

'Do I hear fifty?' he asked. The silence indicated no. 'Ten?' he asked. 'Come on, we're dealing in a psychosexually historical area here in a never-to-be-repeated offer.' More silence. 'Let's hear it for the little lady' – he began to do Archie Rice imitations in an all-out effort to loosen up the crowd. 'Will the beautiful woman in the front row come up and model this for us.' Silence again. Desperate measures were called for. Somebody in the back bid ten shillings. Mitchell laughed, but it was cut short by another bid of 10s. 6d. 'You must be joking,' he snarled. I raised my hand, just to keep the bidding going, but it didn't do any good. Mitchell was forced to knock down the bra to, as he said, 'the connoisseur' in the front row, namely me. Mitchell's finest hour was throwing me the bra with the line, 'Oh, how the mighty have fallen.' Years later, Hanya confessed it wasn't Christine's bra, but one of her own. 'Christine doesn't wear a bra,' she said sheepishly, 'but I thought the deception was justified for a good cause.'

Matusow was not a man to be ignored. He showed up again with his extravaganza, ICES, the International Carnival of Experimental Sounds. Again he called on me for help. When he explained the scope of the event 'with performers from all over the world participating', I knew the American translation was, 'Could you put some of the artists up during their stay?' His benefit for Mailer should have taught me to beware of his projects, but I had to say yes, lest Cosmo report me to the Arts Council for bourgeois tendencies.

Into our lives came American cellist Charlotte Moorman and her partner, Nam June Paik. They looked like the usual mismatched, attractive, urban couple, but their act was from Mars. Charlotte was famous for her annual parade of *avant-garde* happenings in

New York. Paik was an electronic genius, who had designed the world's first television bra – a marvel of engineering – especially for Charlotte. It featured two miniature television sets projecting from already ample breasts which could present *News at Ten* and a BBC documentary simultaneously.

A dress rehearsal was held in our living-room to a very mixed reaction from the Landesman family. Miles's tongue was hanging out; Cosmo's scepticism was showing. Fran and I worried about the fuses blowing. After a period of major adjustments, including artistic differences, pandemonium broke out when one of the sets short-circuited while strapped to Charlotte's breasts. Accusations of unprofessionalism flew, but nothing short of a total black-out could have stayed them from their mission.

On the night of her performance in London, except for some minor bra slippage, the event went off without a hitch. For an encore, Charlotte turned her breasts on the audience and replayed on the twin televisions their stunned reaction. The tabloids covering the event – rumour had it the picture editor of the *Sun* was in attendance – had a field day. The caption to the *Daily Mirror's* picture was 'A Girl with Two Points of View'.

One night we came home to find Charlotte had left the television bra in the living-room. I suggested to Fran that she slip into something uncomfortable. 'It might save the marriage,' I said. I got a cold reception. To her dismay, I slipped it on and turned the knobs, but disappointment reigned – I couldn't get a clear picture.

When ICES moved to the Edinburgh Festival, Matusow rented a train with ten carriages to transport the equipment, artists and their groupies. Fran and I went along because we like train journeys. And what a ride it was! No Paul Theroux or Miles Kington sentimental journey on the iron horse. The only normal thing on the whole trip was the British Rail coffee. In charge of catering was a performing artist whose speciality was putting the fun back into food. My purple *baguette* with blue mince filling tasted peculiar, but, as a pioneer in the natural food world, I was no stranger to innovations. Fran picked a green biscuit with a striped orange coating which co-ordinated with her outfit, but, instead of eating it, style-conscious girl that she is, she wore it.

Those familiar with 'experimental inter-media ramifications' were treated to non-stop seminars, therapy workshops, rolling psychic jam sessions and impromptu tarot readings. The beautiful experimental film-maker and performing artist Carolee Schneemann's performance piece raised a few eyebrows as she roller-skated through the coaches wearing only a smile. There was critical comment on her skating technique, but other passengers were less fussy. Just in case anyone missed any of the train's events, there was a newspaper printed and distributed en route by another performing artist, the King of the Gestetner Duplicator, Felipe Ehrenberg. Naturally the events at the Festival couldn't compete with the train ride we had just experienced – all the fun was in getting there. We did take in a Polish play, but regretted it.

My affair with the *avant-garde* covers many gruelling years, so I should have been prepared for Charlotte Moorman's *pièce de résistance* at the Roundhouse the following week. Bare-breasted, she performed on a cello made of ice with a glass bow an entire Saint-Saens cello concerto in pantomine until the cello melted. At the conclusion of the concert, she rushed backstage in a panic – an asbestos pad had slipped. 'Is there a doctor in the house?' she cried. 'I think my left tit is frost-bitten.'

Charlotte died of cancer at the age of 57 in a Manhattan hospital in 1991. Her obituary in *The Times* filled in some missing colourful bits of her life:

She played in the orchestra under Leopold Stokowski and for five years was a member of Jacob Glick's Boccherini Players. And then, in 1963, something happened. She explained it herself by saying that one day she became bored with a Kabalevsky cello piece, and someone suggested that she try playing John Cage's *26 Minutes, 1.1499 Seconds for a String Player*. This, among other things, requires the cellist to prepare and eat mushrooms during the performance. From this point on, the avant-garde became her life. That same year she founded the annual New York Avant-Garde Festival – which did not, of course, take place annually. Nevertheless, she presided over fifteen festivals during the ensuing nineteen years, attracting big audiences to such unlikely locations as the Grand Central Terminal and the Staten Island Ferry . . . The composer Edgard Varese once called Moorman 'the Jeanne d'Arc of new music' (though at this distance 'the Lady Godiva of music' might seem a more appropriate description). John G. Hanhardt, curator of film and video at the Whitney Museum of American Art, said on hearing of her death: 'She will be seen as very important to the history of video and performance art. She was a vital presence and had a passionate commitment to the avant-garde.

It was right after ICES that we began seriously to look around for another place to settle. England was sliding into economic disaster. Friends were leaving London for Paris and points east. In the back of our minds we never saw London as permanent. When the opportunity to buy a vintage Art Deco bus for peanuts came up, it seemed logically sound to have the means to escape in style. Turning the bus into a mobile Hilton, with chemical toilet, fitted kitchen, refrigeration, a dynamic sound system and generous sleeping arrangements, we were ready for any contingency.

CHAPTER ELEVEN

A few successful trial runs with our bus convinced us the Greyhound people in America had got it right – it was the only way to travel. Its advantages were self-evident. We were able to cook our meals and pick our scenic spots to park overnight, but its main attraction was that Fran's bed-life was uninterrupted. The bus had large windows in the sides of the roof, enabling her to see the sunset lying on her back. It made us independent of the usual travel nightmares. We set our sights on France. We had been there a number of times, always regretting our inability to master the language for the full flavour of the country. The time had come for us to go back to school.

We jumped in at the deep end, signing up for a term at the Lycée Français even though it was on the other side of town, in South Kensington. We needed the discipline of a classroom and a stern teacher. The trip across town would have been a drag had we not travelled in our bus. Driving through the early morning freshness of Hyde Park was the perfect hangover remedy. We must have looked like two delinquent schoolkids on their way to a picnic. Overtaking cars honked and waved their approval.

Our class was small enough for us to receive the kind of special attention required by two genetically handicapped pupils. Neither of us had mastered the tools of learning when we were young; Fran never learned how to link up letters in her progressive school, and I was hopeless at everything except geography. The only thing that made us think we had a chance was our dedication. I took work home every night. I played tapes of the day's session. I bought books and records in French. Fran and I tried to speak nothing but French, but that proved impractical, if we didn't augment the exchange with a heavy dose of sign language. Fran was making progress. The teacher was impressed with Fran's explanation of why we were late one day: '*Le chien a mangé mon mari,*' she said confidently.

To be honest, we didn't learn much French, but we were popular after class at the local *pâtisserie*. Those sessions were so animated with lively, sometimes revealing conversation that it was a great temptation to turn the class into an encounter group and forget the French lessons entirely. There was one girl who showed signs that a little therapy would not go amiss. She was, naturally, the most beautiful girl in the class, but her self-confidence was as inadequate as my knowledge of French verbs. She invited us to a party at her parents' house somewhere in the stockbroker belt. We were older than her parents, but not nearly as good looking. Nor did we have a yacht, vintage champagne, servants, and a swimming-pool. The party, of course, was a complete bore, which encouraged us to invite her to try our world for a real change of pace. It did cross my mind it was time for Cosmo to meet some new friends who were not reading Kafka.

We gave a small party with a cross-section of younger and more adventurous misfits (some of Miles' friends) who wouldn't think of improving a pretty girl's mind. Cosmo was not one of them. Over the years I had built up an indentikit picture of the perfect girl for Cosmo. She must have read Nietzsche by the time she started menstruating. A familiarity with the essays of Alexander Pope was not a necessity, but would help break the ice. She should be about six feet tall, wear dark prescription glasses, and have dirty fingernails. She should have hair long enough to whip him with, or none at all so he could worship her as some bald-headed goddess. Fortunately, this girl didn't meet a single requirement. I don't know what made me think she'd be suitable for Cosmo, but I personally can't resist a beautiful girl with a problem. Cosmo could and did, and was quite annoyed at my meddling. By the end of the term I can honestly say my only accomplishment was to be able to pronounce, in perfect French, the phrase 'the soles of my shoes have holes'.

Getting accredited to the Cannes Film Festival was harder than getting into Oxford. I had to ask the newspaper publisher Joseph Pulitzer to use his influence with his city editor and send me a letter saying I was going to write the best-ever column on the Cannes Film Festival because I was going down there in my bus and would invite the whole festival to tea. I received the letter, but no expenses, even for tea bags.

For added insurance, we took Hanya with us. She had worked in films in Rome, Paris and London, spoke four or five languages, and had many friends in the business. Our finding a place to park was due more to Hanya's good looks and French accent than to luck. Her way with the police was so enchanting that they stopped the traffic so we could make a triumphant entrance into the best parking space in town. The Palais was on one side of the street and *de luxe* municipal toilet facilities stood on the other.

That was the year the film industry discovered the Sexual Revolution. If the films featured at Cannes that year were anything to go by, soft core pornography was in for a long run. Late-night movie houses which once specialized in quirky or *avant-garde* films now showed erotic feature films of dubious cinematic value. Once again it brought up the question: was Hollywood reflecting the times or exploiting them? Cannes wasn't in the same league as the Wet Dream Film Festival, but the distributors were licking their lips in anticipation of finding a formula that worked miracles at the box office. At one of the French press conferences a reporter asked one of the distributors why all the relationships in his film were purely sexual. The film's star jumped in with a snappy reply: 'Come on, you old bag. Remember orgasms? Ain't they great?' Linda Lovelace didn't show up the first day, but Divine – who, in *Pink Flamingos*, actually ate some dog turds on camera – was in attendance.

A note of humour was struck by Manouche, doyen of the French criminal set. 'I've been coming to the festival for forty years and I love it – it's full of queers, so there are no screaming brats on the beaches. I'm here for Mastroianni's movie *La Grande Bouffe*. I'm godmother to the film and for the opening I'm going to dress up as *sauerkraut* with a sausage head-dress.'

Our own version of a banquet was a simple meal of rice, beans, vegetables, garlic and onions cooked in our *wok* in the bus. It may not have won any prizes, but as the smell of frying onions and garlic permeated the air, it endeared us to the local policeman. He mimed the raising of a wine glass to our health accompanied by an audible, '*Bon appétit.*'

The press conferences were often more exciting than some of the films. Alexandro Jodorowsky, director of *The Holy Mountain*, one of the festival's most talked about films, gave a sensationally hostile press conference at which he managed to alienate everyone with his views on violence, power, murder, sex, film and food. 'Why do you use so many cripples in your films?' asked a journalist. 'I use these monsters to show how monstrous humanity is,' he said. I introduced myself after the conference and congratulated him on his mentioning the influence of macrobiotics on his films. I invited him to have some brown rice on the bus; he, in turn, invited me to have a drink on his yacht. Unfortunately he didn't mention its name. Discreet inquiries proved useless. Fran warned me not to continue with my cry of, 'Alexandro Jodorowsky, where are you?' along the waterfront. When we finally found it, we went aboard only to discover he wasn't there, but his butler gave us a refreshing organic drink.

Cannes was the last place I ever thought I'd see Groucho Marx. I don't remember why he was there – he certainly hadn't made a film in years – but his press conference was a lively affair, full of irreverent throw-away lines. Groucho was old and rather deaf by then. A black reporter at the back asked him what he thought of the Black Power movement in America. He leaned over to a press officer and asked, 'What did the *schwatza* say?' Whether that was his way of answering the question or he really didn't hear it, no one will ever know, but he caught a lot of flak for the remark, which did not enhance his standing with anyone except those with a sense of humour that matched his.

A big problem for Fran and Hanya was what to wear. The post-hippy gear they'd brought was completely out of fashion, so they spent most of their time improvizing night-time outfits. I often ended up escorting two Vivienne Westwood lookalikes on the way to a psychedelic reunion. One of the films was directed by John Frankenheimer. At the point where the depressed hero considers cutting his throat, I turned to the woman next to me and said, a little too loudly, 'Do it, for Christ's sake, and let's get the fuck out of this movie.' To my surprise, the audience picked up on the suggestion and chimed in with the volley of loud, 'Do it's' as he agonized over his decision. It built a certain solidarity between us, much to the annoyance of Fran and Hanya. My neighbour turned out to be Eleanor Perry, who wrote the screenplay for one of our favourite films, *David and Lisa*. Our friend Victor Herbert, the last of the great philanthropists, was so impressed with meeting her, that he sprung for a fabulous dinner in an ethnic restaurant out of the high rent district, where we had more fun than we'd have had in the grand ballroom of the Majestic Hotel filled with celebs.

The bus, its sleek Deco lines gleaming in the sun, aroused some curiosity. The French are not the only ones who appreciate a vintage as rare as our temporary home. I won't go so far as to say it was competition for the topless parade of starlets on the beach, but people did peer into the windows to see who its lucky occupants were.

As we settled in, we felt that we were ready to entertain. I heard that movie critic Rex Reed was in residence. His scathing film criticisms in America were as notorious as his disparaging reviews of the festival antics. We had never met him, but we knew from Jackie and Roy, two of his favourite recording artists, that he admired Fran's 'sophisticated view of life through her lyrics'. He never dreamed he'd be invited to meet her in the middle of Cannes playing the role of Hostess to the Bus-Set.

Once he had settled down on the bus mattress with a nice cup of tea, he confessed to Fran in his soft Southern accent: 'I never expected to meet somebody like you under these peculiar circumstances. I thought you'd be on some *chaise longue* with a cigarette holder a foot long, drinking champagne, with a couple of Borzoi dogs at your feet, and entertaining the cream of society. It's a most original approach to the festival.' Even though tidbits of gossip flowed from his lips like sweet grape wine, I don't think he ever got over his illusion that sophisticated song-writers do not park outside the Palais and hold court in an ancient bus.

Our next guest was an old friend from our Greenwich Village days, Paul Mazursky, whose film *Blume in Love* was showing. We hadn't seen each other since 1955, when he played our club as part of the comic team Igor and H. (Herb Hartig). Paul was eager to meet us and had no trouble adapting to bus life, although he was staying in the plushest hotel in Cannes. 'I've been keeping in touch with your exploits, Jay. I've heard about your diet. I, too, have been following a special diet. For the past year I have been eating nothing but' – he paused like the master of timing he was – 'pastrami.'

It wasn't a surprise when he mentioned how alienated he felt in Cannes. I told him it was a far cry from his *Next Stop Greenwich Village*. 'Jay, my suite at the Majestic is making me nervous. Let me know when you have a vacancy, I'd like to move in – that is, if you take children. I have my daughter with me.'

After three days, there was hardly room for me and Fran. Once word got around about our 'hospitality bus', we'd have people coming around in the afternoon for tea and post-mortems on the previous night's indiscretions; at night they'd crash in the aisle. Privacy was at a premium. I felt like putting up one of those 'No Vacancy' signs so popular with guest houses.

It was something of a treat to escape to the posh hotels to catch a glimpse of the stars relaxing, but all we ever caught were people like us looking for the same thing. In short, we were not hounded by the paparazzi, but I talked a roving photographer from *Women's Wear Daily* into taking a shot of me throwing myself into the arms of a beautiful black American model who just happened to be passing. The photo turned up in a full page of shots of 'celebrities at Cannes', which included our Hanya, who made a small contribution by declaring that Bergman's *Cries and Whispers* was a film about lesbianism.

When we returned to London, I wrote a light-hearted article on how it felt not to be discovered in Cannes and not to be able to find where the orgies were. The article was rejected, which temporarily halted a promising career in journalism and future visits to Cannes. Returning to Duncan Terrace was always the best part of any trip. Just seeing that tree-lined street or the familiar face of the newsagent welcoming us home recharged our batteries as much as the trip had.

Duncan Terrace had been undergoing gentrification for some time, but now it was in danger of losing many of the characters which made it so colourful. At one end the artist Tom Espley was doing his best to hold back any signs of progress, which he saw as the ruin of mankind. Although he was relatively young, his heart was in the nineteenth century. His way of life, starting from the front-door bell that had to be pulled rather than pushed, was a homage to post-World War I standards. There were no mod. cons at his place – even a radio was considered too radical. What a pleasure it was having dinner there: the guests served themselves from a sideboard of old-fashioned English recipes to the soothing music of 'Whispering' Jack Smith on old 78s.

Guests' conversation never went beyond the relative merits of Prime Minister Baldwin's contribution to world order. Espley ignored the following decades as if they had been a temporary aberration. Although he was a teacher at Camberwell Art College, his main source of income was special commissions to copy paintings, nothing later than the Victorian period. Having him as anchorman of the terrace was uniquely comforting and I suspect it was because of his house and way of life that the Department of Environment classified the block as one of historic interest.

On one side of our house lived the vicar, and on the other there was Andrais, whom we called 'the Smiler'. He sat patiently at his window throughout the seasons, watching the passing parade. He had been invisible for most of his life, but his constant smile let the world know he was now accessible. There were those who felt sorry for him and who would return his cheerful smile, but others crossed the street to avoid his frightening set of National Health dentures. His was the first face we saw as we left the house in the morning, which I always enjoyed, but Fran's, 'I don't want to get involved,' showed a certain lack of neighbourliness.

'He's a creep,' our children said. 'He's always pestering young girls.' I didn't want to believe it. I asked a young sociology student who lived up the street if that was her experience. 'Don't you know?' she said. 'I used to stop and chat with him. He said he used to work in a sweat shop in the East End until he lost his job. One day he asked me if I would like to have a cup of tea. I'd had such a nice day, I thought the least I could do was to make his day a little nicer and accept. His little room was full of bleeding heart Jesus posters, so I didn't think anything was wrong with his asking me if I would like to see some frocks he used to make. He opened a cupboard door where they were kept. The frocks were innocent-looking enough, but what set off alarms in my head was the collection of nude photographs pasted inside the cupboard door. When he made it plain that I could have one of the frocks at 'a give-away price', I didn't wait for the kettle to boil. Does that answer your question? By the way, my mother wouldn't have worn them to a jumble sale.' Her startling revelation only made me feel sadder for him; I made a point of asking him if there was anything I could get him from the market.

Just the idea of living next to a vicar seemed exotic to a nice Jewish boy like me. I took great pride in informing guests of that fact, hoping that my proximity to such goodness would impress. If parties grew too loud, too wild or too long, I'd use the vicar as an excuse to slow down the action. 'Morning, Vicar,' was not my style, but I never failed to say hello to his big toothy wife – the kind of woman no scandal could ever touch. We kept up friendly appearances, but maintained a discreet distance until one night, way past midnight, we invited them in for a nightcap, never dreaming they would accept. We were with Rosie Boycott at the time, who whispered, 'He's cute for a vicar.'

The first brandy did little to break the ice, but they learned that Rosie had started *Spare Rib* and I learned that the wife played trombone in West End musicals. By the second brandy – Fran was showing signs of flaking – Rosie had begun a long dissertation on the role of vicars in English literature; the vicar seemed pleased, but it was a subject that sent Fran scurrying to bed. A delicate balance of intention hovered over the four of us as they accepted a third brandy. Was this the woman next door who constantly complained of our children's loud and often bad language in front of her two young brats? I was slightly drunk by now, so her smile struck me as an invitation to mischief. Testing an old theory, I started playing kneesies with her under the table. At least I thought that was what I was doing. There was no resistance as I stepped up enough pressure to crack a kneecap; it was embarrassing to discover the knee cap that was cracking was mine – against the leg of a very badly designed table. To salvage the evening, I promised the vicar I would be attending one of his sermons any day now.

If England's economy was under pressure, its emotional life was under siege. London was about to have a new communications centre. They called it Global Village. Three giant arches under Charing Cross railway station were transformed into an elaborate set for an English person to shed his or her inhibitions and get with it at the same time. Sounds, images, live theatre, organic food, ethnic dancers, loving hands' products, *avant-garde* films, expensive words and gentle touches were the basic ingredients for a unique environmental bill of fare. Global Village had everything money could buy to heighten the sensory perception of a nation of people not particularly interested.

Like most innovations in London life at the time, the energy and money came from America; close to $1 million was spent to give Londoners a chance to ease the pain of ordinary existence and let themselves go. It was a place where you could walk in as a tired, defeated, contemporary person, go through the processes and facilities of passing from one set of hands to the next, experiencing the softness of young flesh against your cheek, the blowing of sweet breath in your ear, the kiss of both female and male guides as they welcomed you into the world of games for grown-ups. You were expected to emerge a relaxed, informed, satisfied, organically fed and clothed human being of the future.

The last time Fran and I tried such a leap into the future in London was an encounter group that proved somewhat less engrossing. Our leader, a trendy dentist, was unsympathetic to my up-front American approach when challenged to come clean about the sadistic nature of dentistry. Shocked at such brazen tactics, he asked me to leave *pronto*. 'Nuts', I said. 'Put it to a vote. I signed up for the full twenty-four-hour treatment.' After the group voted for me to stay, I did my best to smooth things over, but it was obvious to everyone that the dentist's future did not lie in the New Age techniques for bringing people together.

After the Global Village session, we decided that the whisper of young flesh against the cheek and strange people of both sexes offering waspish lips to kiss was not the most meaningful experience we had ever had. Cosmo was somewhat more direct when we took him to an evening performance. 'What happens to a person who leaves this fantasy?' he asked the Global Village's high-powered public relations chief, Robin Green. 'How does he relate to the world outside after experiencing your environment? Do you care? Do your actors turn into probation officers to check up on audiences that have been through your three-hour jail sentence?' He was trying to tell the chief the Global Village was a rip-off, a Utopia taken over by a consumer society mentality.

Green did a masterful job of leading Cosmo through a philosophical justification that had its basis in the ideas of Marshall McLuhan, Buckminster Fuller and a dash of Joan Littlewood's Fun Palace, but Cosmo wasn't buying. 'I would have liked to have enjoyed the experiences offered tonight. I didn't.'

'That is the price you pay, Cosmo, for being such a cynic,' he replied.

When it became evident that the Global Village's dream of an alternative approach to leisure and learning was a complete disaster, the owners sold the lease to Richard Branson, the entrepreneur who founded Virgin Records. Global Village was renamed Heaven, a disco that was to become one of the great successes of the 1970s, especially with gays.

The collapse of Global Village's utopian dream was the last sign that the Sixties hippy-dippy world was finished. G. Legman's prediction that the 'fake revolt' was going to open the flood gates to excesses beyond anything ever seen was happening. 'Sex came out of the closet. There was nothing to be ashamed of anymore,' wrote 'Dee Flowheart' in a glossy magazine. 'Sex became a political matter ('Make Love. Not War'), a rallying point.' In 1971 America already had its first Sexual Freedom League. Women's liberation showed all the signs of future militancy with its demand that men became 'cunt-positive'. The clitoris was at last receiving the attention it deserved. Family taboos were breaking down. 'Miss Flowheart' quotes a passage from Jim Haynes's *Hello I Love You* about a mother supervising the initiation of her fifteen-year-old daughter into lovemaking:

> I talked to my lover; he was apprehensive at first, but we decided that if the whole thing was done in a very loving way we could show her together how to make love with a man. So I taught her how to get an erection on a man, and showed her where the sensuous areas are, and how to suck his cock. Everything was presented in a very beautiful way and with the understanding that it was natural and good. I had her take his come off my hand, smell it and taste it, so she never got any feeling other than of beauty. She watched Paul and me make love, and he didn't fuck her, but he played with her and petted her, and gave her a feeling of his love.

And people thought Fran and I were far out!

CHAPTER TWELVE

Bearing a famous name has one obvious advantage: head waiters in smart restaurants do not ask you to repeat it. It also has enormous disadvantages, as was brought home to me when I opened the door to one of its victims. He had a sheaf of foreign-looking flutes hanging from his shoulder, some penny-whistles in his shirt pocket, a beard and gold-framed glasses.

'Hello. I'm John Steinbeck Junior, a friend of John Simon's. Can I crash for a couple of nights?'

'Yeah,' I said, 'if you promise never to play those flutes in the house.'

He laughed, walked into our living-room, looked around for a second and said 'I like it. I think I'll stick around.'

Most people forgive the trespasses of the sons and daughters of the famous. They ignore their flaws and arrogance. Steinbeck's excesses would hardly classify him as the perfect guest; I never saw him wash a dish, cook a meal or even clear the table. However, I must give him credit for grinding the roasted sesame seeds we used as a seasoning. After three nights on the living-room mattress, he suggested the spare room might be more accommodating. I asked him, 'To whom?' He laughed and moved in that night.

During our afternoon drinking sessions, I came to know him. He was not bashful about talking about himself, a trait that endeared him to me. He had been around, displaying a finely-honed breed of irreverence. His faults were too numerous to mention. Fran wrote a poem about him that summed up the burden of carrying a famous name:

. . . The people ask you questions about your father's life
His habits and his pastimes, his crazy second wife
You answer them with patience, supply the missing link
The only thing you ask them is buy another drink . . .

Although we had much in common, it was our relentless pursuit of projects that bound us together. His projects were more ambitious than mine. There were movies to be made from the various short stories by his father that he controlled, but they never came off; there were novels to write which never got started. On one of those days that begin at noon with a liquid lunch and end up at three o'clock in the morning trying to remember the lyrics to obscure Cole Porter songs, Steinbeck and I managed to lay the ground work for a project to end all projects: an anti-talent agency.

It began by my saying I could straighten out his life if I were his business manager. (The Steinbeck name was his most valuable asset.) We ended up forming an agency for seriously flawed writers, actors and artists. We called it Creative Arts Liberated (CAL). It was dedicated to liberating the artist from becoming depressed about having the talent, but not the competitive spirit. 'We take the sting out of success and put the fun back in failure' was our motto. We promised prospective clients that we would never get them a job, but that, if one came along, we'd give it consideration. This appealed to Steinbeck's Zen sense of humour. On top of all his problems, he claimed to be a practising Buddhist.

Jordon Reynolds came back on the scene with perfect timing. He had found a building in Kentish Town in which squatted Christof, a young, poetic-looking Polish aristocrat. The three of us inspected the new premises, which Christof grandly christened the Poly-tantric Building. It was not an impressive structure, but big enough to turn into a multi-anti-energy centre. It had the feel of a building that was about to come to life. There was already a store on the ground floor which gave away clothing and household items. It was doing a flourishing business – the only store I had ever heard of that didn't need a cash register. The upstairs rooms housed a variety of alternative enterprises, including a primal scream room and a large area turned into a martial arts gymnasium. In the basement was a disused printing press, and a stage which had once displayed gas cookers was turned into a cabaret for emerging rock groups and needy poets.

With the offices fitted out from local skips and stationery printed on the reconditioned printing press in the basement, CAL was in business. We gave a cocktail party launch, inviting potential clients. These included the local bikers and tradesmen from the area. The star of the party was an American girl called Doshin, who was breaking in her act as the first *kung-fu* stripper, an act incorporating poetry as well as stripping. Her songwriting talent was not going to give Fran any competition:

> Sadie Mae
> Oh oh oh oh
> Sadie Mae can you come out to play?
> We're revving our bikes in black leather spikes
> You know you look divine
> Strung out on the back of mine
> We'll have a strapping bad time.

William Berger, an American actor based in Rome, came to town to promote *City of Angels*, a book Timothy Wilson had written about his plight. Berger was well known for his panache in spaghetti westerns, and his other crime was leading a life-style unacceptable to the Italian police of Positano. The police watched with horror as Berger turned his house in Positano into a hippy enclave. His wife was a member of the Living Theatre, whose antics the authorities already had under surveillance. When the bust came, he and his wife were jailed, physically mistreated, harassed and threatened. The police refused to allow his wife the medical attention she needed; a cruel decision to withhold her medicine resulted in her death.

His career in ruins, he arrived in London anxious to relaunch it here. Becoming a client of CAL was not the wisest course. With all my connections, the only exposure I could obtain for him was an interview in the Underground paper IT, and even they seemed sceptical. The book died. He was impressed by our monumental failure to get his career back on the boards, but reluctant to indulge in self-pity.

By now both Berger and Hanya were staying with us, and it looked as though Berger was going to get lucky. Hanya and Hugh had split up some time ago, leaving her with an unemployed heart. 'I like him too,' I said, 'but he's not for you.' She got pregnant that same night.

Berger left for Sardinia to build a new commune for losers, but, before he left, he asked what he could do for CAL. 'For openers, how about paying CAL's phone bill?' He gave us a cheque that would cover it for some time. 'I only wish I could stick around and see CAL take over William Morris,' was his parting remark.

Steinbeck and I had weekly conferences on the progress of his professional career; it was not going well, which suited him, but not me. I had come to appreciate his talent for conning people into thinking he was going to outclass his father some day by writing the big one. The best I could do for him was to introduce him to Rosie Boycott. They made an instant connection. It was as if they had been waiting years to meet. On the next day, Rosie reports in her book, *A Nice Girl Like Me*, they took some acid in an open field of cows. Steinbeck did a number with the cows, playing his flute; they gathered around him as if he were the Pied Piper. Later, at lunch, Steinbeck told her he loved her and moved into her place. I was glad to see the end of the flutes, but I missed our ridiculous daily conferences. As a parting gesture to express his thanks for our hospitality, he gave me a hug which bruised my entire rib-cage.

As the Polytantric's most successful tenant, I was called upon to officiate at the ribbon-cutting ceremony opening the newly decor-ated tea house on the ground floor. On the great day, it was discovered that the gas had been cut off and they had forgotten to have it restored. Worse, there was no ribbon or gas cylinder to be had on a Sunday. Christof, a master of *ad-hoc*-ism, stretched blue toilet paper across the entrance in such abundance that it proved difficult to cut through with the blunt scissors I was given. While trying to get the kettle on, Christof discovered the electricity had been shut off. We borrowed a blowtorch from the bikers and held it under the kettle. With all problems solved, the only thing which kept it from being a memorable day was that nobody showed up for the ceremony.

A much larger crisis loomed with the arrival of a producer who wanted Steinbeck as technical advisor on a film he was shooting in Vietnam. The fee was impressive enough for Steinbeck to consider taking the assignment in spite of what such a success would do to CAL's reputation. He took the money, but, instead of returning to Vietnam, he ended up going to India with Rosie on a motorbike to help a dying friend find a miracle-working guru. His departure marked the beginning of the end for CAL. How fitting that it should have done so on such a romantic and loyal gesture.

CAL was still operating, but along more conventional agency lines. One of my clients was Timothy Leary, whose literary efforts were in disarray. He had written a science fiction novel on the ultimate space journey. I thought, with his reputation in that field, it would be a natural to sell to English publishers, but it turned out to be too spaced out even for the most courageous of them.

My other client was Fran, whose career had taken a strange turn. She had been invited to read some of her poetry at a special event in the crypt of St Martin-in-the-Fields organized by Satish, an Indian who had just walked around the world for peace. She had her doubts about reading poems that rhymed to an audience used to free verse, but she thought it would look good on her CV. To her astonishment, she got through it in record time, to a receptive audience which included some hard-bitten poets and Michael Horovitz, who set up her next gig at the Three Horseshoes in Hampstead.

By now she displayed a cool, self-deprecating, quirky charm that enchanted the audience. Her poems were reminiscent of desperate conversations held in smart bars or brooded about in lonely rooms. After it was over, Brian Patten, who had been performing with success for years, came up to her and said by way of appreciation just two words: 'Et cetera.' 'Does that mean you liked my act?' Fran asked. His answer was a big hug. I was so impressed with her

124

subsequent performances, I decided to put a number of the poems and her lyrics into a pamphlet to give to friends for Christmas. Song-writer Johnny Mercer's annual Christmas card in rhyme, which Fran enjoyed so much, was the inspiration. Although the pamphlet was a lousy job of production, Fran's wry observations on life read well in print. People liked them and, to our surprise, asked for more.

It so happened that a printing and graphics co-operative moved into the Polytantric building, offering their services for practically nothing just to get their name established. Their designer was a woman who loved Fran's work; the printing was done by a Buddhist centre in Purley, who didn't understand a line, but whose price was right. The book, called *The Ballad of the Sad Young Men and Other Verse*, was dedicated to the people who had recorded her songs – Chet Baker, Shirley Bassey, Tony Bennett, Betty Carter, Petula Clark, Miles Davis, Gil Evans, Ella Fitzgerald, Roberta Flack, Stan Getz, Cleo Laine, Carmen McCrae, Rod McKuen, Mabel Mercer, Anthony Newley, Anita O'Day, Zoot Sims, Sarah Vaughan, and Nancy Wilson – as well as Fran's collaborator, Tommy Wolf, and 'Jackie and Roy, who were the first to record my work'.

This time the production was professional, looking like a real book. Fran was delighted with my first effort as a publisher. I was very proud of it too, until Jeremy Brooks, who was the first person to see a finished copy, called. 'Loved the book, Jay,' he said, 'but did you know the author's name on the cover is misspelled?' Being in love with failure dies hard, but I honestly wanted this book to be a success and came up with an idea that salvaged the project. I had a metal dye made which cut out the misspelled name on the cover, leaving a blank space on the fly leaf for Fran to write in her signature. It lent a personal touch as well as a three-dimensional look, unique for its time. The only complaint from Fran was an aching right hand from signing 500 numbered copies.

With her reputation firmly established now, it was easy for me to get her gigs at arts centres, jazz festivals, universities, workshops and theatre clubs all over England. When Michael Kustow, then director of special projects at the National Theatre, invited her to

125

do a platform performance at the Lyttelton Theatre, she felt she had arrived. There were some who thought her sitting down on the apron of the stage like Judy Garland was a bit much, but it was this theatrical touch which enlivened her act. In fact, Kustow invited her back to play the Olivier Theatre to another enthusiastic audience.

She was now CAL's only client, but a valuable one who needed constant attention. I began to slip into the role of her personal manager, something that required getting used to since I was the one who usually received all the attention. Her success was not of the kind that turned into jealousy on my part. I was proud of what she was accomplishing, but I couldn't reconcile the fact it wasn't making her any easier to live with. She still felt she wasn't really doing what she did best, which was writing lyrics for Broadway or at least a West End musical.

When I came back from the office, I often found her on the bed, depressed. At those times I questioned the value of devoting all my time and energy to promoting her. 'What the hell do you want? I'm doing everything I can to make you happy and what thanks do I get? After a hard day at the office devoted to your interests, what do I come home to? A depressed, *angst*-ridden wife.'

'I'm a poet, I'm Russian. What do you expect?' was her only explanation.

It wasn't enough for me. Whether from jealousy or envy, I decided it was time for positive action. I wasn't about to become Fran's husband, Jay, after a lifetime of her being Jay's wife, Fran. The next day I started on my memoirs. I wrote to a widely read columnist in St Louis that, if anybody remembered what I had been doing between 1934 and 1964, I would like to hear from them. I received a reply from one of my teachers, who said I wasn't 'particularly literate'. The other reply was from a boyhood friend, who reminded me I used to be called 'Butch'.

A third of the way through the book, I realized I was writing in the wrong voice. Envy and all its side effects swept through me, colouring my story a shade of emotional puce that was most unattractive. I put the manuscript in the overcrowded trunk and forgot that I had a past.

My future was in doubt too, but, thanks to my past, a challenge came from the most unexpected source. The St Louis City Fathers had been trying for years to do something about restoring a historical area on the banks of the Mississippi; the area had been ripe for redevelopment for years, but had proved too big an undertaking for local planners. My only experience up till then had been the successful development of a three-block area. Turning some twenty-six blocks of historical significance into another successful Gaslight Square was a formidable task. It was obvious they wanted to pick my brains when no cheque or contract accompanied their letter. Nevertheless, the offer was a perfect opportunity to improvize on some of my old theories of environmental engineering on a grand scale.

Finding someone in London interested enough in the idea seemed unlikely. I consulted the *Yellow Pages* in search of a 'Genius', but discovered they were a breed that didn't advertise. I found instead an organization called Environmental Consulting Service. It sounded perfect, but from its fancy address I imagined it to be too chic for a collaboration on a project which offered no front money and little chance of success. I couldn't have been more wrong. Its director, Gerry Carter, was a full-time architect and part-time prophet who, I was sure, after seeing some of the models of his grandiose schemes, had some astral connection with the building of the pyramids. One meeting was enough to establish that we were made for each other.

Working from data, aerial photographs, historical backgrounds, and my personal knowledge of St Louis, we conceived the idea of a walled city, five storeys high and five storeys below the surface, recreating St Louis at its peak – 'to enshrine its past and ensure it a future'. The whole project was conceived as a film set, a vast stage where the people were the actors and the large spaces became whole changing environments through which tourists and natives would pass, experiencing a series of environmental surprises which included trolley cars, a horse and buggy, telegraph poles and gaslight clusters – 'revolving nostalgia' we called it. There would be speakeasys, hanging gardens, a spectacular waterfall, flea markets, boutiques, workshops, restaurants, bars, a paddle steamer, jazz shrines, pop festivals, parade grounds, a race track and an outdoor auditorium. We aimed for a commercial enterprise to cater for the explosive growth in leisure time and, at the same time, give new heart and pride in history to St Louis.

After months of work, armed with a slick, professional presentation, I arranged to go to St Louis and present the proposal to the City Fathers. I wasn't expecting to win their approval on the first presentation, but felt we had developed a bold enough programme for them to take it seriously. Some did, and asked me to stick around for further discussions. Worried, I consulted the architectural critic for the *Post-Dispatch*, George McCue, for some idea of what to expect. He complimented me on the boldness of the plan, but raised the problem of a walled city at a time of racial tension, when any innocent gesture would be interpreted as a provocative act. I didn't wait for further meetings, but packed up the 'dream city' and returned to London – not a wiser man, but one of the first victims of political correctness.

I wasn't out of projects long. Into my life came Gary Davis, a hero of my youth and the original architect of World Citizenship, an organization about as obscure (and successful) as a school for Esperanto. Davis was in London to set into motion the British branch of what he called his party, a collection of people who held world citizenship passports.

Once a USAF bomber pilot, Gary became world famous when he pitched a tent in Paris, where the United Nations were meeting for the first time and declared himself World Citizen Number One. The newsreel shots of him tearing up his American passport on the steps of the United States Congress were an inspiration to my generation, starved of a little post-war rebellion. Since then, he has travelled on a world passport, which he designed and printed himself, and which was his only source of income costing £4 a go. It looked like a passport, felt like a passport, and to some immigration officials it passed for one. Eight countries have recognized his one-man sovereignty, and many more, mostly in the Third World with unpronounceable names, validated his passport.

When he showed up that day, he was a bald, bearded, paunchy looking salesman with a briefcase which contained detailed plans for a world government, including a new currency, a world mutual bank, an institute for economic justice, and a fixed rate of exchange – more or less what is being proposed today by the Euro-planners. I liked the idea. Fran warned me against ending as Sancho Panza to his Don Quixote.

I invited him to dinner. His plans sounded good over the hors d'oeuvre, but by dessert it had all turned into a scenario for a world bureaucracy, and he had clearly cast himself as the lone saviour of civilization. Fran thought he lacked the humility of Don Quixote. I thought his scam was so nutty that it might be fun to see how far he could take it. From the very first press conference, well attended, where he announced the opening of the headquarters for the British branch of his phantom world government, I knew the media would pick up on him. It was summer, the beginning of the silly season.

What was even sillier was his offer to appoint me as the party's British Ambassador to the Court of St James. My house was to become the diplomatic headquarters for the party. The only other time I had ever served in an official capacity had been as a judge in the Gaslight Square beauty contest. I told Cosmo and Miles that at last I was going straight, but Cosmo saw it as another attempt to humiliate him. Miles rather liked the idea of the family car having CD plates and Thames Television coming to record the flag raising ceremony. We had the World flag, but no flagpole. Panic set in.

As the television crew set up the cameras for the historic event, I grabbed a mop from the kitchen, broke off the mop head, tied the flag to the handle and triumphantly waved it outside the bedroom window. The party's anthem, *My Country is the World*, with lyrics by Fran and music by Paul Jones, had been recorded by him and we broadcast it over a borrowed ghetto-blaster. The cameras were rolling. The television crew couldn't keep a straight face. Later, Fran and I were interviewed in the doorway of the new diplomatic nerve centre of Islington. The presenter, whose tongue was firmly in his cheek, asked about my qualifications for such high office.

'I have all the right clothes necessary to fulfil the appointment,' I said, looking to Fran for verification. She was too stunned to answer. Her eyes glazed over as I put my arm around her affectionately.

'And who is the lovely lady?' he asked.

'This is my Ambassadorable,' I said somewhat sombrely.

'Cut,' cried the presenter, breaking into uncontrollable giggles.

That night the whole sequence was at the end of the news. A friend who was in hospital called me from his bed. 'You son of a bitch,' he yelled. 'I just saw you on the news. I laughed so hard my stitches broke. Now I have to stay here another two days.'

I never made it to the Court of St James, but I was given an honorary passport should I ever want to leave the country. Davis finally returned to his headquarters in Berne, to be hounded by the French Government for passport forgery. The London World Citizenship passport division was taken over by Jordon Reynolds, who finally found a lost cause that was profitable.

CHAPTER THIRTEEN

When I heard that Cutie was near the end, I flew to St Louis to be with her. I had some unfinished business which needed sorting out. At her bedside, I adopted what I thought was a light-hearted approach to death.

'Well, Cutie, are you satisfied with the way life turned out for you?'

She gave me that look of hers which said, 'What a question to ask at a time like this.' With a great effort, she raised her eyebrows and a suggestion of a smile crossed her ancient lips. 'I stayed out of jail, didn't I?' I couldn't help but laugh. Did she think that to show any vulnerability was a crime?

The turn-out for her funeral was disappointing. I thought her act would have put bums on temple seats, but box office she wasn't. Hardly anybody showed except a few old-time customers and a couple of the dealers she had spent a lifetime bargaining with. Where was the Sisterhood of Temple Israel, whose members she had poured thousands of cups of tea for over the years? I felt sorry for the Rabbi, who struggled valiantly to say some nice things about her.

My brother Gene was there with a camera, which I thought was in doubtful taste. 'Hey, Gene, it's a funeral, not a wedding.' Gene always had his own way of handling Cutie, with no quarter given or taken. Ordinarily, Gene was the quiet Landesman. I was shocked when he gave the camera to someone to take his picture making the v for victory sign over the casket. He may have come to terms with Cutie, but I never did. All I ever wanted from her was a letter that said her baby, Jay Irving, was OK, but I knew she would never sign it now. She was a tough bird, but I loved her toughness.

I was just beginning to feel comfortable in the Svengali role with Fran, when she accepted an invitation to tea that turned out to be an invitation to change my life – again! I went to pick her up at Jill Neville's house. While waiting, I spotted a lonely looking manuscript among the dozens of books lying around the room that Jill was reviewing for the *Sunday Times*. It was a collection of poems by Elizabeth Smart. I thought they were terrific and told Jill they should be published.

I had met Elizabeth the first week I came to London, and had had a crush on her ever since. I was one of the 300 people at the launch of the paperback edition of *By Grand Central Station I Sat Down and Wept* at the Roundhouse in 1966. The setting might have been designed by Jean Cocteau, except for all the mini-skirts and flowing Indian dresses. The party had lasted until 2.30 am, clearly enjoyed by all her publishing friends, family and drinking chums from Soho. Over 100 glasses were broken, a sure sign that the launch had been a success.

Jill told me Elizabeth had been living in obscurity in a remote part of Suffolk taking care of her grandchildren, cultivating her garden – a miniature Sissinghurst – and trying to cope with a classic case of writer's block. In spite of the favourable reviews, nothing much had happened after the paperback publication, but, unknown to her, the book had become an underground classic. Had it been published a couple of years later, its timing would have been perfect for the Women's Movement.

By now she had such a solid reputation that I was convinced all she had to do was let any publisher know she had something new and they would snap it up. I learned from Rosemary Sullivan's recent biography of Elizabeth, however, that one of the contributing factors to her writer's block was not having a sympathetic publisher to encourage her.

'You're the first to see these poems, Jay. Why don't you publish them? You did such a good job on Fran's book,' said Jill.

I was sure she would want someone more experienced than I to relaunch her career after thirty dry years.

'But Elizabeth doesn't want to bother with a big publisher. She doesn't like all the hassle you get from them. She wants them published quickly. You two would make a perfect team.' I hesitated. 'Call her up right now and tell her how much you like the poems and that you want to publish them. I'll bet you anything she'll say yes. And I tell you this confidentially, *By Grand Central Station* is available too. She got back the rights.'

The idea of publishing it was reason enough to go into the publishing business. I made the call. When I told Elizabeth that I wanted to publish the poems, she thought I was being 'too kind'. I wrote to explain my position:

Dear Elizabeth,
As you know, I want to publish your book of poems, but I think I should tell you something about the way I plan to operate. I am not a professional. That is to let you know I don't believe in contract ceremonies, but I do hold great store in a handshake. I only do things that are fun to do; the minute it becomes a hassle, I'm not interested. If you think I will do a good job on just my word then you should publish with me – it will be more fun. If you require all the trappings of a big company, I am not for you. I am prepared to give you an advance of £100 . . . I like to keep the business details to a minimum. You will get a good shake . . .
Fondly,
Jay.

I was nervous about the meeting with Elizabeth, but it was nothing compared to her nervousness. We met at the French Pub, familiar ground for both of us. I had seen her many times there, often wishing I were one of the lucky ones in whose company she was usually found. Although we always exchanged hellos and sometimes bought each other drinks, I never felt I was one of her inner circle. After a few drinks, she relaxed enough to take my arm as we skipped around to Wheelers, where she was greeted like a long lost friend by the knowing head waiter, a gesture I appreciated more than she did. I ordered some champagne to begin with, playing the role of the City publisher with the little country girl at his mercy.

By the end of the lunch, I discovered she knew a lot more about publishing than I did; she suggested some kind of contract would be appropriate to cover foreign, American, and paperback rights. I promised I'd try to find a contract form somewhere that would give me some idea of how to arrange those things.

Peter Owen, one of the most successful independent publishers, tried to dampen my enthusiasm for publishing. 'Don't publish any poetry or novels, biographies and satire,' he warned me, but he had a great deal of respect for Elizabeth Smart. If anyone knew about how to run a small successful publishing company, it was Peter Owen. A regular at the French, it was through him that I learned the most important detail of a contract – give very little to the author. In Elizabeth's case I'd make an exception.

I found the perfect office in a squat in Maida Vale. It was on a street controlled by squatters, a highly streetwise group of entrepreneurs, including Winston Churchill's grand-daughter Arabella. When I learned she operated the local vegetarian restaurant, I volunteered my services, but her five-year-old son was already employed as the added attraction – he looked exactly like his great-grandfather. Arabella, unlike some of the family, avoided any attempts to capitalize on the Churchill name. The neighbourhood accepted her without reservation. When she organized the block party to celebrate the Queen's Silver Jubilee, it was heartwarming to see the poor, the dispossessed and the junkies waving the flag of the Empire and dancing in the street under a balloon-hung sky.

My office was the size of the waiting-room of an unsuccessful dentist, yet it seemed big enough for a publisher who only had a contract for one book of poetry and the possibility of another. The first thing I did was to subscribe to the *Bookseller*. From it, I discovered the basic information required to make my first move – get the book into the bookshops before the reviews. The first person I saw was John Hyams, the buyer for W. H. Smith, whose fondness for poetry, I was led to believe, stopped with Pam Ayres. He actually read a couple of Elizabeth's poems in my presence. I was very nervous until I heard a laugh – he liked them and gave me a firm order for 350 copies, unheard of for a W. H. Smith book buyer in 1977.

Encouraged by his act of faith, I hit upon the idea of dealing directly with distributors and bookshop owners whenever possible. Those in London I called on personally; out-of-town dealers I called on the phone, using the same approach. I was surprised so many booksellers knew of Elizabeth Smart. Those who did, I told about a new hardback edition of her novel which would be available soon. The telephone technique was so successful that it became my trademark.

Producing a book and promoting an author aren't that different from producing a show, and showbiz was my biz. I rallied all the friends I had made in the media over the last fourteen years to help bring in a hit. On the day the book came out, Julian Holland, an editor on BBC Radio 4's *PM* news programme, featured an interview with Elizabeth. Many of her admirers in the literary world followed up with interviews and reviews which gave Elizabeth's first work in thirty years the attention she deserved and badly needed. That all the publicity sold out the first edition of 2,500 copies was 'a bonus', which was the title of her book. In those days a slim volume of verse which sold 500 copies was considered a best-seller.

It was time to talk about a new hardback edition of *Grand Central Station*. When I suggested she might want a more serious publisher who could do a better job, she insisted she didn't want anything to do with the professionals. '*Grand Central Station* took thirty years for people to appreciate, through no help from them. I like the way you get things done without a fuss. I have another book I just finished that you can have too.' It was a bombshell. I thought I had a temporary licence to print money.

The relationship between writer and publisher flourished. For the cover, she gave me a rare photograph of herself and George Barker, both of them obviously in love, walking hand in hand at night with Grand Central Station in the background. I wanted to maintain that sense of nostalgia and asked her to write out the title in her own handwriting. Consulting Elizabeth on every step of the production gave her the feeling she hadn't lost her 'baby' as she would have with a big publisher. We used to meet whenever she was in London to plan future projects together. A gardening book was outlined. Publishers were eager. Elizabeth was having fun for the first time in years.

I had become hopelessly devoted to her. I told her how brave I thought she and George were to flaunt the conventions of the times. 'You did it in wartime,' I said, 'when it was really tough. Do you realize you two were in pajamas when the rest of America was in uniform? You're pre-Kerouac's *On the Road*.' I continued to guide her as much as she would let me. Sometimes she acted annoyed at having to do radio and press interviews, but never once failed to show up. At the first reading she did – Fran was on the same bill – she got cold feet and wanted her son, Sebastian, to read for her. 'You must read yourself. You'll like it, I promise you,' Fran told her. 'All those young boys coming up to you after the performance telling you how wonderful you are.' Elizabeth was terrified. According to Rosemary Sullivan, she likened reading in public to 'sitting in a gas chamber', but, once she was in the spotlight, old Dr Footlights came to her rescue and she performed like a veteran.

I thought, when the *Observer* gave her the Literary Comeback of the Year Award for 1977, she was on her way. I stepped up my lunch dates with publishers and the media, which led to the sale of the paperback rights to Nick Webb at Panther. The advance was unheard of for a cult author. I got to know the wonderful world of Tom Maschler at Jonathan Cape, who undertook the distribution of the second edition of *A Bonus* and made a co-publishing deal for Elizabeth's new novel, *The Assumption of the Rogues and Rascals*.

There were good reviews for the latter, but the major ones were literary muggings. 'What's it all about?' asked Auberon Waugh. When I was doing background material on the book, I asked her the same question. She wrote back: '*The Assumption of the Rogues and Rascals* is the story of a person (female) who has been shattered by an experience and is resolved to get on with survival, work, bringing up children, etc. She is consoled by friends, drink, nature, observations, etc; she learns compassion for other people; she wants to make something (write sometime), to capture the past, to encapsulate the present, to make sense of being alive. She tries the various other ways of life, but finds they won't do. She goes on, and on, and gets a glimpse of a meaning. She is purified (accepts the will of God as some people would say). Or – it is about being a woman, unprotected. Or – it is about being alive without telling lies.' She added a postscript: 'But if it were easy to tell what it's about, I wouldn't need to have written it, would I?'

'Heroine in a Terrible Mess' Waugh's caption writer concluded after reading his copy. Elizabeth was very hurt – no, she was furious. Jeremy Treglown's review in the *New Statesman* convinced her son Sebastian that he should be challenged, but Elizabeth would not permit it. On the day Waugh's review came out, I happened to run into him at the French Pub. Without mentioning his awful review, I asked him how much influence he thought a bad review had on the sales of a book. 'Not much, 200 or 300 copies,' he said. I didn't buy him a drink, but I didn't throw the one I had in his face.

In spite of the poor reviews, Elizabeth was in demand. *Grand Central Station* was dramatized by the BBC, with Maureen O'Brien winning the prize that year for the best radio performance. A stage dramatization was presented in an off-off Broadway production. Elizabeth was tickled that someone wanted to turn it into a musical. She went as far as writing a lyric:

> By Grand Central Station I sat down and wept
> Because of the date that you never kept
> By Grand Central Station I sat down and said
> Being in love is worse than being dead.
>
> Chorus: Boohoo hoo hoo
> Choo choo choo choo
> Wish I could lose
> Those Grand Central Station blues.

He was bad
But I loved him like mad
I have to cry
Because that dirty double-crosser has said goodbye

(Chorus)

I cry and cry and cry
'Cause love and all its trimmings is a great big lie
I cry all night and I take a train at dawn
Lovers' meetings end but the journey goes on

(Chorus)

I liked it so much I gave it to Brian Gascoyne to set and record. Of course nothing came of it, but Elizabeth was having fun again. All her books were in print. She had eclipsed George Barker as a literary figure.

There seemed little more I could do for her until some time later, when Metropolis Films (London) wanted an option to make *GCS* into a feature film. She didn't like the idea, but I talked her into taking the money and guided her through three options. Just before the last option was about to run out, I received a serious call from Timothy Burrill, a high-profile English producer who, after a very successful meeting with Elizabeth, was prepared to make it his number one project. I notified Metropolis Films that I had other interests, never thinking they would pick up the final bill, a £17,000 payment for the complete rights, but they did.

This did not make Elizabeth happy. She resented my encouraging her on the whole film project, accusing me of conspiring to invade her privacy. 'I sold them the rights to my book,' she told a friend, 'not to my life.' In spite of all the encouragement she received from friends to keep writing, she returned to a solitary life, reading her journals, contemplating whether she should write her autobiography. We drifted apart. I went to her funeral, held in a village church near her home. As they lowered her casket, there was hardly a dry eye among all the rogues and rascals from Soho who, in the end, were her real friends. I counted myself lucky to have known her.

CHAPTER FOURTEEN

I was fifty-eight years old. Fran and I had been married for twenty-seven years. Our children hadn't become junkies. For the first time since coming to England thirteen years previously, I was doing something I was good at and having fun too. In spite of Peter Owen's dire predictions, I published the kind of books he had warned me against. 'Who knows,' I told Fran, 'we might break even in this game.' I had certainly got off to a flying start with Elizabeth Smart. 'Now that I'm a real publisher,' I said, 'it's time I got a real office.' It meant dipping into what little capital we had.

Fran backed me up all the way and even told me how proud she was of me. 'Who knows' – she parodied my earlier remark – 'I might even let you publish my next book.'

Finding a seedy-beyond-belief office on Wardour Street for £15 a week plus a modest key fee was my second coup in publishing. It was a salubrious location, adjacent to a sex cinema called Spankorama. (I went to see a demonstration of the fifty-nine different ways to spank, and left convinced that all my past troubles had sprung from not being spanked properly by Cutie.) What really turned me on was telling prospective visitors my address. '159 Wardour Street, you know, right next to Spankorama, one floor up.' Built before America's Civil War, it was the perfect background for the Gentleman Publisher, Jay Landesman Limited. My new logo was a spilt bottle of ink.

A pattern was beginning to emerge – get the books out fast, give small advances and big promises, and maximize the promotion of the book and myself. Discovering writers was the exciting part of the operation; promoting them was the next objective. Heathcote Williams could have gone to any publisher with the manuscript for his new play *Hancock's Last Half-Hour*. Instead, he offered it to me, because he said he liked the way I got my books into bookshops. I think the real reason was because I was the only publisher who would publicize his lurid, flamboyant past exploits:

> Heathcote Williams is the author of the play *AC/DC*, *The Speakers*, a documentary novel about the Hyde Park Corner orators, *The Local Stigmatic*, *The Truth Dentist*, and the orgiastic opera *The Supernatural Doctor*; and as a partner in the Ruff Tuff Cream Puff Estate Agency, which provides free accommodation for the homeless, he's been involved in various enlightened crimes, such as opening up the Palm Court Hotel for the battered wives and children of Chiswick Women's Aid; the Albion Free State Meat Roxy, a former bingo hall in the Ladbroke Archipelago, where he organized free days and nights of nameless wildness. A volume of his essays, manifestos, and graffiti on God, Sex, Death, squatting, Beasts Liberation, Plant Lib., suing the Chief Constable of Windsor, etc., to be entitled *Severe Joy* is to appear soon.

In one week my telephoning around brought in over 750 orders, but it could have been a sign of the affection British bookdealers had for Hancock. (Of course, they know Heathcote Williams as the best-selling saviour of elephants, whales and dolphins.) Louis Baum, who was deputy editor of the *Bookseller* at the time, was so intrigued with my operation that he asked me to write up my experiences for the magazine. Thus began a series of occasional articles on the trials and tribulations of a very small publisher. It gave me national recognition and Baum said it put a sense of fun into a very straight-laced business.

And business was good. I could no longer do everything; I needed a Girl Friday. The last one I'd had was a groupie of Miles's band, a fifteen-year-old with a literary bent. Coming to work after school in her uniform, throwing down her homework and making me a cup of tea, she never failed to top up an already exciting day. She refused to join me in the move to Soho lest she run into a family connection, Lucien Freud, who she implied was very strict. I didn't believe her until Freud deliberately kicked me in the shins outside the French Pub. He must have heard I was not as strict as he was.

I suppose I should have gone to Help The Aged to look for a Girl Friday to fit in with the office's character, but I hired 'Jumble' Annie instead. I called her Jumble because she was one of those women who looked good in anything, but especially good in the kind of things bought at jumble sales. She possessed a droll wit and the lines of a woman who had enjoyed a misspent youth. She was brilliant at everything, often surprising me with how much she could accomplish on a salary of £12 a week. She loved her work – at least until I turned over the promotion via the telephone to her. Listening to her attempts to pitch a book or an author was a highlight of my day.

'Ummm . . . umm . . . is that er? This is Um . . . Annie Sheldon-Williams. You won't have heard of me . . . you have? How extraordinary – it must be my husband you know . . . I am representing Landesman Limited. We are a very small publisher, you certainly can't know about us – we're very insignificant, we've never done anything particularly exciting . . . *Grand Central Station*? Well, I am surprised! . . . Well . . . er . . . er . . . forgive me for bothering you, I know you have much better things to do with your time – but I'd like to tell you about our new book, though it won't interest you much, I'm afraid . . . thank you for being so patient . . . It's called . . . forgive me for just a moment while I look it up, sorry to be so stupid . . . Do you really want to know? . . . It's a silly title, don't you think? Just wait till you see the cover – that's even worse . . . I think the author's quite talented, but then I'm usually wrong about everything . . . Shall I send you a copy? Though you might not think it's worth the trouble to read . . . Oh, very well, with pleasure . . . I'm so grateful – though I know you're just being kind. Our phone number? Just a second . . . I've got it here somewhere . . . '

Most of her calls, for reasons that escaped me, proved to be extremely effective.

What appealed to me most was getting a book out of someone who never thought of writing one. 'Everyone has a story,' as Tyrone Power said in *Nightmare Alley*, and I believed him. Everyone was a potential prospect. My opening line at the French Pub to anyone who looked as though he or she had led an interesting life was, 'Have you ever thought of writing your memoirs?'

I wasn't the only publisher who used the pub as a likely source for material. Peter Owen actually published the memoirs of the publican of his local pub, who went on to write another book. Like me, Peter was always on the look-out. A kind of competition developed between us as we surveyed the talent available.

When I told him I was dickering with one of the regulars at the French Pub, Paul Potts, Peter warned me that he was a literary scrounger and would never come up with the goods. I was so fond of Potts that I wanted to do something to revive his career. Unbeknowst to me, someone else had had the same idea. An unsung surrealist poet Charlie Graham, who published an arcane magazine, *Tuba*, felt that Paul's work had been neglected and republished his book of poems *Instead of a Sonnet*. For a few weeks Potts was the toast of the French, but then the book, Potts and Charles Graham returned to an undeserved anonymity. In Potts' case it looked as though it would be terminal. I let him know how much I regretted his not letting me do something for him, reminding him of what I had done for Elizabeth Smart.

'It's not too late, Jay, old boy,' he said over the drink I had just bought him. 'I have an idea that will make us both a lot of money. Let me edit an anthology of poems for you. I've got a great title: *Poems for Poor People*.' In the old days he was tagged 'the People's Poet'. 'The only difference between me and a great artist is that I am not one,' he used to say.

His enthusiasm for the project increased in direct ratio to the drinks I was buying. Before the afternoon was over, we had the golden handshake. His advance was possibly the lowest in publishing history – £5 and free Guinness whenever I was in the French. We both knew the book would never happen, but I enjoyed the liquid negotiations. Sometimes he'd ask for a cash advance – a quid or two – which made him feel he wasn't being taken advantage of. He became my personal charity; over the years I suspect he got a larger advance than any of my legitimate authors.

My next book was discovered by the mother of fourteen-year-old Gideon Sams. He was the son of Ann and Craig Sams, whom I had worked with during my macrobiotic days. His mother noticed the exercise book in a rubbish bin while she was tidying up his room. 'It looks interesting,' she said to me. 'He wrote it as a school project. His teacher thought it showed promise. Would you like to see it?' I immediately saw its potential. It was a short account of the punk scene, which was breaking big around that time. To publish the world's first punk novel would be a coup as well as commercially viable. Most of all, it would be a lot of fun to upset the publishing trade with a well-written book on such a disgusting subject.

'This is where you meet the great safety pin in the sky, punk.' He drove the knife into the punk's arm. Blood poured out at an amazingly fast rate, but still the punk had some fight left in him. He lunged out at Ned and caught him in the nose with a bottle. The Ted's head fell back against the wall with a thud, as blood emptied from Ned's nostrils. 'You bloody rat! You gonna die for this.'

Not exactly the poetic prose of Elizabeth Smart, but it had immediacy and enough violence to satisfy the most blood-thirsty reader. What made it so interesting was that Gideon had unconsciously rewritten the Romeo and Juliet story in punk terms, with plenty of blood and tears (just like the original) which gave it a contemporary flavour.

Filling only one exercise book, however, it was hardly enough to make the shortest of novellas. I offered some editorial advice and told him I'd publish it if he could lengthen it to about sixty pages. A couple of weeks later, he turned in a typewritten manuscript of sixty-two pages which did not need any copy editing. Instead of a cash advance, I gave Gideon a pair of cowboy boots. I had the book in print in three weeks. I would have had it out sooner, but was held up for a few days searching for the right size safety pin to put through the nose of the Johnny Rotten clone on the cover.

At the book launch, Gideon played his part to perfection, insulting the press, stuffing himself with smoked salmon and being generally obnoxious. By the end of the party he was pissed, which everybody thought was cute – for a punk. As we left, he swiped a bottle of vodka and ran for a cab. The bottle fell out of his leather jacket, smashing on the pavement. 'There goes your first royalty cheque, punk,' I shouted as he got into the cab.

Interviews and features appeared in *Melody Maker*, *Record Mirror*, the *Evening News*, *Evening Standard*, *Daily Mirror*, *New Musical Express*, the *Sunday Times*, and the *Observer*. His performance on *Nationwide* reading some of his prose was reviewed by Clive James for the *Observer*: 'Gideon's appearance gave the lie to his professed attitudes. Far from being a spotty oik with razorblade earrings and a bolt through his neck, Gideon was a fresh-faced, cleancut youth with a nice smile which failed hopelessly at trying to look wicked. Only fourteen and already on *Nationwide*. (His ambition, it transpired, is to be a brain surgeon.)'

At only fourteen, Gideon was an expert at taking the piss out of the media. He had written the book with tongue in cheek, but decided to play it like a punk, which was difficult with his angelic face. He was much better with insults. When he was asked his opinion of a professor's rap on the same programme, Gideon sneered directly into the camera: 'What a bunch of crud.' The *Sunday Times* asked him his views on dating: 'I don't mind girls; girls aren't that important to me really. I used to get really infatuated about a year or two ago. But now I've got more important things to do. Fun first, then the girls. That's my philosophy.'

Meanwhile, he was working in his father's bakery, making wholewheat pizzas. 'I've never been a punk; it doesn't appeal to me. I'd rather be rich and decadent, like Mick Jagger.' And he almost was. I sold the book to Corgi paperbacks, who rushed into an initial print run of 50,000, but without the safety pin I felt it was like Faust without the devil. Film director Mike Sarne optioned it for £2,000 in advance. According to Sarne, the producer of one of Hollywood's most controversial films, *Myra Breckenridge*: 'My only problem is to persuade the stars to put safety pins through their noses.' The book sold to a dozen magazines and publishers in Europe. The only place it didn't sell was in America, where they thought it was too violent.

Fran and I saw Gideon a number of years later in Greenwich Village. We were standing in line to see *Blue Velvet* when he came over to say hello. He was a handsome young man, looking quite grown up in a snap-brim hat, a button-down shirt and a tie. The only thing that hadn't changed was his famous sneer. 'You won't like *Blue Velvet*. It's for grown-ups.' He told us that New York was his apple and that he hadn't been so happy since the day he swiped that bottle of vodka. He had become a stationery salesman and was about to take on a new job. It was a short reunion, but a very heartwarming one.

A few months later we heard he had died of a bronchial illness he had refused to take seriously. How I wish he had lived long enough to hear the news that Mike Sarne had started production on the film of his book. He would have sneered at the prospect.

I had been warned that books about libraries were death. The image of libraries was boring; they were places where nothing happens. Then I saw a letter from a librarian in the National Book League's newsletter about economy cuts in library budgets. It made me laugh; I realized I had come across a budding novelist. I was convinced when I saw the author's note about himself: 'Barry Bowles is the Punk Correspondent of the *New Library World*.' I wrote and asked him to tell me more. I received the following:

> Barry Bowles is a resident lecturer in frustration at north London bus stops. In 1963 he dropped biochemistry and headed south for loneliness and libraries, where in fifteen short years he rose from assistant librarian to older assistant. Meantime Ambit published his poetry at the insistence of London Transport, who wished to avoid a body on the track. He succeeded in getting married, and having a brief affair with a hat stand on a drunken night. Eventual breakthrough came with a Radio Merseyside

145

broadcast and from then on it was all down hill with stories in *Knave*, *Men Only*, *Penthouse*, and *Fiesta*, under the name of Captain Lust.

He finished the novel in record time. *Between the Stacks* might change the image of libraries and librarians, but would it sell to the public? Promoting is only an art when you sell something nobody wants. Instead of aiming the book at the public, I concentrated on promoting it to the library trade, who were very protective of their image. 'We'll take a look, but no promises,' they said. I had Barry write a 2,000-word piece in the *Library Association Record*, which broke the ice. 'Very amusing,' they said.

I rushed the book into print. I had a button made that said 'Get it! Between the Stacks' and sent it to librarians around the country with a note: 'I hope to see all right-minded librarians wearing this button with pride in knowing that they are at the forefront of the battle to make librarians interesting.'

I scrapped the cover I had planned in favour of one I considered would destroy for ever the image of librarians as a dull lot. I hired a tall, beautiful model, put a pair of horn-rimmed spectacles on her, asked her to adopt an expression of bliss, and posed her between stacks of books. Instead of a skirt, she wore sexy Janet Reger knickers. It was a great success with libraries, who bought out the first edition, but it did little to change their image with the public, who bought very few copies.

My reputation as an original publisher was growing. The range of subjects, the unconventional promotional drive behind them, amused and impressed other publishers, the trade and the public. My appearances in the media created a sense that publishing had room for a maverick. With all the publicity, business increased so much that I decided to turn over the details of administration to the professionals. For the first time I had genuine overheads and an overdraft, and I wasn't looking too well either.

I would have kept Annie on if she hadn't introduced her friend Pamela into my life. Little did she suspect that the woman who showed up at the office to say hello in a tight pair of blue jeans and high 'fuck me' boots would be my next employee. Annie was busy at the time of Pamela's entrance, and said in her sweet, motherly fashion, 'You two go out and have fun.' She'd catch up with us later.

Three hours later we returned. Annie was not pleased to see Pamela collapse in a corner, throw up in the waste bin and pass out. I thought it showed a certain amount of flair, especially since she had spent most of her time telling me of her qualifications for a job in publishing. She had worked with Tessa Sayle, one of the top literary agents handling foreign rights for best-selling authors. When Annie went on a holiday, I asked Pamela to fill in for her. When she returned, I had a difficult time explaining why I thought Pamela was right for Jay Landesman Limited without telling her I had started an affair with her best friend.

CHAPTER FIFTEEN

With Pamela ensconced at the reception desk which doubled as a bar and a platform for her views on life, the traffic in and out of the office increased to an alarming level. Since we were in the heart of Soho's naughty strip and only one flight up, a steady stream of misguided enquiries – 'Vere is de Sauna?' – was a constant source of irritation to Pamela, whose denial of any such activity was usually met with a lewd wink and the offer of a £10 note for further information. The girl could have made a fortune if she hadn't been so intent on helping me spend one.

This wild flower I had picked as Annie's replacement turned out to be a great believer in establishing the image of a serious publishing company, even though she was aware that it was eccentricity which had given Jay Landesman Ltd its singular reputation. Her requests for a budget to provide new fixtures, office equipment, decorating or larger authors' advances were systematically refused. Her demands for heat in the winter, fans in the summer, respect for holiday plans, a good grade of toilet tissue in the bog, and plenty of ice cubes in the fridge did not seem unreasonable and were granted forthwith.

Most publishers would need a new book to justify a party; Pamela needed no such excuse. She organized small parties on national holidays and obscure literary anniversaries, and would often lobby for a bash just for the hell of it. They were never the cheese and plonk launches most publishers had, but full-scale rehearsals for *La Grande Bouffe*. Luckily I had a bent smoked salmon connection on Meard Street who knew me only by the codename Operation Banquet.

Pamela's guests were mostly my friends, chosen by her for their inability to get us any publicity. Peter Cook was not known for his book reviews. Asheton Gordon, who had been the art director for *Dearest Dracula*, was too handsome to be excluded. Alan Brien could have given us some publicity, but it would have been of the negative variety. Jeffrey Bernard came for the vodka. (He didn't approve of my attempt to go straight.) I assume Tom Maschler showed because it was lunchtime and he wanted a change from the egg salad sandwiches he used to eat at his desk. Reporter Sally Vincent dropped by in the hope of picking up a story. R. D. Laing came to get away from listening to all those tales of upper-middle-class *angst*. Peter Dunbar was looking for a little action. Peter Owen warned me I'd go bankrupt if I continued to indulge in such hedonism. 'Fran will end up in a bedsit in Finchley,' he warned. They must have been good parties because nobody wanted to go back to work, even after the booze ran out. Often a guest would initiate a whip round for more drink, which would keep the party going until the Swiss Disco in the basement opened for business.

Unfortunately there was a serious facet to Pamela. She enrolled in the London College of Printing to learn the technical side of publishing; the results proved to be provocative and irritating. No longer could I get away with my customary haphazard method of publishing a book in six weeks. With her new grasp of technology, it took twelve weeks. Slowly our romantic conversations over a drink at the end of the day turned into a printing seminar. I was confronted with an expert on type-buying, six-colour covers, paper variations and technical terms which had escaped my attention, but which added enormously to my anxiety. Then she introduced me to one Richard Minsky, an American bookbinder who was lecturing at her school and needed a place to live.

Minsky's last major project before he came to London had been to bind an edition of Buckminster Fuller's *Tetrascroll*, a forty-three-foot-long book of three-foot triangular pages folding into an equilateral tetrahedron. As a result of his creative approach to bookbinding he was given a US/UK fellowship of $16,895 to go and play in London for nine months, and that was what he was doing when Pamela announced that the top floor of my house was available.

It was rumoured that he had chosen England for its emerging punk scene. 'My sole purpose for being in England is to bind Patti Smith's poetry in rat skins and safety pins.' To Minsky, English Punk was so full of energy, even black was bright. With his eccentricity, Minsky gave the English some competition. According to Pamela More in her introduction to Minsky's book, *Minsky In London* – a hand-made edition of twenty-five, priced at $500 a copy – the more outrageous aspects of his image 'included a Lapland hat, cyclamen hair, a Neanderthal style of dancing, a Marilyn Monroe jacket, a rhinestone tie, and fast and blunt conversation. Despite the formality of their structures and traditions, the British sense of humour allowed Minsky enough latitude to play with their rules.'

His book was a departure from the established style of autobiography. He sent a letter to forty people who had crossed his path during his stay in Britain, asking them to describe him in any terms they saw fit. My contribution was the first entry:

As Richard Minsky's landlord during his stay in London, he had had quite an influence on my opinion of artists in residence. He paid his rent promptly and, when unable to pay it, he sold me a pair of shoes, his Marilyn Monroe jacket, some painting (?) and took out the balance in bookbinding. In the latter field he did a fantastic job for me and I have received many compliments on his work, both here and in America. He terrorized the house with his definite statements about art, music, literature, sex, and personal daintiness. His eyes twinkled on occasion, and the only negative aspect of his stay was to lower real estate values in the neighbourhood with his tinted hair. His violin playing was most welcome, as I like to cry late at night and his music was perfect for that hobby. I was impressed with his ability to make friends with the corner grocer and other locals. He was kind to a band of new wave musicians that used the premises; he was a generous host, but his menu got a little repetitive – how much bean sprout can one handle? He talked big and was big, but his word was not God. In the end he vandalized the wall of his quarters with a self-portrait that I had to have the exterminators in to obliterate. He is the kind of person I would most like to meet in a dark alley, late at night, and in need of a friend. He did not try to seduce my children or wife, which I find it difficult to forgive him for; nor did he try to seduce me. His great value lies in his ability to judge a situation and act out the most practical way of surviving. I have no doubts that he will survive. In fact, if nothing serious happens to him he will be back, some day, asking for his quarters back and I shall be happy to accommodate him if they are available. Incidentally, he is inclined to be serious, his only flaw.

(When the book came out in 1980, I bought a copy as a present to Pamela. Years later I discovered she had used it to prop up the foot of her bed high enough to relieve a women's complaint.)

At the height of the punk music scene, Miles and his group, now called Miles Over Matter, were a nightly fixture in the basement, blasting away for hours with unrelenting high energy sounds. Just as he was about to sign the big contract, the band broke up. Miles became the unofficial roadie for the all-girl group The Slits, and laid plans for a triumphant return to music.

Our traditional New Year's Day party did not look promising, although it was an opportunity to renew old friendships which had languished over the years; something was missing. There was no doubt that I had found publishing fulfilling, but not without sacrificing a certain amount of the irresponsibility which used to fuel my many absurd projects. Now I felt I was in danger of growing up – particularly when I saw my bank statement. Towards the end of the party, Miles' friends The Slits made a dramatic appearance with the professional irritant of the punk world, Johnny Rotten. 'My Gawd,' Fenella Fielding said, turning to me as if to ask why she was being subjected to this gothic nightmare.

Mr Rotten was like a high-octane fuel injection into a garage full of Morris Minors. Suddenly the party came alive and I wasn't ready for nighty-nights. He was just what I needed – somebody to get silly with at the start of the New Year. I took great pleasure in seeing him squirm as I introduced him to our friends, who must have looked to him like out patients at St Bart's. Fran was up in her room talking with a Slit, who insisted on referring to her as the 'the Mama Punk'. Rotten deserved some decent Scotch, which I had stashed up on the top floor. He accompanied me, paying the price by putting up with a great deal of metaphysical babble on the way.

As we passed Miles on the way down, Rotten called out to him like a drowning man: 'Hey, your old man is crazy. Get him off my back.'

I let him off the hook by guiding him into Fran's room. She was lying in her usual position and smiling a delicious smile, which Mr Rotten completely misinterpreted. I was familiar with that particular Cheshire-cat gesture, having been a victim of it for many years. What Mr Rotten didn't know was that Fran had recently written a poem about him that she was very pleased with. The opportunity to recite it to him was irresistible. He was lying on the *chaise longue* opposite her, with his bottle of Scotch as a security blanket when she began:

> . . . We know you're gonna make it
> But maybe it's too late
> If by the time you make it
> You're what you used to hate
> You'll end up fat and frightened
> And cut off like the King
> With yes men to protect you
> And nothing left to sing
>
> Mr Rotten, why be a hit?
> When you're Top of the Pops
> Then you're right in the shit
> They'll process your protest
> And fuck up your view
> They're gonna make a sausage out of you . . .

Rotten listened attentively and, when it was over, said through clenched teeth, 'It's going to give me great pleasure to prove you wrong.' He got up and left the room.

A short time later his entry into the punk market in America was a self-made disaster. Much to the shock of his American promoters, he refused to compromise his anarchic stand. He did not go down well in Topeka, Kansas. He returned to England disillusioned; the Sex Pistols broke up and Mr Rotten went back to being plain John Lydon. He did, indeed, prove Fran wrong.

Fran's career was continuing with some modest success, but not enough to satisfy her. She still felt she was Mrs Someone instead of Someone. However, her status as 'Jay's wife' was seriously threatened when Tom Maschler at Cape decided to publish her second book, *Invade My Privacy*. My grand design was to co-ordinate the publication of her book with negotiations for Fran's appearance at Ronnie Scott's. There was resistance from Ronnie's partner, Pete King, who lacked enthusiasm for the idea of a middle-aged woman reading poems without music. He relented under steady pressure from both Ronnie and me. On a Bank Holiday weekend, she opened on a bill with Dexter Gordon, and came on around midnight. The place was filled with inscrutable Japanese and drunken English businessmen. The occasional boo during her performance was more a product of alcohol than an aesthetic judgment. Dexter was out in the audience supporting her with unremitting laughter. By the end of the two-week engagement the jazz *cognoscenti* had given the performance their seal of approval.

'For years I sat in the dark watching other people in the spotlight doing my material. Now I ask myself why I waited so long. I just love going out there, giving of myself and receiving all that love and energy. I may start to work with an accompanist, try and sing more seriously. I want to go on tour. I want to make an album. I want to be a star,' she told Michael Zwerin, the music critic who was covering the event for the *International Herald Tribune*.

The next time Fran played at Ronnie's, Tom Waits was in town playing at the London Palladium. We had previously met when he was a jazz cult singer doing his gravel-voice imitations of Jack Kerouac and Neal Cassady at Ronnie's. It was the Beat connection that brought us together. Waits would sit at our table in his funky cloth cap, his double-jointed dirty fingers hugging a Budweiser, a cigarette hanging from his chapped lips as I recounted stories of those Beat nights that I thought people had forgotten. While he was still at Ronnie's, Fran laid her latest book on him. He told her later that he was so inspired by her poems he couldn't stop writing for the rest of his gig. Fran was flattered, but what really knocked her out was to read, in an interview he gave to *Melody Maker*, that she was one of his heroes.

Waits went on to become a major draw. After his show at the London Palladium, he rushed over to Ronnie's to catch Fran's act. He was just in time to see her give one of the least successful performances of her career; everything had gone wrong. The microphone was set too high and proved too difficult for her to adjust. She had worked her way out of the spotlight. Doing her act in the dark lent it a ghoulish air. 'What's the matter with that girl?' he whispered to me. 'Doesn't she know about lights?' Waits could stand it no longer. 'For Christ's sake, get into the spotlight, girl,' he rasped, loud enough for her to hear him. She desperately tried to obey, but seemed unable to find where the light was coming from.

We saw Waits once again backstage at the Dominion Theatre. Married by this time, travelling with his wife and baby, he presented us with a picture of domestic bliss that would have been inconceivable a few years back. His act, by the way, had developed into a theatrical pastiche of the music of the Weimar Republic and choreography out of a Magritte painting as directed by Fassbinder. I still couldn't decipher his coded lyrics, but I'm sure they had something to do with urban despair.

When Fran appeared at the Edinburgh Festival that summer of 1978 her wry observations on love, death, drugs and sex had trouble finding an audience. Her venue, Better Books, was off the beaten track and it looked as though she wouldn't have a quorum for her debut. It was my job to see that she did. I stood outside on the pavement doing an imitation of a crazed carnival barker, hustling the passing crowd with come colourful commentary on what they might expect to see if they 'stepped inside' and caught the act of 'the tough little lady direct from New York . . . ' By the time she was ready to go on, there were bums on seats and critics poised for either praise or poison. When a review by Allan Massie appeared in the *Scotsman* proclaiming her lyrics to be 'wittier and truer than Sondheim, more rhythmical, more alert, and more sensitive', my job was made a lot easier. By the end of the first week she was playing to packed houses. I didn't see any need to hang around for the final week.

Edinburgh was a turning point for Fran. For the first time she had a taste of what it was like to be accepted unconditionally. Students, middle-aged mums, punks, other performers told her how much they loved her work. Everywhere she went people smiled and she smiled back. Suddenly the 'crippled girl' walked – it was just like the movies – all over Edinburgh, and by herself. She even bought a ticket to someone else's show, all on her own. Finally, she discovered what it was like to have that feeling of being Someone.

Returning from such a success to a mundane business of being just another housewife presented problems. Fran always believed there had to be more to marriage than two people locking each other in a cage for the rest of their lives. Her dim view of marriage had been instilled in her by her mother and nurtured by her search for her own identity. She saw her marriage to me as a good first one that she could dump with ease if it didn't work out. 'I always knew,' she once wrote, 'I ought to get a divorce. I would have looked so good on the witness stand in an understated outfit. The only sticky bit would be going home without you.' In spite of her unconventional life, she had a regular daily routine any *hausfrau* would envy. If I were to ask her to include me in her catering plans for the odd lunch, she'd say, 'I married you for better or worse, but not for lunch. Sorry.'

Sally Vincent was doing a series of articles for the *Observer* on couples who lived unconventional lives within the framework of a conventional marriage. She chose us as two people who stabilize each other's adventures. After the interview, she asked us to write an account of our day; a real picture of our life as a couple emerged:

FRAN'S DAY:

My day starts here in this lovely bedroom when Jay comes in with a tray. I like to sleep late so I probably wouldn't have breakfast, but Jay likes to talk in the morning. He's charming and he's really funny; when everybody else is sort of grouchy, he's looking out in the garden saying, 'Good morning world, good morning flowers,' and having incredible conversations with the cat. So I let him wake me up and have this breakfast and I laugh at all his jokes and as soon as he walks out the door I go right back to sleep again. I drag myself out of bed at eleven and that's really an hour before I'm good and ready. And that's my worst time, somehow. No matter what kind of a good time I've had with Jay I just notice everything that's wrong, and where the kids have made a mess, and I just whinge about everything and it's not till I get dressed and walk up to the market that the bad things start to go away. So I do the grocery shopping and go to the bank and the post office, all that, and I come back and make lunch. I'm very scheduled. My son Cosmo is usually here and we used to have a social time at lunch, but lately I get the feeling he'd just as soon read, so a lot of the time I just take my lunch and have it right here in this bed, which is where I feel most comfortable. I prefer not to see my friends in the daytime. I like to be in bed and do a bit of scribbling or some correspondence or reading or something . . . Or I like to do a bit of dinner preparation before people start coming in around five or six. I like to do that by myself in the kitchen listening to one of those plays that's on the radio that makes me blissfully happy except that I'm kind of praying nobody's going to ring my doorbell or call me on the telephone. I don't like to use the phone; I much rather drop somebody a note. I like to have a lot of people at the dinner table. The four of us and usually some lodgers as well and anybody who calls by, and then I can easily stay up all night. Even if nobody's here the night's the best time for me. It's being in this room where nobody can get at me and nobody's going to make any demands and I can watch my television or read or do anything I want to do. I feel like Queen Victoria in that old Helen Hayes movie where they come and tell her she's the Queen and she says, 'Right, now I'm having a room and a bed to myself,' and chucked her mother out.

JAY'S DAY:

I'm an early riser. Early to bed, early to rise, eye on the ball, concentrate on one thing, do not pass GO. I've started to practice all the things my mother taught me would make me successful, and I'm getting to be quite a dull man. So I get up and make breakfast for Fran and take it up to her and that's the best part of my whole life . . . It's the only time we can be really silly and honest and laugh and feel no pressure. I get to my office about eight o'clock and I have this problem always, wondering how a guy from the banks of the Mississippi came to wind up on the first floor next to the renamed Finger Tips Massage Parlour in London. Then I warm up thinking about how other publishers do their days. I think about all the agents' manuscripts piled on their tables, all the left-over editorial letters they have to write and I think 'Wow! Gee! How lucky I am not to be bothered by anything like that.' What I do is try to create an environment I can function in because, well, it's much more fun than being in someone else's movie. Books are just other worlds so I try to think up some interesting areas that nobody else has covered, like, for instance, the series of books I'm doing on boring people. I try to get authors who have a way of turning bores into fascinating people because it's just a little opposed to the regular biographical style which turns fascinating people into bores. I try to match up the book with the person. Like I've got this idea for a book to reappraise the problem of cowardice. Or the definitive book on crying, called *Boo-Hoo, The Complete Criers Companion*. That's the creative side of publishing. I feel it sets me apart from all decent, civilized, good-thinking, logical publishers. I get home and Fran doesn't ask me how things went at the office. Our living-room has gotten to be like a Chekhov drama, everybody talks non-stop and their subjects are never related. So I end up in this Chekhov play at night, and, like the drunken uncle, I retire early to bed. For a major theme I'd stay up but I never seem to find one to keep me up after eight-thirty.

Sally's article got into the eye of the hurricane of our marriage:

All this talk about Having Fun, as though it was nothing to be ashamed of, is enough to make you nervous of what might be expected of you. But there's a real coal fire in the grate and the cat is laundering herself in front of it, somebody is strumming a guitar, somebody else has gone gracefully into the wind and bluster for *doner kebabs*, and what you mostly feel here is cared for . . . Like the fabric of their home, the Landesman life is either a terrible mess in need of major repair, and a good clean-up, or it's eccentrically, humanely, bravely and infinitely generously disposed . . . 'Suburban Swingers', Jay says, relaxed as spaghetti, but bordering on scornful, 'always abuse the thing they take to be their freedom. They go about having fun like they were boy-scout leaders on a mission. They can't have a simple little affair without sighing about running away together like what they're really doing is trying to find a way out of their misery. So they play all these yukky games throwing their shoes or their keys into a heap and then obliging each other to fornicate with whoever picks them up. They don't even take any responsibility for what they're up to.'

At the time of the interview, Fran was having an affair with a brooding Australian iconoclast, whose depressing views on the human condition – 'the world is my ashtray' – were a source of some of Fran's more cynical verses. 'Have fun, sweetheart,' Sally quotes Fran as saying as I prepared to leave for a meeting with Pamela. Fran wrote a poem that filled in some missing spaces Sally left blank:

> Don't change
> Stay the way that you are
> Don't change
> You were always a star

It's marvelous to see you coming
Arrayed in splendor, cheering up the street
A Jewish prince who's done a little slumming
Like Fred Astaire, you never miss a beat

Don't leave
For the world that's so wide
I'd grieve
Without you by my side

Time marches on but you're still dancing
Still trying to extend your range
Technology may keep advancing
And things and people grow more strange
But please don't go too far.

Just stay the way you are
Don't change!

CHAPTER SIXTEEN

By 1980 I had a collection of writers unsurpassed for eccentricity who were no strangers to failure. A drinking session at the Colony Room with Dan Farson led to a collaboration between a gullible publisher and successful author which, on the surface, looked promising. Jeremy Thorpe had been front-page news for the better part of a year. By the time of his trial, he was red hot. The idea of writing the story of what really went on while the trial was in progress and having it in the book stores on the day the case went to the jury held no terror for either of us. Farson was a fast writer, I was a faster publisher. When he outlined what he had in mind, I saw promotional potential, as well as another publishing first. Since the setting was North Devon – Farson territory – he knew all the participants in the tragi-comedy well enough to write the inside story, only no newspaper – not even a sleazy tabloid – would dare print it.

In order to avoid libel, he'd tell the story from a dog's point of view, with all the dogs based on the real-life characters. He had a simple plot. Max Von Fleet, top dog in his district, has hopes of winning at Crufts. His chances are threatened by the arrival of a silly poodle called Maisie, who keeps barking her mouth off about an earlier liaison with the 'great dog' and its consequences lead to his trial. Farson sent me weekly instalments. I was impressed – it was satire at its best. Unfortunately disaster struck when the jury returned a not guilty verdict on the day the book was published.

Farson had assumed that Thorpe would go down, so to speak. However, the book was well received by the critics. 'Long after the exact events it parallels have faded from our memory, [*The Dog Who Knew Too Much*] will survive on its own merits. The mark of first-class satire is that it has a universal as well as a contemporary point . . . this book passes that test,' George Melly concluded in a review in *New Society*. Farson and I were proud that we had broken fresh ground, but heartbroken that the jury's verdict had rendered the book dead on arrival.

This disaster left its mark. I took a serious look at mainstream publishing: books that attempted to expand the mind or at least improve it were in fashion. In my attempt to follow suit, my literary standards began to slip. Nothing could have pleased me more than to receive the manuscript of the world's first cookbook devoted to canine gastronomy, using food appealing to both man and beast. Author Richard Graham regarded himself as an authority on food and wine, having eaten and drunk nearly every day since he was born. A writer for *The Times* and *The Good Food Guide*, he was a passionate lover of dogs, particularly his Lulu, to whom he dedicated his book:

> I want to thank my dog for his endless patience and under-standing through the long hours I have slaved over a hot stove during the preparation of this work; for the encouragement he has given me when sometimes I have felt unequal to the task, and for the infinite trouble he has gone to in sampling and commenting on the wide variety of dishes I have had to prepare . . . The fact that he has not typed the manuscript and read the proofs has only been due to circumstances which I hope will be rectified when we publish a companion volume in this series to be entitled *Secretarial Skills For Dogs*.

With Don Grant's clever illustrations, and cover quotes by Elaine Stritch ('My dog loved this book so much she ate it'), Robert Carrier ('Menus to make Fido blush with pleasure') and Jilly Cooper ('It is a must for all four stockings this Xmas'), the book earned that choice place next to the cash register in many a bookshop across the nation. It went into a second printing before publication.

To coincide with the London Book Fair we set up a publicity stunt for the *Sun*'s reporter, who was fascinated with the social implications of the canine party we planned:

The first dinner party for dogs was a glittering Chelsea occasion spoiled only by legs cocked against a cocktail cabinet and a fight breaking out under the table. 'Dogs dinner parties will take a little time before proper codes of behaviour are established,' the author said. He had to round up a collection of dogs for the occasion, some of dubious background. Midge was an Islington alley dog, described by her owner as an 'unmarried mother of fourteen,' who stood around eyeing the dustbin instead of the delicacies. 'I think dog dinners will catch on. I would like to cater for some. Perhaps I will put an advertisement in *The Times*,' Graham said. Lulu formed a relationship with Rumble, while Midge sat near the door like an Eliza Doolittle who knew she did not bark properly. When the chef emerged from the kitchen two hours later with a hot *boeuf bourguignon*, a fight broke out between Rumble and Lulu, with Lulu grumbling like Penelope Keith eating at a works canteen. Midge looked on disapprovingly of their middle-class behaviour. 'I suppose really we could have started off with a savoury and mushroom dish,' said the chef at the end of the meal.

There are some publishers who have been in business for years without getting a front window display at Foyle's. Knowing of Christina Foyle's love of dogs, I sent her a copy. She responded with a display devoted to Lulu, making the book one of the hits of the shop's Christmas season. At last I had a book I could make a killing on. I decided to take a small booth at the Frankfurt Book Fair, where world rights are bought and sold. I asked Pamela along to help set up the appointments with foreign publishers who I was sure would be lining up to buy. I didn't tell her I would need her assistance in the kitchen for the cooking of a dog's dinner.

Frankfurt, the world's biggest book fair, was the great test – a challenge that made me throw caution to the winds. I was determined to get my share of attention. A friend who lived there came by with his huge Pyrenean mountain dog, which was perfect for my stunt. I asked Pamela to help cook a meal for the dog. You would have thought I was asking her to perform an obscene act. When she saw me in a chef's hat, she said it was not her idea of how a publisher should behave. It was too complicated for me to make a meal without her assistance, so I decided to wear the chef's cap and take the dog on a parade through the halls. Not only did it offer a temporary *divertissement* for the bored stall-minders, I sold the rights to seven countries including Japan, whose publisher thought it was a book about how to cook dogs. When I set up the dog's bowl soliciting contributions for a Home for Aged Gourmet Dogs, it proved all too much for Pamela. She packed up and left Frankfurt, an act which, I told her, would seriously affect our future relationship. 'Who wants a relationship with a chef's cap?' she said.

I was sorry to lose Pamela, but what price romance when a potential best-seller was on the horizon? Graham came up with the idea of a book about cuisine for cats that would be even more popular than the dog cookbook. In the meantime he produced *The Good Dog's Guide to Better Living*. This incorporated ideas for careers for the ambitious canine, good dog etiquette and essentials for your dog's education.

By Christmas I was so busy, I didn't have time to choose a decent present for Pamela. She had bought me a non-stick pan as a joke. When she saw my present to her, a redundancy notice, we had a row that led to my hasty departure, narrowly avoiding injury from a pot which flew out of a window aimed at my head.

With the success of the dog and cat books, I was in a position to take more chances. What could be more chancy than a biography of an ex-Communist, homosexual, illegitimate, lapsed Catholic poet who had a drinking problem? In 1970 Eddie Linden started a magazine called *Aquarius* with a capital investment of £4. He had a talent for getting other people to do the magazine's actual production while he hustled the Arts Council and friends for money to keep it going. (John Betjeman used to send him a fiver every Christmas.) To support himself he charred for friends. BBC's

Frank Delaney dubbed Eddie 'the Butler to Literature'. The book, *Who Is Eddie Linden?*, was written with the full co-operation of the subject by Sebastian Barker, who had known Eddie all his life.

How bad a hand can life deal a man? Surely he deserved some kind of recognition. 'In Eddie's own poems,' Sebastian wrote, 'he shows us the inner life of an intolerably sad and lonely man who has made it his business to hide the fact in his service to others.' Eddie went to all his famous friends asking for jacket quotes. There emerged a picture of Eddie Linden as a cross between Captain Courageous and a performing artist. 'Eddie is a talisman of youthful hope . . . he has never given up, nor should we,' Peter Porter wrote. Brian Patten: 'If Eddie didn't exist, no one would have dared to invent him.' Harold Pinter was as terse as usual: 'There is no one like Eddie.' It was John Montague who summed Eddie up for me: 'Eddie Linden is a human event.'

Eddie asked his friend Ralph Steadman to do the cover. Steadman produced an Eddie holding a tartan cap for contributions of any nature. It was so biting a caricature I thought it might put off the book-buying public, but Eddie appreciated the recognition. He was delighted when I suggested that he deliver his review copies of the book in person to the likely literary editors, including those in Scotland and Ireland, who might put it out for review.

I don't know what he threatened them with, but reviews appeared in the *Literary Review*, the *Tablet*, the *Listener*, the *Evening Standard*, *Tribune*, *Books and Bookmen*, the *Scotsman*, *New Society*, the *Glasgow Herald*, the *Observer*, *Ambit*, the *Guardian*, the *Spectator*, *Cork Examiner*, *Gay News*, *Hampstead & Highgate Express*, the *Irish Post*, *New Edinburgh Review*, *Books in Scotland*, *Cyphers*, *World Reviews*, *Cencrastus* and *Lambda* (an alternative journal of the Italian gay movement).

The book almost sold out its first printing. Gus MacDonald at Granada TV loved it so much he optioned it twice. He saw Eddie as some kind of Scottish folk hero; I saw him as a poor man's Quentin Crisp; Eddie, for the first time in his life, saw himself on the verge of success. All those perceptions were true, but would we ever prove he was bankable? He wasn't.

Eddie's optimism never flagged. He still comes around regularly for a cuppa and a chat, and asks the same question: 'Have you heard anything from the wee Scottish producer?'

With our careers in top gear, Fran and I saw less of each other than ever before. What limited success we had seemed to strengthen the marriage and, most important, Fran's feeling about herself. She wrote even more frankly about the ups and downs of her life, but now without any regrets:

> I devote myself to making small jokes and screwing
> And I spend my spare time polishing my art
> And you ask me if I'm happy in what I'm doing
> I ought to be – I wrote the part.

I was as proud of Fran's accomplishments as she was of mine, especially when I published her third volume of verse, *More Truth Than Poetry*. After appearing in features in all the slick woman's magazines, she was in danger of believing her publicity. She was attracting the kind of adulation few poets ever receive. She was especially chuffed when it came from people she respected. When Bette Davis was in London in 1975, we couldn't get tickets to her sold-out performance. Fenella Fielding, who was at the concert, told Fran that Miss Davis was going to record *Ballad of the Sad Young Men*. Fran sent her a copy of *Invade My Privacy*. Miss Davis wrote her a note: 'Your lyrics of *Sad Young Men* plus Mabel Mercer's record have haunted me for years. I am so thrilled to be allowed by EMI to have it part of my LP. Your book of verse is sensational. We must meet! Call me next Friday. What a talented person you are. *Most* sincerely, Bette Davis.'

She called Miss Davis and we were invited to have tea with her at Grosvenor House, which must have been the highlight of that or any other year for Fran. She met us at the door in a pink-flowered housecoat which I thought any male over fifty-eight would appreciate. Once all the niceties were exchanged, she became the vinegary Bette Davis we knew and loved. She was completely open about her liaisons with the Hollywood Casanovas and her failed marriages. Even when I put my hand on her knee to ask her an intimate question, she did not seem offended. Only when I asked about Joan Crawford did she draw herself up and remove my hand delicately. 'That we will not discuss.'

By 1980 publishing was becoming more a part of show business each day. The book fairs in Frankfurt, London and the States, with their dazzling promotions of best-selling authors, left little room for the small independent publisher. Ironically, many a small publisher lived in hope of finding the big one. I was among them with my quirky but money-making books on dogs and cats, but I hadn't hit the best-seller list. With the foundation for expansion firmly in place, I invited Cosmo to help. He was now an ambitious twenty-seven-year-old, whose life was grounded in literary bric-à-brac. He had the title of Commissioning Editor; his salary was of secondary importance, but on a par with Jumble Annie's.

His first suggestion was to put Jeffrey Bernard between hard covers, something I'd long wanted to do, but I knew Jeffrey had driven many a publisher with the same idea to aphasia waiting for a manuscript. He had mastered the art of writing 750 words, often sober; any more would, he said, be self-indulgent. (Once he wrote his column in the office at 10 am. Cosmo and I were transfixed as he typed out his 750 words without once looking up at the ceiling for inspiration as the other master columnist, Keith Waterhouse, did.)

'Let's do the best of High Life and Low Life columns from the *Spectator*,' said Cosmo. I agreed, as did Jeffrey, but I didn't know about Taki, who wrote the High Life column. To my surprise, Taki invited me to lunch at his gambling club, Aspinalls, to talk it over. Intimidated by the rarefied atmosphere of the club, I was embarrassed to offer him any advance, especially since the bill for lunch topped the £100 I had in mind. He thought it would be fun and accepted.

High Life, Low Life was greeted warmly by the media. Auberon Waugh, who had mugged Elizabeth Smart for making such a mess of her life, now gave me a rave quotation for two men who had made a profession of messing up their lives. 'They have more to say about contemporary society than Gibbon in his *Decline and Fall of the Roman Empire*,' he wrote. With Jeffrey between hard covers at last, a second and a third printing, and a paperback sale to Unwin, his fortunes changed overnight. Suddenly he was in demand, doing A Life in the Day Of . . . profile and putting up with BBC camera crews who followed him around Soho as he tried to explain his 'useless' life. 'By and large I've met a better class of person in the gutter than I have in the drawing-room,' he once wrote. Now that success was unavoidable, he was out of the gutter. It would have been an appropriate time to remind him of Graham Greene's dictum: 'Fame is a temporary postponement of failure.'

Meanwhile, Taki wrote from New York that Tom Wolfe was going to review the book for the *American Spectator*, a rare event since Wolfe never did book reviews. Taki, whose knowledge of the book business was on a par with that of a Greek waiter, demanded that I give them an advertisement as well. It proved to be too expensive for me, but for a rich publisher it would have been peanuts. Instead, I tried to negotiate a commission deal with the magazine, but was getting nowhere. Taki got wind of this. Feeling betrayed, the angry rich kid sent me a telegram: 'I am shocked to hear that you did exactly the opposite of what I asked you to do. The *American Spectator* is not an Eastside rag to bargain with you. Either pay for the advertisement or let's drop the whole thing. Your pettishness and Bush-League antics make me regret the day that I agreed to be published by you. Taki.'

I wrote back:

Received your telegram written, no doubt, in the heat of battle. I've always tried to do what is best for the promotion of the book, even humbling myself three times before the owner of the only book shop in Gstaad at your suggestion, only to be ignored . . . I am at a loss to understand why you're so outraged. I hope this error can be forgiven. In spite of my Bush-League handling of this project, I shall continue to promote the book . . . You have been most helpful and generous in the past and there is nothing I can do to erase that from my memory, but if you insist on holding this against me, you prick, we're through.

The list of books that Cosmo wanted to commission was a perfect formula for either a brilliant future or bankruptcy. They were so intriguing I couldn't wait to risk it. Who would resist a book titled

The Good Guide to Joyless Sex – 'a book guaranteed to take the joy out of sex'. Unable to find an author to tackle the subject, Cosmo attempted to undertake the research himself, but couldn't find a partner who would put up with his basic premise. *Teach Yourself Duelling* – 'a book for anyone who cares about chivalry and romance . . . A humorous and historical look at duelling practices and how they can be applied to combat the insults and abuse we face daily. Head waiters be warned!' It was the first sign that Cosmo had bankruptcy in mind. I came up with an idea. *So You Think You'll Never Make It* – 'the stories of how people who had been dismissed as losers overcame unanimous rejection to achieve their goals'. 'The story of your life, huh, Jay?' queried Cosmo.

I chose instead to publish a scholarly bibliography of the collection of erotica in the British Library, which they kept locked up unknown to the public. Scholars and collectors of the genre knew of its existence, but were seldom able to study its contents. Peter Fryer had written a book entitled *Private Case, Public Scandal* which caused a small earthquake. No one had ever catalogued the complete collection until my new author, Patrick J. Kearney, decided it must be done. A picture editor by profession, he devoted every free moment to the task, which should have been done by the British Library itself.

The potential market for such a bibliography was limited to reference libraries, antiquarian booksellers and collectors of erotica. With this in mind, I produced a limited edition of 1,000 numbered copies, beautifully designed and printed on expensive paper, and bound in a special cloth which some joker claimed looked like foreskins. The price of £45 ensured that the book wouldn't get into the hands of sensation-seekers.

When the book was published, England's library budgets were drastically cut, making many librarians reluctant to order a book on such a specialized subject. Nevertheless, thanks to a well-targeted campaign, the book sold over 450 copies in the first three months. (I was particularly delighted when Hull's most famous librarian, Philip Larkin, ordered a copy.) Financially secure again, I felt it was time to take more chances.

Browsing through the small publishers' section at America's

largest book convention, I came across a tall, middle-aged, sombre-looking man playing free-form jazz on a soprano saxophone in front of his booth. I knew at once that Martin Shepard was a class publisher and someone I could do business with. He had just created a new imprint, the Second Chance Press, and was looking for an adventurous co-publisher and distributor to implement an original concept. 'Each year many books are condemned to die, struck down by such diseases as neglect, bad timing or lack of exposure. Quality books are an endangered species. There are special groups for saving everything from whales to historic landmarks. Why not books?' he asked. I agreed and signed up.

An announcement in the *Bookseller* warned the trade that Landesman was getting serious. 'I want to bring back to the literary mainstream the big ones that got away.' Second Chance Press and Jay Landesman Ltd published an initial list of six titles, which I distributed in Britain with some modest success. Some ten titles later I went off the idea of bringing literary orphans to Britain. However, Martin and Judy Shepard went on to become successful in America, admired by writers, booksellers and reviewers.

One of our titles, *The History of Pornography*, caught the attention of a book packager named Michael Rainbird. He introduced us to the profit motive, an element which had always eluded me. In packaging, a book is treated as a product. Instead of selling it to the public, the packager sells the finished book to another publisher. We were so taken by the prospect that we spent a fortune on dummies which we then took to the Frankfurt Book Fair. We had forgotten that packaging called for an illustrated product. We did sell a cartoon cat book titled *Pur-plexities*. The other titles were shredded.

Then there was Landesman's last stand, literally, at the London Book Fair. 'The Risk that Paid Off' was the headline in the *Bookseller* reviewing my last act in publishing:

The reward for the most eye-catching stand at the fair must surely go to that veteran of publishing showmanship, Jay Landesman. It was difficult to tell who was attracting more attention – himself, attired in white linen suit, or the dark beauty looking like a member of a harem lounging on a *chaise longue* passing out pieces of Turkish Delight on a silver tray, surrounded by cardboard eunuchs and leopards – all to promote *The Bedside Book of Erotica*.

There was a lot of action around the stand, all very promising, but nothing materialized. I folded up the stand and my future, and sadly stole away. I sold my lease on the Wardour Street office, bade farewell to the girls in the sex show next door, and moved the remaining stock to the basement of Duncan Terrace. I ran into Peter Owen at the French Pub and asked him if there was a home for the rehabilitation of chronic sufferers from Micawberism.

CHAPTER SEVENTEEN

A show written by Fran with music by her new collaborator, Jason McAuliffe, had just opened at the White Barn, a pre-New York try-out venue in Connecticut. It was to be the perfect showcase for the new collaboration with McAuliffe. He was a fan of Fran's who had set music to her four volumes of verse without having met her. From the first time Fran heard his toe-tapping melodies, she knew she had found the perfect collaborator. Big things were predicted for them, if audience reaction and hard-nosed critics' notices were to be believed:

> *Loose Connections* is a total musical experience, much in the manner of Jacques Brel. It is made up of forty songs that have, without the use of dialogue, been woven together to form a remarkably penetrating study of men and women: how they see themselves, how they see one another, and what does or does not happen when they go about the business of communicating . . . made the audience laugh continuously at the parade of false values and collisions of life objectives which we all encounter along the way to maturity.

Negotiations for an off-Broadway production of *Loose Connections* began to heat up; so did their collaboration when Jason came to London to work on the show. McAuliffe was an actor, with Broadway credits and a sound musical background. That he was the most talented, charming and hopelessly romantic collaborator a woman could ever wish for gave Fran the kind of fundamental support she felt she never received from me. He was in his twenties and Fran was in her fifties, but both were grounded in the past.

Having wound up the publishing business and written its obituary, 'Mr Micawber on Grub Street', for the *Bookseller*, I was at a loose end. It seemed the perfect time to retrieve the manuscript of the memoirs I had started years ago. I sat down in front of my ancient Smith-Corona. Before I had finished a paragraph I got the feeling that the typewriter didn't like me any more – it made ugly noises on the carriage return, kept interpolating the letter к, and farted. I must have spent more money maintaining that machine over the years than I spent on any mistress. I decided to scrap it and buy a word processor.

When news got around that I was writing my memoirs, friends divided into two camps: those who thought I was presumptuous – 'Who wants to read the memoirs of a Mr Nobody?' – and those who thought it was a good idea – 'Tell the truth and you've got a good story.'

Writing about myself for eight hours a day, seven days a week, and then talking about it for a couple of hours with friends and family was not a bad way to spend time. The only difficult part was trying to remember did that come before this or what happened at that party? Organizing the scenes of a life dedicated to enlightened chaos was tricky. What to leave out became a bigger problem than what to put in. Luckily I had Fran as an editor – she proved to be an expert at spotting any false notes.

I was miserable company for the next few months, but Fran didn't notice. One evening I had the blues and Cosmo happened to be around. I did the whole *angst* number for him with a little boo-hooing thrown in. He made a few sympathetic noises. Fran walked in unexpectedly.

'Has anybody seen my lead sheets?' she asked.

'Lead sheets?' Cosmo shouted. 'You talk of lead sheets at a time like this? Look at this man, for God's sake. He's breaking up before your eyes.'

Fran stopped looking through a pile of papers long enough to come over and look at me. 'Have you seen my lead sheets?' she pleaded.

Since our break-up, Pamela had written several articles on the role of the modern mistress for *The Times* and *Time Out*. It led to *Forty Minutes* doing a BBC documentary on how she coped with the role. A book on the subject was her work in progress, which led me to believe she had turned being a mistress into a cottage industry. The first draft of my book *Rebel Without Applause* finished, I couldn't wait to show it to somebody other than the family. Pamela was the first guinea pig.

'You want to know what I think of it?' I noticed a hint of displeasure in her voice. 'Here's what I think of it,' she said, trying to tear the manuscript in half, as strong men do with telephone books.

I leaped in and saved what was left. 'Why did you do that?' I asked. (I had another copy, but she didn't know that.)

She lit a cigarette, inhaled Bette Davis style and then let me have it. '*I,I,I,I* and *Me, Me, Me*. There's too much of you in it,' she said. Reminding her that it was, after all, an autobiography made no impression.

Nevertheless, I sent the manuscript off to Sterling Lord, a leading New York agent, whom I knew from the old days when he handled the unknown Jack Kerouac. There it stayed unopened for seven weeks, which friends in New York assured me was normal. Finally I received a call from Sterling while I was in Fran's room. She was watching television and did not welcome my carrying on a conversation in her viewing time. His opening was, 'Jay, you've written a beautiful book.'

I tried to give the thumbs-up sign to Fran, but I couldn't attract her attention. Phone call over, I collapsed on the bed. 'I did it,' I shouted. 'He loves it.'

She actually gave me a big hug. 'I'm happy for you,' she said, and went back to her viewing. I wanted to celebrate, but there was no one to celebrate with.

The problem was solved the next night. Carolyn Cassady, Neal Cassady's wife and Kerouac's lover stayed over on one of her rare departures from her cottage in Winchelsea, East Sussex. She was a complete Anglophile, in love with English tradition and reckoned she was related to Sir Walter Scott. It was hard to come to terms with the idea that she was once the wife of the 'Dean Moriarity' of *On The Road* fame. It was an intimate evening with just the three of us. Carolyn was mellow enough to let down her hair and tell us what it was really like to be a victim of Cassady's notoriety. Since Jack's and Neal's deaths, she had been trying to correct the prevailing distortions and lies with little success.

A section from her then unpublished autobiography was picked up by Hollywood. Even Nick Nolte and Sissy Spacek couldn't save *Heartbeat*. 'They got it all wrong,' she said. 'They hired me to be the advisor on the film, and then completely ignored my advice.' I told her I thought it was a good picture and only wished it could have happened to me, as long as they spelled my name right. We did agree that the Beat Generation had been misinterpreted by Hollywood as well. She finally got the chance to tell her story properly. I brought it to the attention of a new tasty London publisher, Simon Pettifar of Black Springs Press. They brought out *Off The Road: Twenty Years With Cassady, Kerouac and Ginsberg*, which made an impact both here and in the States. 'Carolyn Cassady's book is the one that I have been waiting to read for the past forty years, the one that sets the record straight for the first time . . . this is a book about the end of innocence in America. It's one hell of a story,' I wrote in my review of the book for the *Sunday Times*.

We had a delayed celebration. I opened a bottle of champagne and put on an old Artie Shaw record, *Begin the Beguine*, and asked her for a dance – the way we used to at high school proms. To me, she was the best dancer in the class of 1938. The only thing missing was the gardenia corsage that a pretty girl was always given by an admiring boyfriend.

I spent half of the summer avoiding American tourists and the other half waiting for word on the book. I had been down in a cold, damp basement for the last two years typing away my life. Fran had been up in her beautiful bedroom with the sun streaming through the large french windows, her beloved Radio 4 at her side, all the mementoes of her past holding the room together, yet she suffered from backache, sinus problems, sensitive teeth and a heavy heart. In spite of the good critical reception *Loose Connections* received, the New York production failed to materialize. It died along with the romance of the collaborators.

On my sixty-fifth birthday, the only thing that I had to look forward to was obtaining my OAP bus pass. I showed it to my friendly newsagent. 'Congratulations. Too bad you don't have any friends to visit,' he said. I thought he was very perceptive. I didn't know what to do with my idle hands. I decided on gardening. Going to the flower market early on Sundays I purchased instant colour to brighten up a garden which had been an object of ridicule since it was first conceived. Fran called it a perfect example of Japanese-Jewish design – 'a lot of rocks and weeds that didn't cost anything'. I couldn't take gardening seriously, but at least I had something to keep me from writing one of those suicide notes Cosmo talked of anthologizing. Waiting for a progress report on *Rebel* was a full-time anxiety-ridden job.

It probably caused the infection which sent me scurrying to the dentist. I was lucky to emerge from the ordeal alive. A dose of penicillin sent me into a coma. The dentist told me later that my blood pressure had dropped to zero; had he not administered oxygen and mercury, and called an ambulance, I would have ended up as a corpse on his front lawn, which, he said, would have been bad for business.

A letter from Sterling Lord played more havoc with my blood pressure than the penicillin. He had spent the summer sending the book around. After a series of rejections, Sterling wrote, 'We really have some marketing problems here.' A rejection from Joyce Johnson, who at the time was executive editor at Doubleday as well as being an accomplished writer, read: 'Landesman is a rather obscure figure for American readers and the book would have to be sensationally written in order to have much of a chance.' Another publisher had an original twist: 'Although Mr Landesman played an interesting role in the Beat period, he doesn't focus enough on it here. A book about his publishing life and his friendship with the writers of the period could be very worthwhile, but it would have to be written with the intention of giving his special perspective on these people and events.' Maybe the dentist could have done me a favour that day.

Discouraged with the New York reaction, I asked Tom Maschler of Cape if he would like to have a look. He wrote back: 'We would very much like to read it. I've seen you in action on the promotional front and the notion of working together with you on your own book is enormously appealing.' I heard from Liz Calder, then Cape's editor-in-chief, that the book had a wonderful report from one of their readers. I wondered how long it would take Maschler to get around to reading the report, much less the book.

The house took on an empty look without any friends (or lovers), or Cosmo or Miles. Their luck wasn't any better than mine as they drifted through their various pursuits. (I felt a certain gratification that they hadn't strayed from the Landesman credo of putting the fun back in failure.) Cosmo was eking out a living as a freelance critic. (Fran said that if she had known he was going to be a critic, she'd have snuffed him at birth.) Miles was a salesman for Boy on Kings Road, but still working nights at becoming a rock star. I had published a small book of his rock lyrics as a gesture of support. Cosmo wrote a biography of him for the back cover:

Miles Davis Landesman was born in St Louis in 1958. He came to London in 1964, when his showbiz parents were forced into exile by indifferent notices. Educated in the worst schools, he left formal education at fourteen and had many jobs, including Problem Child and Messenger Boy. Music has always been his first passion and he has played such distinguished venues as the National Theatre and the Hope and Anchor. Miles, an early pioneer in the head-banging rock genre, has over 300 unreleased demo-tapes to his credit. He is currently playing in his new group, Miles Over Matter and in his spare time prays for a record contract. As well as music, Miles has also been involved in the theatre. He is the author of two plays, *The Lost Messenger Boy* and *The Final Circumcision* – a Jewish rock horror.

Cosmo's only accomplishment in life up till then had been making an art form out of mixing the perfect martini and getting a Ph.D. – in party talk. His biggest crisis was deciding what colour socks to wear to a book launch. Then, one day, he planted a time-bomb in our life – its name was Julie Burchill. The affair had been going on for some time, but Fran and Cosmo, knowing of my loose lips, didn't dare tell me. It was only when they showed up at our front door, seeking sanctuary from her irate husband, that I discovered they were serious.

I couldn't have been more pleased. Next to Cosmo, I was probably her biggest fan. I had been reading her notices of public executions in her columns in *Time Out* and the *Sunday Times*, wallowing in her outrageous, but incisive views on the manners and morals of her time. It reminded me of my *Neurotica* days when I did the same.

The only space available was Cosmo's old work room, a level up from the basement. The room had been turned into a storage area for broken things. Although it overlooked the garden, the view was hidden by a tangle of ivy. Bars across the window gave it a jail-like atmosphere, which was perfect for the prisoners of love.

With two professional critics on the premises, Fran and I felt like the homosexual couple in *La Cage aux Folles* who try to clean up their act when the son brings his girlfriend home. Cosmo had already warned us that Julie knew all about us, having read the Sally Vincent piece when she was sixteen years old. She hated hippies, ex-hippies, food freaks, open marriages and, worst of all, old people. She let us know right at the beginning that she didn't think sex was a laughing matter. The only thing she liked about us was that we were Jewish.

It didn't take long to discover that this raving revolutionary was an old-fashioned girl in a bright, new, alluring package – a designer rebel who yearned for bourgeois respectability. I had to make sure.

'Do you get down on your knees when you scrub a floor?' I asked.

'Yes, it's the only way to do the job properly.'

'Do you know the secrets of polishing?'

'Yes, I do it every day.'

I deliberately sounded like a KGB interrogator to play up to her Stalinist leanings. 'She hates cooking,' Cosmo added. 'She doesn't use public transport either.'

With four writers under one roof, the house was alive with the sound of life-styles clashing. Julie's vocabulary consisted of two words – 'rubbish' and 'horrid' – both intimidating conversation stoppers. She made it plain from the start that she intended to make Cosmo over into a real working-class hero. When he went out to the pub with their only friend, Toby Young, leaving her at home, she simply said: 'I'll be waiting up for you, dear – with a rolling pin.' I asked what would happen if she went out and left Cosmo at home. 'Girls shouldn't go out. That's what boys do.' Toby was at a loss to understand her relationship with us. He had a theory that she was a spy in the house of worn-out images gathering information and would later bring us up on charges of wanton libertinism.

After their first few weeks of residence, I wondered if there was any connection between Fran's new bout of illness and the entrance of Julie into our lives. Since we shared the kitchen, the first sour note was her introducing white bread into the house. Cosmo, who hadn't seen any white bread since puberty, thought it was exotic. Her provocative column one Sunday claimed that the Ten Commandments weren't for Christians – 'After all, they were given to Mr Moses.' It made me proud to think that I might have a daughter-in-law to carry on upsetting the Judaeo-Christian apple-cart when my licence expired. But she could go too far. One night Fran went to the theatre and I was under the impression that Cosmo, Julie and I would be dining together. I made a ceremonious entry in a neat smoking jacket, prepared for a stimulating evening, only to find them dressed up, drinking martinis. I was told they were going out to dinner – and I wasn't invited. I ate my monklike meal of rice and beans alone. When Fran returned, I told her about it.

'We've got to get used to the fact that we're just a couple of old folks to them,' she said, rather sadly.

'Speak for yourself,' I answered.

The obvious affection between the two of them led me to lament the lack of it in my own life. For a moment I thought it might be because I had just got my OAP travel permit, but I suspected it went deeper. It seemed that all the attention we craved and sometimes got only made us more lonely when we were together. Dinner with just the two of us was a lonesome affair. Big table, bigger silences. 'Am I interesting any more?' I asked. 'Do I bore you?' she asked. There were times we both had a compulsion to express tender feelings, but we were victims of the cool world of the Fifties when expressing such emotions was uncool.

I called Pamela. 'I've forgotten how to wink,' I said, 'What'll I do?' I knew I could count on her to say something nasty. 'You've had a good run, you old geezer. Why don't you just stay laid back, look dirty and depraved. They'll come to you.'

I took her advice. For the next few weeks I was seldom seen at the French without my dirty Humphrey Bogart Burberry. Drinking Pernod and hiding behind my heavily-tinted glasses, I looked as depraved as Picasso's absinthe drinkers. I broke into a conversation Gaston, the owner of the French, who was, as usual, having with the prettiest girl in the room.

'May I buy you a drink, Gaston?' I asked, looking directly at the girl.

'What a good idea', she said. 'We only drink champagne though.'

I ordered a large bottle, noticing that they were drinking splits. When she came up to the bar to collect it, she seemed even sexier. She snuggled up so close to me, I thought my dirty Burberry was going to fall in love with her.

'We've met before,' she said. 'I'm a friend of Ian Dunlop. He introduced you as the publisher of the Sears Roebuck catalogue. It intrigued me at the time. You looked so unlike a publisher.'

We fell into a lively exchange of attitudes that passed for conversation:

'I like your dialogue. It goes with the coat.'

'Do you ever do anything silly?'

'Not if I can help it.'

'Do you realize that we have never had a serious discussion since we met?'

'Let's keep it that way.'

'Did you ever have them with your other lovers?'

'Yes. That's why they all ended in failure.'

'What do you expect out of this meeting?'

'The same as you.'

'I want a beautiful young girl. This could be my last affair, so please be cruel.'

'You're too old to fall in love.'

'And you're too nice.'

'What makes you think I'm nice?'

It was too late to call Fran and tell her I wasn't coming home to dinner. (I hadn't stood her up in ages.) A delicious wave of irresponsibility swept over me, filling me with the promise of an interesting evening. I was afraid she might decline my invitation to dinner, but the offer of more champagne brought her to her senses.

At the end of dinner I asked what she did when she wasn't picking up dirty old men. 'If you must know, I work for the Girl Guides. Isn't it a shame?' I thought she was going to fall into the mustard sauce on her plate after confessing to such a corny job. I had once corrupted a Boy Scout den mother, but this promised something more exotic.

'I think you'd better put me in a taxi,' she said at last, which came as a surprise. She reached into her purse for her keys and gave me her card. 'Call me next time you're in town. You're quite amusing.'

I gave her my card, the one that still claimed I was a publisher. I found her a taxi and was tempted at the last moment to join her. When she didn't offer a friendly goodnight kiss, I slammed the door and turned to the driver. 'Royal College of Needlework and drive like hell.' Like me, it was an old joke, but it got the best laugh of the night – from the driver.

When I dropped in on Gaston the next day, he chided me on being taken for a sucker. I didn't tell him I had called her that morning. She made a tentative date to resume the conversation when she returned from her holiday. I didn't know what I was getting into, but by now, I didn't much care.

180

CHAPTER EIGHTEEN

Our first dinner with Cosmo and Julie was almost a success. We got a rave review from Cosmo on the artichokes, but not from Julie, who had never seen one before, and who said it looked nasty. He guided her through the ceremony without winning her gratitude.

Julie was slowly winning us over with her Hoovering skills, although I could have given her some tips on furniture polishing technique – she was no Marlene Dietrich. Her pillow fluffing was beyond reproach, but I suspect that was Cosmo's influence – he had had the job for two decades. Her biggest success was with Marlene, the cat. 'We're really great friends,' she bragged. I complained about Marlene's lack of appetite; Julie offered a solution. 'Get her a companion. Not a young cat who will only want to play with her, or a tom who will bring up territorial problems, but someone her own sex, age, and spayed.' As if I didn't have enough problems with my book languishing in limbo and Fran's mounting depression, I now had to find a lesbian relationship for Marlene.

Worried about Julie's and Cosmo's lack of social stimuli, I gave a party for them, much against their wishes. Julie relented when I said there would be some teenagers she could relate to. She had let us know early in the relationship how she felt about being in the same room with anyone over thirty. I didn't dare tell her Fenella Fielding and Sylvia Syms were coming too. Sylvia, who had never met Fran, had been doing some of Fran's poems in her readings. Nothing could have pleased Fran more than to know she was gaining exposure in Milton Keynes through the still glamorous, if somewhat nervous, ex-movie star. 'I stood outside your door doing deep-breathing exercises for ten minutes before I could get up enough nerve to face anyone,' Sylvia confessed when they met.

The wild-haired, leather-clad, anorexic poet John Cooper Clarke, with whom Fran had shared many a platform-reading, went into shock when Julie walked in with Cosmo. 'I hate him,' he growled. He was green with envy at Cosmo's good fortune at having snared the one girl he admired above all others. 'Don't introduce me to her. I can't talk to her,' he told Fran. I introduced him instead to Sylvia, who was still recovering from meeting Fran. Julie was too shy to meet anyone. Armed with a collection of records, she headed for the dentist's chair, next to the record player, feeling that her only chance of survival would be to ignore everyone and hide behind the 45s. It worked until Sylvia got her brass back and confronted Julie.

'I know who you are so would you mind my asking you a question?'

I saw Julie's eyes drop.

'I know who you are too,' Julie said.

'Why aren't young people interested in politics?' Sylvia asked, not waiting for permission to speak. Julie looked at her incredulously.

'Because they're all wimps.'

Sylvia was smart enough to leave it at that and return to Johnny Clarke.

Julie's vocabulary had widened to include some new words inspired by the party – 'nightmare', 'shameless', 'grotesque' and 'ugly'. We thought the party had been a great success. Johnny Clarke stuck around for a post-mortem. He asked for a bowl and some milk for the sugar-coated cornflakes he had carried with him since he began to appear on those television cornflake commercials. Fran, Miles and I had a dance: 'A family that dances together has fun together,' was Miles' goodnight kiss to Fran, who was still suffering from party nerves.

The next day, on the way to my office in the basement, I had to pass the love nest. Despite accusations that I have no respect for privacy, I always ignored the exotic noises coming from their cell. On this occasion, their door was open. Cosmo was in bed reading the Sunday papers, smoking a fag, having a cup of coffee, his breakfast tray by his side. 'Get yourself a working-class girl, mate, they know how to treat a man,' he said. It was the first sign that Cosmo's sense of humour had returned. Shopping in Marks & Spencer's food department seemed to be Julie's idea of heaven. She called them 'the genius of the kitchen'.

They seemed deliriously happy, even though Cosmo hadn't touched a typewriter since she came into his life – unless he made out his shopping list on one. When I asked how the novel was going, Julie jumped to his defence. 'He's too beautiful and too talented to work,' she said, gazing at him with a look she usually reserved for Joseph Stalin.

To keep up the illusion that we had something in common, I suggested we go out on a double date – dinner at the Ritz to see our friend, cabaret artist Steve Ross. For Julie it was an evening of high embarrassment. The table setting at the Ritz had such a variety of silverware, it left her no alternative but to eat with her fingers. During the music, her small fists were clenched so tight that her knuckles turned white.

Cosmo spent most of his time trying to catch the attention of the waiters to keep the drinks coming. They watched with horror as Fran went into a trance during Steve's singing. Her smile could be seen in the dark. 'Here's a song for the Duncan Terrace contingent,' Steve announced. Afterwards, he came over to tell Fran how much it meant to him to have her in the audience. Julie and Cosmo looked as though they wanted to crawl under the tablecloth. The evening proved we had little in common, but Cosmo complimented me on my restraint in not doing my usual table-hopping.

I refused to recognize that we didn't have something to attract their company socially. (Fran reminded me of how badly we had behaved when her parents had attempted to integrate us in their social life.) Worse, I failed to notice that Fran was miserable. Hutchinson had rejected her new book of verse, a collection of all the ways love can go wrong. The writer's block was back. And she had lost Cosmo. All their affectionate exchanges over a bowl of lunchtime rice had ceased. She felt she had been reduced to the status of a landlady. Her temper, always under control in the past, flared up at the slightest provocation. She exploded when I forgot to tune back the television channel she had been watching. 'I've missed the credits,' she cried.

Worried, I described to the brats Fran's sense of isolation. Julie responded sympathetically with a short history of the politics of *angst*.

'Where there is stability there is happiness; where there is happiness there are no problems; where there are no problems people develop *angst*. It is a sensual pleasure that only happy people can afford. People with problems don't commit suicide. There are no suicides in El Salvador, where people are fighting for their lives every minute of the day.'

Reassuring as this sounded, I recalled that *angst* had developed around the height of the Habsburg empire, when people developed the fine art of the waltz and suicide simultanously.

'Unfortunately, Fran's a happy girl,' Julie continued. 'She has accepted she no longer wants to have affairs, which is a great relief to a woman who's become ashamed of her body, and those kind of scars never heal. She is a happy woman who's growing old and is in a constant rage. It's the price she must pay for the life she's led.'

'Heavy shit,' I said, 'but you might be right.'

It happened so quickly I could hardly believe it. Fran was cooking her lunch; Julie and I were talking about middle-class values; Cosmo was reading; Marlene was sleeping. I mentioned that the Kray brothers' downfall had been caused by aspiring to middle-class values. 'They object to girls swearing in their presence.' This only made Julie defend them more.

'What's so nice about girls swearing?' she asked.

From the kitchen came Fran's vigorous defence of my observation. 'Yeah, gangsters don't mind killing a few people, but object to swearing. Some sense of values they have.'

Julie continued to defend the Krays. Fran snapped.

'I wouldn't want to live in a world where your values ruled.'

Julie made a dash for the door, slamming it so violently it woke Marlene. Fran finished her cooking, took her bowl of rice up to her room without saying another word.

'Now do you wonder why nobody wants to be around Fran?' Cosmo began to pace the floor. 'That's twice she's snapped at Julie this week. You weren't around when Fran said she didn't want to hear any more "fucking ageist talk" from Julie while she's a guest in her house. I think we've been here too long. It's time to move on.'

Reassuring him that they were welcome as long as they wanted to be, I suggested that Fran's feelings ought to be taken into consideration as much as Julie's.

'We better make plans to move,' was his solution.

I went up to see Fran who was trying to put on some make-up; we had a date with the Notting Hill carnival.

'They're spoiled brats, just like we were,' I said.

She stopped doing her eyes which couldn't contain her tears. 'I can hear my mother's voice in mine, full of rage. Now I'm doing the same things and I hate myself for it, but I can't control it. I'm getting old, Jay. It's awful.' She was so confused and helpless I felt great compassion for her.

'I'm on your side no matter what happens,' I said. 'We'll work this out together. I think it would help if you apologize, even though we both know Julie's the one who should apologize to you.'

On the way out, Fran did apologize. Julie wasn't very gracious, but Fran was relieved; she had established the right to say what she wanted to in her own home.

Forty-eight hours later, Cosmo had found a flat. Fran said she was sorry they were leaving.

'I hope we can still be friends,' she said to Julie.

'You don't think, once we've left the house, we'd ever come back voluntarily,' Julie said in her wicked baby voice. At one time, Fran would have understood her joke, but under the circumstances it misfired.

I told Cosmo that I thought he had handled us very badly. He rejected the charge vehemently.

'I'm tired of hearing about you and your wife's career problems.'

It was sad to contemplate how things had deteriorated between us. Once, there had been nothing I wouldn't do to help him; now there was nothing I could do. Fran said it might be a good thing. 'He finally has something to rebel against now,' she said, hoping it would help me come to terms with the problem.

Cosmo wrote a thinly disguised portrait of me in his column in the *Literary Review*, which scholars of patricidal literature would have appreciated more than I did:

I went to see my parents over the weekend. They live in a big rambling house in Hampstead. They are old literary bohemians. Their world stopped in 1968. Some say it was the drugs; others the notices of father's first novel. One critic wrote: 'If the novel is not dead, this one will kill it.' My father was a schizophrenic, alcoholic junkie – but after the reviews he just went to pieces. Father was in the studio, surrounded by his mementoes of a literary life: a letter from Pound begging him not to visit – Pound feared for his sanity – the stuffed lobster of Gerard de Nerval, the upper bridgework of Genet and a signed first edition of Cocteau's shopping list. Great stacks of yellowing manuscripts grew in every available inch of space like Triffids of type. The room was dimly lit so as not to reveal his tear-stained mascara. Father was in such an advanced state of decomposition that he made Burroughs look like Arnold Schwarzenegger. Behind a great desk he sat in his wheelchair, with hose and plastic bag in one hand, a microphone in the other. For the past twenty-five years he had come to this room to dictate his memoirs. When I pointed out that the tape machine had not been plugged in, the shock of twenty-five years of memoirs down the drain brought an attack of epilepsy. I left him twitching to visit mother . . . eventually when I made my escape I looked back at the house. Through the large french windows I saw two figures silhouetted by the light: a man slumped in a wheelchair and a woman in a rage; two of the best minds of a generation destroyed by failure . . .

Cosmo's appraisal of my condition wasn't too far fetched. An avalanche of rejections all the way up to Christmas ensured that it wouldn't be a merry one for me. Maschler finally got around to returning my manuscript with egg salad sandwich stains, which mysteriously stopped around the third chapter. Sterling Lord was still having marketing problems. I gave it to London agent Richard Gollner, who knew something about eccentric authors, having Quentin Crisp as one of his most successful clients. He didn't bother to read it, but had the *chutzpah* to send me his reader's report: 'Mr Landesman is all mouth, a disembodied voice so concerned with what is going on around him that the centre of the book is a void. Reading it is like being chained to a stool of a bar-fly, trapped in a life with a terminal bore. A little Rebel goes a very long way. And yet not far enough.'

I did find someone in London who was starting up a new publishing company that might be interested. I used to drink with Edmund Fisher at the French when I was in publishing. I asked him to give me a brutally frank opinion. He had been a director of Michael Joseph and had a reputation for spotting a winner. He wrote me a note after reading it in record time:

> You have written something which has given me more pleasure than any manuscript I can remember for a very long time. It is a nervous and stimulating piece of compulsive reading, which I suspect was not compulsively but painstakingly written, and which is originally funny. It is also honest, to a fault, but beyond reasonable expectation. If it isn't honest, not only have you got Fisher fooled, but you could give lessons to Phineas Barnum and David Ogilvy.

He would have been the perfect publisher if he hadn't gone broke before he published his first book. I tried to hide the disappointment in my voice when I told Fran the news. 'Oh, well, another blow.' She came over to sit on my lap and give me a hug. 'What does it matter? We have our house, each other . . . ' but she couldn't go on. Neither could I.

I received a card from Pompeii, but I couldn't read the signature. The detail from a mural showed two lovers, both male, in a passionate embrace. Whoever sent it had had the good taste not to write, 'Having a wonderful time. Wish you were here.' It was much more cryptic. I recognized the word 'flashing', a word I associated with dirty old men in old Burberrys, and knew immediately it was from the Girl Guide. According to the postmark, it had taken a month to arrive, which accounted for my not hearing from her after her holiday. I had given up on ever seeing her again. Now I was ready for a holiday myself – a holiday from rejection.

Her phone call later lightened a heavy day spent staring down a word processor. 'I missed your coat,' were her first words, said so sincerely I almost believed her. 'When I didn't hear from you, I wondered if you were offended by the postcard.'

I told her I was and asked her to meet me at the Soho Brasserie. 'There's a dinner involved,' I said, hopefully. It had been so long since I'd seen her, I wondered if I'd recognize her without the mustard sauce on her face. By the time she showed up, I had become involved with Al, an actor friend who was in *Evita*, playing across the street from the Brasserie. He was telling me of his plans to do a one-man show on the life of Nelson Eddy. When GG showed up, I managed to escape the details of the caponized lover's career. She thought it was bad taste of Al to offer us tickets for that night's performance, after she'd said how much she loathed Andrew Lloyd Webber. After a bottle of champagne, a compromise was reached. We'd go back-stage with him, but we didn't have to watch his performance. It wasn't the kind of evening I had planned, but GG insisted, claiming to be fascinated with 'back-street life', a curious Freudian slip if I ever heard one.

'Perfect,' Al said. 'I don't go on until the second act.' He was playing the Argentine dictator, Peron, which I thought showed a certain amount of creative casting, since he had the face of a Jewish pawnbroker.

I noticed there wasn't a silver star on the door of his dressing-room, nor even a yellow one. He opened a bottle of champagne claiming it always improved his performance. 'Mine too,' GG said, already a little giggly, anticipating, no doubt, another misspent evening with my Burberry. People kept popping in and out of Al's dressing-room with frantic messages, hazy instructions and rumours of minor calamaties, as if in a Marx brothers movie. GG was enjoying the chaos, particularly when the sound man fitted her up with the mike intended for the General. By the time they were finished with Al, he was the embodiment of an Aryan superman in full uniform and a completely new nose. He looked in the mirror, snapped his heels together smartly, and raised his right arm in a Nazi salute. 'Heil Hitler,' he said in a Jewish accent. 'I'm on.' He slipped me the joint he had been smoking. 'Enjoy, enjoy,' he said.

'That was fascinating. We must do it again,' GG said afterwards, as we drank more champagne at the Brasserie. 'I like your friends. I thought there was a dinner involved,' she remarked.

'I lied,' I said. 'Let me take you home. You're pissed.' She accepted a ride in my Bentley.

'Now that's what I call a car,' she said. She admired every inch of its interior down to the cracked leather upholstery. When we drew near her place, I could see she was getting nervous – but a perfect parking place right outside her door left no doubt the gods were smiling.

She changed into something more comfortable – a man's frayed bathrobe – and started to drink Irish whiskey straight from the bottle, a gesture I admired enormously. I lit up a joint.

'How old are you?' she asked. Now I knew why she needed the whiskey.

'Would you believe me if I told you I was seventy-five?' I answered.

For a horrible moment she looked as if she did, but remained silent. She stared at me as though to analyse my chances of surviving the rest of the evening.

'You're almost as old as both my parents. How sweet.'

'Are you trying to tell me something?' I asked. 'If you are, I must tell you that it has long been my cherished hope to die in the saddle.' I pulled her down to the floor, dying to kiss her. The only thing that stopped me was hearing my heart go funny. I dismissed it as the power of suggestion, but as a precaution I kept my tongue in a very dry mouth – mine.

I was too stoned to go home. I settled for a foetal position on her sofa until her alarm bell went off at six-thirty. The next thing I remembered was a figure dressed in a houndstooth jacket, a young boy's shirt and a red bow tie offering me a thimble of liquid with a shaking hand. It could have been an eye-wash, but she insisted it was peppermint tea, She led me to a sleazy café near her office and we had what I described as a naughty breakfast – white bread toast, greasy chips, fatty bacon, yesterday's sausage and battery eggs.

'Perfect,' I said, mopping up what was left of the Daddie's sauce. 'We must do this again some time.'

She took another look at the Bentley, seeing all its scars. 'I hope you're in better shape than your car,' she whispered in my ear. 'I really had a delightful evening.'

Fran's weeks of rattling around the big, empty house and my frequent absences from it required a friendly therapy session.

'The only thing that cheers me up these days is the thought of knocking myself off,' she said. It hardly seemed an appropriate time to tell her I had started an affair with a twenty-seven-year-old.

'What's the chances of your developing some interests outside your career?' I asked. To Fran that meant only lunches with the girls and more calories.

'I'm not happy with anything I have to say these days. It's all so boring. I'd be surprised if anyone would want to have lunch with me. I need a gig.'

Since I was busy launching my own career, it was difficult to imagine who would look after hers. Fran's market was shrinking; she couldn't compete with younger performing poets.

'Something's always bothered me,' I began very tentatively. 'How is it that you can't put the bite and wit that you put in your verse into your life?'

'I'm not really witty. I'm just a good rhymer.' She looked sad.

'I don't accept that,' I said, trying to lighten the scene. 'We couldn't have lasted as long as we have if you hadn't had a sense of the absurd. Our marriage worked because we didn't take ourselves too seriously.'

She lightened up.

'I'm going to make a comeback. First thing I'm going to do is be nice to people on the phone.' I knew she was serious when she gave up control of her television that evening. We switched back

190

and forth between movies, trying to find a more dramatic scene than the one we had just played. I noticed the next morning she put a reminder on her mirror: 'Don't take yourself so seriously.'

We weren't actually invited to dinner at Julie's and Cosmo's new flat, but we did drop in on them while they were eating, and they spared no effort to make us feel welcome. Julie offered us a house tour.

'This is the kitchen,' she said with pride. 'Notice the little dryer and that's a little washing machine. Isn't it cute?' It was over in a minute, but I wouldn't have missed it for anything. It backed up my theory that she was, like Miss Dietrich, just another talented *hausfrau* who happened to get paid very well for doing what she was very good at doing.

I thought of taking GG home for dinner, but decided she should meet Miles first; he was always good for a laugh. He was in Boy's stall in the basement, unloading their unsold gear. Miles in a kilt could pass for normal, but in chains, spikes, rubber thongs as well, he was one hell of an advertisement for S & M. (Cosmo and Julie once told me they were taken to Skin Two, where that sort of thing is the entertainment, only to discover that it was Miles who was doing the entertaining. 'It was so boring,' Miles said, 'I thought I'd liven up the bill.' It was the kind of excuse I wished I was capable of making up on the spur of the moment.)

I asked him if he had anything a Girl Guide could wear.

'Right this way,' he said, leading us to the T-shirt rack and picking one out at random. The message on the T-shirt was plain: 'Fuck me, suck me, whip me, piss on me, and come all over my face and then get the fuck out of here.'

'Do you have anything less casual?' GG asked. 'He's certainly a "Landesman",' she said after we left. 'He talks out of the side of his mouth exactly like you.'

From past experience, introducing a new girl to Fran was important. Fran liked to know what the competition was like. Dinner was a success. When GG asked for seconds, I knew they were going to hit it off. My worry was that they would become great mates and I would become the odd man out. (The one thing that gave Fran a sense of confidence was knowing that I would never leave her for another woman. She told this to Pamela the first time they met and Pamela never forgot it.) We went upstairs to Fran's room after dinner to watch television.

Fran's room was the showplace of the house. It reflected her personality perfectly. Her walls were plastered with pictures and trays covered with fluorescent butterfly wings under glass. Her mantelpiece was a dumping ground for the *kitsch* in her life: memorabilia from parties, picnics, and old lovers. The mirror above it was framed with picture postcards sent by long lost friends. Her bedside table was a miniature pharmacy, the nerve centre of the room. Every surface was covered with *bibelots*. Above her bed hung a canopy – an embroidered Chinese shawl which gave anyone under it the feeling of being wrapped in a cocoon. It was unmistakably a room within a womb.

Lying all together on Fran's bed watching Bo Derek meet Tarzan was not everyone's idea of marriage building, but the fact that GG fell asleep before the movie was over only proved how comfortable she felt in a new environment.

The highest compliment that can be paid to a wife by a mistress is to adopt the wife's look. Fran introduced GG to her beloved Spastic shop, the Bloomingdales of Islington charity shops. GG walked into the shop a well-dressed career woman; under Fran's tutelage, she walked out looking like a baggy Charlie Chaplin. As a token of her appreciation GG turned Fran on to her latest anti-histamine pill. It changed Fran from a whingeing hypochondriac into a normal one, grateful for the relief.

Having a new mistress in the family prompted me to see the world through a new pair of eyes. GG introduced me to opera and I introduced her to Pappa Gus's restaurant, the Beggar's Banquet. I never took Fran there because his food was so distorted by excesses of spice and salt it would have given her chronic indigestion. Other people must have felt the same way because I never saw more than one or two couples there, even at the height of the dinner hour. On the day I took GG, however, a private wedding party was over-flowing the restaurant.

Gus was in a panic. He had turned the cooking of the wedding dinner over to his washer-up, who had never so much as heated a croissant, in order to join us. 'My good nature is being taken advantage of,' he said. 'God, I hate crowds.' My reminding him that a crowded restaurant was likely to become a successful one only depressed him.

The kitchen was in total disarray. The washer-up was in despair. 'Please Papa Gus,' he cried, 'come back.' GG tried to be helpful. 'You've got to do something, Gus, before this crowd turns ugly.' Ignoring her advice, he settled down to make romantic overtures to her. The musicians hired especially for the wedding had been playing non-stop, sensing that, if they did stop, the room would panic.

GG was not a Girl Guide for nothing. She led Gus by the hand into the kitchen and warned him that, unless he started cooking something, anything, the restless crowd would revolt. The musicians had collapsed by now, giving an opportunity for the best man to take over and lead the guests in community singing. Chairs were pushed aside; people began to dance and to chant, 'We want food. We want food,' like characters in a Buñuel movie. Sizing up the situation as hopeless, GG decided we should get out while we could.

'Gus loathes success more than you do,' she said.

'Not many of us success haters left,' I said, as we ran for the exit.

I had dinner at GG's flat: left-over rabbit stew and candlelight. We were celebrating our second month together. Fran admitted that GG was an asset when she saw her high up one of our trees, sawing away the dead branches. 'A Grade One preservation order should be put on that girl,' she said. I agreed. What other woman would spend Boxing Day collecting manure from the City Farm and then spend the next day spreading it in our garden?

CHAPTER NINETEEN

At Pamela's party, Fran remarked on how terrific she was looking. 'Having a man of her own has done wonders for her self-esteem,' I said, admiring Pamela's legs under her white leather mini-skirt. She looked happy and trim for one who had just hit forty. 'The years spent with your husband,' she had told Fran, 'haven't been a complete waste of time. He gave me a lot of confidence. I'm definitely through with the mistress role.'

Pamela made it a point to introduce Robyn Wallis, the BBC producer of her mistress documentary, to Fran. Pamela explained that Robyn was doing another on the eternal triangle – this time the wife. 'You should talk to Fran,' Pamela had suggested to her. 'Their marriage would be perfect for what you have in mind.'

Pamela's attempt to draw Fran into the project was handled very cleverly, appealing to Fran's obsession with television. 'You'll look beautiful on the box, Fran, dressed in your bangles and beads, lying on your famous bed telling your side of the story. It's fun, you know; I enjoyed all the attention.'

Fran thought the project was interesting, but resisted. 'I don't think I'm up to it at the moment,' she told Robyn Wallis. On the way home Fran asked me what I thought of the idea. 'Level with me,' she pleaded.

'It's up to you,' I said. 'Four books of verse, some 150 songs and years of poetry readings – I should have thought you'd already told your side of the story. It's a very interesting offer, though.'

Before I put the key in the door, I knew she was in two minds. Fran was thinking more of what Cosmo would say about yet another public exposure of our marriage. 'Not again, for God's sake. I'm already known as "Son of Open Marriage",' he once said. Yet the television exposure might help to get her limping career off its plateau.

Robyn made a date to talk to Fran about her availability for the documentary. Fran was still in doubt. The offer whetted her appetite for performing, but the subject matter was a problem. Fran was very naughty. She intrigued Robyn with tantalizing morsels of information about our marriage, but didn't particularly want to share them with the world. Robyn pleaded with her to think it over. 'You hold the key,' she said. 'Where could I find another marriage like yours? I've been looking for years.'

I still didn't think it was a good idea. 'If you tell the truth, you'll end up on the cutting-room floor. If you don't tell the truth, you'll end up looking foolish. Pamela got away with it because she looked so good lying through her teeth. You're not a good liar, so forget it. We don't need the publicity.' I was surprised when she agreed with me – it was the first time in years.

It didn't last long. An agent who specialized in finding engagements for middle-aged women in crisis saw in Fran the perfect client. He made the usual promises, including assigning her career to his top agent, a woman who had masterminded the comeback of several ancient performers. Fran couldn't resist. She told him of the BBC offer. He exploded with greed. 'That kind of publicity is worth a fortune. Call her tomorrow. The timing is perfect.' Fran relented.

I had a lunch date with Julie and Cosmo. While I was at the bar drinking my second martini, I was thinking about Fran's decision to go public again. I remembered all those perfect marriages that had ended in divorce. If we talked about our marriage on television, something might happen to jinx it. I also had second thoughts about the effect it would have on my relationship with GG. I had asked her when I was going to meet her parents. 'Never. I'll introduce you to my dentist – he'd be much more sympathetic, and he's Jewish.' Debating whether I should have another martini, I thought of the old joke about martinis being like a woman's breast – one's not enough, but three's too many.

If Julie hadn't been with Cosmo, I wouldn't have recognized her. She looked almost grown up in her sedate black dress and five-inch stilettos.

'Yeah,' Cosmo said, looking intently at his first martini, 'things have really begun to come together for us. Julie's beginning a column for the *Mail on Sunday* and I'm back at the typewriter.'

The strain between Cosmo and me was still evident. I still felt like an old lover who had been cast aside. I took it out on Julie. 'Don't you ever get bored with putting everything down?' I asked.

'That sounds ridiculous coming from you. You and your generation started undermining the gods long before we were born. Now we're just knocking over a new set of taboos.' She looked to Cosmo for confirmation.

'I didn't take it as seriously as you do,' I said. 'You're a paid assassin. We didn't do it for the money. We were amateurs.'

She smiled for the first time. 'That's why you failed,' she said, pleased with herself.

I decided to introduce GG into the inner circle of our friends at my election day party for Ronald Reagan. I knew it was a dangerous move, but I didn't want to hide any longer my fondness for the President.

'Hey, Jay,' Fran said, 'I don't mind your bringing your mistress into the house – she's so exquisite to look at, but can you spare your friends the agony of having to listen to you drooling over Reagan, that senile old man? You're not going to have a friend left after the party. If you see anybody interesting send them up to my room – that's where I'll be for the evening.'

My American hot dogs and mustard went over big. Nobody minded my having the ex-mistress and the current one sharing the hostess role while Fran was in seclusion. The party, as a political statement, was a disaster, but, if the object was to get a consensus on GG, it was a success with everyone but Pamela. She didn't think GG was ready for the A-team. 'That's what people said about you at the beginning of our affair,' I reminded her.

We dropped in on Fran for a post-mortem on the party. GG thought the political concept was in bad taste, but said she enjoyed meeting Pamela. 'She's so terrific, I don't know what this old man of yours is doing with me.'

It hit the right note for Fran. 'I could kiss you for that, but I'm not too high on affection tonight.'

'Don't bother,' GG said. 'Affection is not a strong point in my family.'

I saw my basement studio taking on the qualities of a slum when Miles began to use it as a storage place for his musical equipment. It was a huge receptacle for broken things, even sadder than the mountain of unsold books which had been staring me in the face. When our lodgers moved out of the top floor, I had second thoughts about renting it out again. It would be much simpler if I moved there instead. It seemed to me I had been living in basements and small rooms since I'd been in London. How nice it would be to have my own set-up and really live semi-detached. I showed the place to GG during a rainstorm. Even the water dripping in through the roof did little to dampen her enthusiasm.

'This place has my name on the door,' I said.

'Mine, too,' she added.

I went shopping with GG at Camden Lock. There I bought two rings – with Fran and GG in mind – at an Oxfam stall for 50p each while she wasn't looking. Our expeditions were often a comedy of errors. Once, at Harvey Nichols, my feminine side erupted. I went out of control at the perfume counter. By the time we hit the second floor – ladies' evening wear – I was smelling like the new Thatcher Rose. When the sales lady asked GG if she'd like to try something on, she said, 'No, thanks, but my father might.'

We arrived back at the house to discover that the BBC was filming Fran. Her room was so crowded with people and equipment, we could hardly get our heads in. Fran was sitting on the bed looking like a young Edith Sitwell without the *Götterdämmerung* overtones. She was colour co-ordinated all the way up to her elbows with bracelets and rings on every finger, which made giving her the ring I had just bought superfluous.

Our unexpected appearance lent an authentic touch to the event. When the cameras started to roll, GG quickly left the room. I stuck around hoping to soak up some of the attention that might be left over from Fran's performance.

'I didn't have any great expectations of marriage,' Fran began. 'I have a very happy marriage. I've been married for thirty-five years to a very funny guy and we make each other laugh. I have my unhappy love affairs on the side.'

I thought Fran looked so self-assured and relaxed, I suspected she had been at the weed. I was on my way out, knowing she'd do a bang-up job of defending her position, until the interviewer asked her why she thought people had affairs. It was something we had talked about for years, but we had never come to any conclusion.

With the wry look I was so familiar with, she explained: 'I know some people think sex is what it's about, but I maintain when you're married a long time, you get so tired of hearing each other's old stories, those polished gems that you've worked a life-time to perfect . . . ' She hesitated a second. 'When you have an affair, you can trot them out again and they sound fresh and exciting to a new person.' She gave a wicked smile to the camera crew. 'I think you'd have to have a tiny shrivelled up heart if there was only place in it for one person for the rest of your life.'

She had displayed an extraordinary directness before the camera, impressing the crew, which is always a sign that it won't impress anyone else. I was about to leave again when Robyn asked if she thought a mistress shored up a marriage. Fran answered with a poem she'd written as Pamela and I were breaking up:

> You come to me complaining about your mistress
> You tell me she's become a nagging wife
> The lady that you said
> Was fabulous in bed
> And brought such sauce and sunshine to your life
>
> You say she's got the bad taste to criticize you
> She makes demands, she cavils and complains

She isn't satisfied with polishing your pride
And keeping your self-image free from stains

Well I know all about you dear
Your boredom and your glory
And I must say I'd like to hear
Miss Pamela's side of the story

You come to me complaining about your mistress
Her lack of tact has cut you like a knife
While I stay safe at home
And write this little poem
And play the part of understanding wife.

'Do you ever feel jealousy?' Robyn asked.

'Yes, I do,' Fran admitted. 'I'm not some kind of superwoman. I'm acquainted with all the illnesses that flesh is heir to. I know what it is to feel possessive and jealous. Horrible is what it feels like. What I advise everybody to do is some kind of exercise. It's like using different kinds of muscles; sometimes you get lazy or prey to those emotions, but if you kind of keep yourself in trim, you can deal with them. And if you have a choice of learning to deal with them or cutting yourself off from all the experiences that make life exciting, I suggest to you – learn to deal with them. The alternative is just too bleak.'

The television crew must have fallen in love with her at that point. She looked simply beautiful against the reflections in the mirror at the back of her famous bed. Her voice was carefully measured, not a word out of place.

'Why do you think you've been able to survive the . . .' Before Robyn could finish the sentence, Fran was quick to cut in. 'How did we manage to get away with it? Is that what you're asking me? Maybe we're not getting away with anything. Looked at from the point of view of society at large, they would say we're getting away with something. There are people who are deeply offended by the way we live. It's weird. I can't understand why. I think everyone should live the way they want to live. Perhaps the kind of marriage I have is all underpinned by the fact that I've

199

been given this gift of rhyming these little poems and I've exercised this art. It has given me much pleasure to share it with other people. The reason people are cruel to each other is the fear of loss, a sense that they don't really like themselves very much. Why should anyone stay with miserable me? I'm just a housewife or whatever. Suddenly, when I was quite old, I had a chance to see myself as something other than that. It gave me tremendous confidence. I don't feel that Jay is going to abandon me.'

She was right about that. In all of our ups and downs neither of us ever thought of running off to Pago-Pago. The next day the crew came back to capture her walking in the garden opposite the house. She looked almost athletic striding among the fading roses, shoulders high and head up – a posture reserved for cameras and personal appearances. I watched from the other side of the garden a different Fran. She was seated in the ideal setting. I wondered at the time if the camera would catch her very secret look as she fondled a faded rose. The camera zoomed in on the rose as though to say, 'Look, she's a survivor'.

With all the attention Fran was receiving, I had to find out if I was still needed. 'You have a Bentley, a wife who is a VIP, a young mistress, and a wonderful unpublished novel, and on a good day, with the light behind you, you'd pass for forty-five,' GG assured me.

A few weeks later GG was visiting my new quarters when Fran appeared. 'You know I've been waiting for the result of my throat biopsy.' She stopped and headed for the door. 'You could have at least shown some concern.' And she left.

'Is she stoned?' GG asked.

I told her about the history of Fran's throat, which we had not taken seriously, but she'd had a biopsy done just to make sure. A very chastened GG wanted to come with me to share responsibility for being so inconsiderate. 'Give me some time alone, and then come in,' I suggested.

Fran and I both had always agreed that consideration for each other's feelings was very important. It was only when I suggested that other people's feelings must be respected too that she listened to my explanation. GG knocked and entered to find herself in the middle of an old-fashioned husband and wife confrontation. She quietly left the room, and Fran and I sat there on the bed, shouting accusations at each other.

Now that GG was spending more time at the house, I pointed out to Fran, we saw more of each other than ever before. She admitted it as evidence, but continued to charge me with neglect. 'Maybe with a little less career talk and a little more interest in other people, including me, we might resolve this.' She confessed to having taken herself too seriously, but blamed it on the hash cookie that she had consumed in an anxious moment. It was the first time she had admitted that drugs had let her down. 'Let's try to make it fun for all of us,' was her way of saying she was sorry.

I went back upstairs to a red-rimmed pair of eyes and a nose to match. GG, with perfect timing, was on her way out to do some shopping. She understood that Fran and I needed more time together to consolidate feelings that had gone off the rails.

A letter that arrived from Robyn helped. 'Dear Fran, Your panache and intelligent comments have delighted everyone around here and I'm sure that many of the listening audience will find your observations full of wisdom and understanding.'

The *Sunday Times* had an amusing review by Byron Rogers. He tagged the three women on the show as the Sad, the Cool, and the Outrageous. 'Outrageous American, a game old trout, married her husband in an attempt to be nice to him. He, in turn, opened a nightclub so she wouldn't feel bored. Just ordinary folks,' he concluded. Fran didn't like the 'old trout' bit, but she really couldn't complain as most of the other reviews were sympathetic. 'Flamboyant Fran admitted that jealousy is a problem in their kind of free-wheeling marriage. But, "If you keep yourself in trim, you can deal with those emotions." ' Even Mary Kenny's review was sympathetic, and quoted one of the poems Fran had recited: 'When love comes along and sings you a song/ It's hard to stay sober and sane/But be on your guard, for out in the yard/Are the terrible tigers of pain.'

Naturally we came under heavy flak from Julie and Cosmo for exposing our private life. We exchanged roles: we were the irresponsible brats and Julie and Cosmo the puritanical parents. They seldom called any more. The only time we saw them was when they accepted an invitation to dinner. Those occasions really turned the clock back. They reminded me so much of the way Fran and I used to go to dinner with her parents when we were young and full of ourselves.

New Year's Day started off with the bad news that Fran's new agency had gone bust before they could get her one gig. It set off a tidal wave of *angst*. Her nightmare of never working again seemed about to come true. I made one more attempt to rescue her. 'Look,' I began in a rabbinical voice that always made her suspicious, 'the only way you're going to beat the game is to make yourself unavailable. Make them come to you.'

It was a piece of advice she was not eager to hear, having heard it so many times before. 'Yeah, I know what you mean. I'm going to be recognized when I'm dead. I can hardly wait. I'd knock myself off if I was sure it would raise my ASCAP royalties.' She thought for a moment. 'You poor boy. You've tried so hard to make it a fun life and I fought you all the way.' We laughed again, otherwise one of us would have ended up crying.

Recounting the scene to GG in one of my rare contemplative moods, I was filled with a perverse kind of optimism. 'It would be a pathetic picture, if it wasn't so funny. Here are these two old farts who have been up at bat so many times without coming up with a winner. The old lady can't get a gig, and I can't get my book published. Pathetic, isn't it?' I wasn't expecting any sympathy, but I was disappointed when she agreed that it was, indeed, pathetic of me to think like that.

'You've got the only marriage I know of that makes sense,' she said, giving me a playful clip on the chin.

'I needed that,' I said.

The two of us spent the weekend chasing Fran's blues away. We cooked all the dinners and I brought her breakfast every morning. We wouldn't let her touch a dish. GG began to see her as some dear old eccentric auntie; I treated her like the Jewish princess I used to know. A visit from her Norwegian collaborators with news that her songs had been featured on Norwegian television cheered her up for a moment. (When Julie heard about it, she said, 'Of course Fran's popular in Norway. They're a deeply melancholy people.')

CHAPTER TWENTY

In the middle of a cruel January, the arrival of Hanya from her home base in Rome was most welcome. It meant we could look forward to her tarot readings, yoga exercises, some laughs and the latest communiqués from the Goddess, who ruled her life. Those were the acceptable aspects; it was the one-woman show she was planning to do at the Old Red Lion that was the hazard. Fran had done her own one-woman show there (*Confessions of a Middle-Aged Juvenile Delinquent*) to a very mixed reception. Like Fran, Hanya was one of the army of middle-aged women who will go anywhere, do anything, under the impression that there is an audience for their life story. For years I had been Hanya's buffer against the harsh realities of life, giving her just enough encouragement to keep her head from Catherine-wheeling all over the place. I'd known a lot of talented men and women whose luck had run out the day they were born, but she was my favourite. (Hanya was once quoted as saying, when she was in films, 'If I'm not told I'm wonderful twenty-five hours a day, I'm lost.')

Although approaching fifty, Hanya still looked like a flower child of the Sixties: a red linen rose on her Italian *borceleno*, a mane of wild, electrified, hennaed hair and a childlike chalk-white face in stark contrast to her coat of many colours. The guitar at her feet completed the picture of a living work of art, slightly abused. Installed in my old room, she appreciated the freshly cut flowers, a Chinese back-scratcher and a tortoiseshell hand mirror.

Nobody knew what to expect on Hanya's opening night. Her friends arrived with all their critical faculties suspended, but by the end of the evening they were impressed. *A Life In Twenty-one Songs* was an incomparable journey, slightly less tragic than the Holocaust, but not as hopeless as *Waiting for Godot*. Had Hanya sung of her nights as a croupier at the Playboy Club while six months' pregnant, and of the days writing a best-selling book on female sexual fantasies (*Freely Female*), there wouldn't have been nights when only a handful of people showed up. In desperation I called Julie and Cosmo, offering them free tickets, dinner and a bottle of champagne – anything they wanted – if they would only catch her act. I didn't want to think of Hanya going through another night without an audience. They admired her courage and professionalism, but were critical of her message, which they had consigned to the compost heap of the Sixties long ago.

We all came back to the house, where Cosmo picked up Hanya's guitar and did a parody of her show, using Fran and me as inspiration. 'My parents' open marriage made me the nervous wreck I am today/they went on television and gave the game away/and now I'm a neurotic psychotic mess . . . ' In a serious post-mortem on her act and Fran's too, Cosmo maintained his reputation for ruthlessness. 'Why don't you people face it? Your act will never appeal to the mainstream of entertainment. Get out of the business. I declare this living-room a creativity-free zone.'

Hanya's Goddess must have taken pity on us. A letter came from a young woman producer in America who wanted to revive *The Nervous Set* in St Louis. We didn't take it too seriously, until she showed up on our doorstep. The saying 'You're getting old when the police begin to look young' applied to producers as well. Hope Wurdack was twenty-five, 4 feet 11 inches tall. Neither jet lag nor the flu could dampen her enthusiasm for the project. 'Everybody I talked to in St Louis flipped out when I said I was considering the show. It seems that most people had seen the original production at least ten times. I knew we had to do it.' (There had been other people interested in reviving it over the years. My nephew Rocco Landesman, who made his debut as a Broadway producer with *Big*

River, did a reading of it for Broadway backers, but no full-scale production came to pass.)

Hope exuded such an air of confidence that Fran and I began to believe in her as well as the Goddess. She left, promising to send a contract, option money and tickets for both of us to attend the opening night. 'I would also like you and Fran to do three nights of cabaret before the show opens. Fran will do her regular act and Jay can read something from his memoirs. It will be great publicity, and help raise money for the production.' I hadn't been back to St Louis for twenty-five years, except for Cutie's funeral and my one abortive environmental presentation. 'We could give you an extra $1,000 for the three nights. You could dance your way back into the hearts of the people who loved the original show.' We had never been offered such a fee for our services.

Hanya confirmed it was the work of her Goddess. When Hope left, we went up to the top floor, to my quarters, to watch the sun set. 'Damn good show,' I said as we watched the sun slip behind the dome of the old Lyons House at the Angel crossroads. We looked at one another and fell into a communal embrace.

GG won Hanya's approval, but was relieved when she left. 'I don't mind sharing you with your wife, but I can't stand feeling like the other woman when you're with Hanya.' By now GG was accepted as a member of the family. Had she looked more Jewish, some would have thought she was.

When GG's landlord demanded possession of her flat in thirty days, we offered the homeless waif temporary residence. Fran had only one practical suggestion: 'Would you mind not putting your laundry in with mine. I don't mind the domestic tranquility of a simple *ménage à trois*, but laundry is always a problem in this kind of arrangement.' That first night GG made a simple cheese soufflé, Fran made the salad and I washed up. 'What a perfect love nest this is going to be,' I said. Once we were alone, GG reminded me that love nests are usually places away from the lover's home. 'I know. That's what is going to make this one so much more fun.'

Browsing around the London market stalls gave me and GG the feeling that we were a couple of newlyweds furnishing our first home. Our tastes were very similar, except for her penchant for overscaled *jardinières*. As spring approached, GG took charge of the garden. She displayed a knowledge of borders, shrubs and wall vines, but her overturning the earth and her judicious pruning were particularly impressive. Her stuffed *crêpes* and grown-up salads brightened the dinners that the three of us shared. GG felt that we'd just about got the recipe for living together right too. 'Nobody is left out, the menus are more varied, the laundry sorted out, a summer garden looks promising, and your wife's going to New York for a gig. What else do you want in life, you lucky Hebrew?' I couldn't spoil her scenario by telling her that my book still hadn't found a publisher.

Julie and Cosmo displayed a peculiar reaction to GG's presence. It had nothing to do with morality. They denounced GG for letting down the image of the mistress by integrating. 'Bring back Pam,' they chanted. 'She knew her place.' It would have been difficult for anyone to understand just why the relationship worked, but one of the main reasons was GG's attitude towards Fran. Unlike Pam, GG saw Fran as a friend, not as a threat or a rival. This had a soothing effect, which often led to amusing exchanges between the two of them. Sometimes GG would pop into Fran's room in the morning on her way to work. 'Have a nice day at the office, dear,' Fran would say, knowing that she would have me for company for the rest of the day, except for lunch.

Originally, when I suggested to Fran that we take GG along with us to St Louis, we both agreed what fun it would be to stir things up a little. I still bore resentment toward the town which had literally driven us into exile. What a lark it would be to return as a *ménage à trois* and show them that we were still high-flying non-conform-ists. As the date of the departure closed in on us, however, I realized Fran was in no condition to handle the situation. I decided not to take GG. Fran was relieved. 'It would have been humiliating for me to try to explain what your mistesss was doing on the journey,' she explained. 'I think you made the right decision.'

Trying to explain this to GG took some doing. She didn't hide her disappointment at my not being more daring. 'All right,' she said, 'but when you come back, we're going on a two-week holiday, you *schmuck*. I don't like to feel left out either.'

Flying back to St Louis, Fran and I didn't know what to expect. We held on to each other long after take-off and landing. We needn't have worried. From the moment we stepped off the plane we were treated like returning heroes. A television camera crew interviewed us as we stepped from the plane and the attention thereafter never flagged. Meeting the cast and holding conferences with the director left us scant time for play. Watching the first run-through, we were struck by the high level of professionalism on display. The two leads captured us perfectly. It was spooky to discover we were still fighting the same issues: Jan, the wife, was complaining about her husband's lack of attention; her husband Brad was trying to get her to be more self-reliant. They drifted apart; he began an affair. Only her attempted suicide at the end brought them together. (Producer Robert Lantz in the Broadway version would not allow a suicide ending; some said his decision ruined the show.)

As accompanist for her act, Fran had the good luck to have Jimmy Williams, who was the show's musical director. He had played the piano in the original production seventeen years previously. I chose to read a section from my memoirs which highlighted the rise and fall of the Crystal Palace. I knew many of the audience would identify with the scene. It was our appearing together at the close of the show that worried me. I can't sing and Fran can't dance except in our living room, and only with me, but that was what we were going to try to do.

Running into friends from the past sometimes proved embarrassing; the names were familiar, but the faces and figures were often unrecognizable. They all looked so grown up, some so blown up. A former waitress at the Crystal Palace waited one night in the parking lot of the theatre as I was on my way to a rehearsal. 'Remember me?' she asked as I passed her car. I stopped and smiled without recognizing her. It was the closest thing to being a movie star I'd ever experienced and frankly I was enjoying it enormously. I even felt like one.

'It's not Terisina,' I asked, recognizing her at last. I leaned through her car window and planted a kiss on her still beautiful face. 'My, you've grown up. Are you coming to the show?' If she wasn't I could understand why. She had caught my act many times on top of the ice cube maker in the back room of the Crystal Palace. 'Sure,' she said. 'Maybe I'll see you after the show.' I knew she wouldn't, but the thought of doing my act in the back seat of her car in the parking lot gave me a thrill.

On the first night of our cabaret, my reading from the memoirs of St Louis days and nights touched an audience whose average age was about the same as mine. They laughed at all the familiar references and, even though I ended on a downbeat note, they gave me a round of applause as if to say they had missed me. Fran's act was received even better. At the end, I joined Fran in the spotlight and the two of us started dancing to a medley of songs from *The Nervous Set*. A big spotlight followed our every move; luckily we were excellent fox-trotters and dip merchants. We danced, holding each other very close. Then, just like in the movies, we broke into one of Fran's songs. Nothing could have summed up our life together as well:

> I wasted my whole life
> Messing up yours
> When I should have been dancing
> I was slamming the doors
>
> I sulked in the spotlight
> Wearing a frown
> When I should have been dancing
> I was putting you down

Then I sang the middle chorus:

> We could have been sensational
> A couple of luminous stars
> Could have been inspirational
> When all those tomorrows were ours

Then both of us, looking straight into each other's eyes:

> I gave you a hard time
> Fighting our wars

209

> When I should have been dancing
> I was settling scores

We stopped dancing. With our arms around each other, we looked out into the audience:

> When I should have been making sense of my life
> I was busy messing up yours

As we kissed in the spotlight, the audience gave us a standing ovation. We took our bows and waved goodbye. Nothing we had ever experienced could capture that moment of complete acceptance. Afterwards, I had a chance to relax for the first time since arriving. The party was so reminiscent of an evening at the Crystal Palace, I had to restrain myself from doing my *maître d'* bit.

By the opening night of *The Nervous Set*, I was still basking in the success of the cabaret. I knew the musical was going to be a good show. I even allowed myself to think that this might be the turning point of both of our careers. For a change I wasn't thinking about my unpublished book languishing in some editor's bottom drawer. I would have liked GG to see what we were like when we were young. I even thought that Cutie would have admitted I was a success. At the intermission, many people came up to express their affection for both the show and us. A young man whom neither of us knew approached us with an outstretched hand. 'I wasn't around when the Landesmans were doing their stuff, but I've heard so much about you all I just wanted to see for myself what all the fuss was about. Now I know,' he said, shaking my hand furiously.

The fact that this triumph failed to bring Fran and me closer together confirmed my theory that success doesn't help. We had one of the biggest fights of our marriage before we left St Louis. So much acceptance had a devastating effect on me. I began to act and talk like the big shot I used to be, which did not go down well with Fran. After a silly argument, I went over the top, feeling I was entitled. I had told Fran so many times in London that if either of us ever made it, the marriage would be in trouble. Now, for the first time, I recognized that moment had arrived. I left the house early

210

the next morning after the fight, hoping things would cool down. Yet, I was filled with a strange kind of excitement. Never in our marriage had I contemplated the idea of a separation.

Over breakfast with my old and dearest friend, Gerry Gadarian, I put forward my plan. 'Why don't I spend a couple of nights at your place? Of course Fran and I will go back to London together,' I told him. 'I look upon this as a practice run.' (I knew what was going through his mind: 'Fran and Jay have the perfect marriage and now this asshole is telling me it's through?') I told him about GG without making it sound like a mid-life crisis. He listened patiently. 'You're engaging in a bit of fantasy, Jayboy,' he warned. 'You could never leave Fran. Nobody would believe you'd be that stupid.' Armenians are said to know the secrets of the human heart and Gadarian was no exception. I went back that morning and made up with Fran. I told our host, Pat Parker I still loved them both.

During the last few days before we left, Alfie Clay, our guardian angel who had raised Cosmo and Miles (and Fran), invited us to her house. As we told her of the adventures of Cosmo and Miles growing up in London, we realized she still approved of us. She set before us a banquet of delicacies one would have thought only the Astors might have served. We had been entertained by the 'best' people, eaten in the poshest restaurants, but nothing compared to Alfie's Maryland golden fried chicken and thick chocolate cake. It was such a contrast to the cocktail food we had been eating, we asked her if we could take some of it home for the boys. 'Not for the dog,' we assured her. Nothing gave Alfie more pleasure. I learned something from Alfie – what a fantasy it was to think of a life without Fran and those memories.

Upon our return to London, we were greeted with the news that GG had missed us. We weren't prepared to hear that we were going to become grandparents. Fran was more ready for the role than I was. 'At least I'll have something to look forward to,' she said. I only wished I could have been as understanding, sympathetic, and caring as Fran seemed to be with Julie during her pregnancy.

My being on holiday with GG for two weeks brought about a change in Fran. At first she dreaded the idea of being alone in the house, even though I arranged for Miles to be on the top floor.

Miles didn't show up half the time; instead of being put out, Fran said she enjoyed being on her own with no one to account to. At the thought of being a grandmother soon, she toughened up. She would damn well do what she wanted to do, and she wasn't going to take any more shit from anyone.

CHAPTER TWENTY-ONE

By now I was so despondent again about *Rebel* not finding a publisher, I needed someone to let me know that I hadn't wasted three years of my life writing the damn thing. I sent copies of the manuscript to the two people I could count on to level with me, Robert Stone and John Clellon Holmes. Stone's novels *Hall of Mirrors*, *A Flag at Sunrise*, *Dog Soldiers*, and *Children of Light* had earned him the reputation of a 'big writer – a writer's writer'. He wrote about men and women who are inexorably drawn to situations they can't handle. With a permissive wife, an unpermissive mistress, a 'professional irritant' daughter-in-law about to make me a grandfather, and an unpublished novel, I was beginning to feel like one of Stone's heroes. His letter came as a great relief: 'I read *Rebel Without Applause* with great pleasure. I think it's an important document. Your book is funny and moving, heartening, tragic and outrageous. To read it is to be present at the invention of contemporary America. Of all the published reminiscences of Bohemian America in the Fifties and Sixties, this is the most revealing and the best . . .'

I showed the letter to Fran – she couldn't have been more pleased; I was practically levitating. The response from Holmes was equally gratifying: 'Your book arrived yesterday, and I peeked in and couldn't stop and read the whole thing in a gulp. You've done it. You've caught the excitement, the fun, the nerves, the aspirations, and the essentially serious thrust of your life and mind . . . Also, very well written – so much of it eloquent, tough, sad, brave and funny.'

Sadly, in another letter Holmes disclosed that he was awaiting operation number three for reconstruction of a cancer-savaged jaw:

> Here's where things stand. I've had two big time operations. They've cut out part of my jaw, and taken tucks in my tongue and borrowed some of my breast muscle to make me a new chin. I've got a steel brace on my chin that makes me talk funny – like 'Ooogla-gurgle-ferkle' – and curse a lot . . . While eating and drinking, I resemble a supra-annuated Gabby Hayes, all a-droll and a-slop. So my trim WASP good looks, never my strong suit anyway, are, shall we say, blurred . . . my public performances are finished.

Ironically, the economic plight that had plagued him throughout his life had been solved by selling his correspondence with Jack Kerouac. In a previous letter he had written of his ideas for a creative retirement – finishing his novel, building an extra room on his house and, most important, getting the taste of twenty years of academia out of his head. 'I'm starved for laughs and truths after years of having to read bullshit for that damn job,' he said. 'What I want is to sit in your living-room, or garden, or bedroom or anywhere and have good vital eccentric talk again and some laughs . . . I miss you both . . . the oldest friendships are the best. Know it or not, pally, you're my oldest, dearest friend . . . I greet you on breaking into the memoir-game with a roll of drums. What you've done is fine.' There's a PS: 'As Phyllis Jackson of MCA used to say: "Now let's go out and make some money." '

We had been in correspondence for over forty years; never was there a touch of self-pity. ('But sing no sad songs for me – remember the movie? Maggie Sullavan starred.') Knowing him and Shirley had kept me creatively alive. Without their support and love, I don't think I would have emotionally survived the journey. I wrote back thanking him for the life-preserver he had thrown me.

Even Cosmo and Julie were impressed with Holmes's letters.

'Now you can stop moaning,' Julie said.

'Does this mean you'd give me a blurb for the book when and if it's ever published?' I asked her.

'I hate to read the work of friends,' she said.

'Well couldn't you make one up something like you do so much of the time?' I asked. I don't know to this day whether she read the manuscript, but she gave me permission to use what she had written:

Jay Landesman's *Rebel Without Applause* is the perfect antidote to all those messianic Beat tales of the Fifties. While Kerouac and Company were busy banging away on their bongoes and going stark raving bonkers, Mr Landesman was cultivating the post-modern life-style thirty years before *The Face* magazine. For an American, he's funny; for a native of St Louis, Mo, he was remarkably hip and for an ex-publisher he's remarkably honest. His marriage resembled a rugby scrum, his morals are low, he is a gossip, a name-dropper and a philanderer – in short, just my kind of writer.

All this acceptance lowered the pressure I had been under the last three years. Trying to get the book published didn't seem so important any more. For the first time I was in the mood to take the advice I had been giving Fran – let it happen; quit trying so hard. If *Rebel* was any good, it would get published some day. Meanwhile, I felt that I was one of the luckiest men in Islington.

When GG wasn't on the scene, Fran and I would make a date to have dinner and spend a rare evening alone. We were like a couple of furtive delinquents – smoking pot, giggling, cracking old jokes, watching television in her room – taking outrageous advantage of GG's absence. We talked a lot about how the forthcoming blessed event might change our lives. Neither of us really wanted to admit that we weren't crazy about becoming grandparents – it would definitely put an end to our illusion that we were still young.

There was no denying that Julie's pregnancy had a salutary effect on our relationship with her and Cosmo. It was as though a moratorium on family differences had been called. They conformed to the traditional role of expectant parents better than we had. When a softer Julie and a caring Cosmo struggled to the surface, it turned us into a reasonable facsimile of a together family with a promising future.

Whether it was God's wrath, divine retribution or plain stupidity, disaster struck during the last months of Julie's pregnancy. The love nest I shared with GG went up in flames. We had been having a cold spell and, fearing that the bathroom pipes would freeze, I left the wall heater on day and night. As a result, the thin wooden wall panels in the lavatory dried out and caught fire. Both GG and I were away at the time; luckily Cosmo was in the house to rescue a frightened Fran from the flames. When I returned home to see the fire engines, my heart sank. I rushed up to a neighbour. 'What's going on?' I asked. 'It's a fire and I'm afraid it's your house,' she said.

I found a distraught Fran sitting in the park opposite in shock. Cosmo told me later, 'She rushed out of the house with three bags of photo albums and two bags of her precious medication, like some old bag lady on speed.'

It was only later that night, alone in a strange hotel room, that we realized how fragile the life we'd built had been: how perishable our pretty kingdom was. Somehow Fran's room had been magically preserved; just outside her door was the bitter burnt smell and the soggy blackened carpet. Inside her room the walls seemed thin as a theatrical scrim. The fire could have poked a hole right through them, allowing the wind and water to rush in. All the lovely objects we'd collected – the clothes, the books, the statues, the diaries and the papers, the records of our victories and defeats – would have been destroyed. Upstairs, in the love nest, the only thing that separated GG and me from the stars was a plastic sheet put there by the firemen. Fran said, 'This must be what they mean when they say, "The world that seems so solid is only an illusion."'

GG and I moved to the basement, while the builders wrestled with the roof. By a strange coincidence, on the day of the fire GG had found a flat she was ready to buy. Had I been more perceptive, I would have realized that both the fire and the impending birth of my first grandchild would affect our relationship. Instead, we carried on as if nothing had happened.

Fran became involved in a project with Nathan Silver, writing lyrics for his original story based on the Tooth Fairy legend. She had a show, *Don't Cry Baby It's Only a Movie*, running at the Old Red Lion Theatre and was writing some of her best lyrics for another one. Her enthusiasm for work was so high she had little time to worry about the problems of the 'lodgers' in the basement.

No matter how cosy a basement is, it is still a basement. Referring to it as a 'love nest' was ridiculous, but GG called it 'Jay's granny flat', which was plain rude. There were other signs that GG's sense of humour had shifted significantly enough to dampen romance. *A Room with a Jew* was her idea of a good title for her memoirs. She began to refer to my forthcoming status as a grandfather and my renewed interest in family matters as though they were signs of approaching senility. I was still worried whether Cosmo and Miles would ever find themselves. 'They could always get a job as living telegrams. Miles would be cute as a Whip-o-gram and Cosmo as a Wimp-o-gram.' I didn't laugh. Her excuse – 'Just trying to keep your sons working' – fell flat, especially since it was St Valentine's Day.

As Julie's pregnancy advanced into its last month, the *ménage à trois* had to fight for space with the imminent birth. Fran's daily visits to the Spastic shop in search of baby paraphernalia became the high point of her day. At times it became a contest to find out who could be the most creative in collecting the artifacts we imagined a baby would require. We kept looking for things we remembered from our day, without any success. We read the tiny signs in newsagents advertising baby carriages, play pens, walking aids, even cribs. Although we knew Julie would never accept anything second hand, we saw it as back-up for when we became ace baby-sitters at home. (The truth was, Fran and I couldn't resist a bargain.) When I saw the baby carriage Julie's mother had bought her, I almost went into a depression. It was about the size of the *Queen Mary*. It didn't matter to Julie that she couldn't get it and herself into the lift at the same time: she knew it was the best and biggest money could buy. 'It's traditional for working-class parents to see their children have the best,' she claimed.

We visited Julie and the Anna Zunz wing of the maternity ward of Middlesex Hospital during her confinement. I brought her a foul collection of magazines and some organic fruit juices. Cosmo was in attendance throughout the day. I saw on the clipboard at the foot of her bed that 'Julie Burchill' had been replaced in Julie's handwriting with 'Mrs Julie Landesman'. I mentioned to Fran that it was a small step for mankind, but a giant one for Landes-mania.

The next day I received a call from Cosmo cancelling our lunch date. 'Julie goes under the knife this afternoon,' he explained, 'and you're in this week's *Private Eye*.' I didn't know which piece of news to be excited about. Ever since I was barred by the ever-popular Norman Balon at the Coach and Horses for 'being boring' – I had dared to exchange a few words with Richard Ingrams at the *Private Eye* table – I had become a target almost as often as my 'Stalinist harpie' daughter-in-law. In the latest piece, *Private Eye* recapped their previous report, which had concerned a mis-understanding between GG and a well-known womanizing MP; they also identified GG as 'the twenty-nine-year-old mistress of the world's most boring publisher, Jay Landesman'. It concluded with a health warning: 'Jay Landesman is eighty-six years old.' On the same day GG had to meet the press to explain away some official foul-up that had resulted in twenty-three Girl Guides ending up in hospital. 'That one I can explain,' she said when I told her the news. 'Just wait until my mother reads you're eighty-six.'

The day was beginning to get complicated. GG returned at about six-thirty with a post-punk haircut – its shock value was ruined when her fringe refused to stay down. By seven we were expecting some news of Julie. We ate dinner early in case a call came. It came at eight. 'It's a boy,' shouted the excited father. 'Thank god it's a baby,' GG said. Fran and I rushed out of the house with a bottle of Dom Perignon for the kid and nothing for Julie.

When we arrived at the hospital, there was the little boy, sleeping peacefully next to Julie, being watched over by a proud Cosmo. A more unlikely picture could not be imagined. For a baby born only a few hours previously, he looked mature enough to recognize his overexcited grandparents. Julie invited Fran to pick Jack up, but she was too scared. The baby's scream, clear and loud, convinced Fran he was healthy with lung-power to spare. Julie was pleased about that too. She smiled peacefully as she held a crying baby aloft for us to admire. We only stayed five minutes, but we knew that we were going to see a lot of baby Jack for the rest of our lives.

'Hello, Gramps,' Fran said as we got into the car.

Meanwhile, the everyday business of living kept me going: replenishing stock from Whole Earth Cash & Carry, going to the Columbia flower market for plants and Camden Lock for clothes on Sundays, dentist appointments, insurance adjuster conferences, visits to the GP, dinner with relatives, lunch with old friends, and household chores. Visits to Jack always redeemed a mundane day. By now Fran had reinvented herself as a dotty grandma out of control. 'When I'm in Jack's company I have tremendous energy and no backache,' she claimed. Her social life picked up; she was nice to people on the telephone.

There were musicians, her sons, her grandchild – all competing for her company. She had something to show off for now. Watching Fran cuddle Jack, I could feel, although I was across the room, the intensity of her affection. I tried to remember if it had been like that with Cosmo. Fran reminded me there were photographs of me holding Cosmo in much the same way. She also slipped into a schoolgirlish crush on Julie; she, too, wanted to appear on *Mastermind* – with Julie as her category.

When Cosmo was a baby, Fran used to say, 'My baby set me free.' Today she says, 'What a relief not to be thinking of myself all the time.' Gone was that striving for attention from the anonymous crowds. Jack was the best audience she had ever had. 'He's better than a Broadway show,' she said – it was a line Cutie had used when she used to babysit for Cosmo. In effect, Fran had a new boyfriend who didn't criticize her, which was her idea of a swell romance. 'We've got seven or eight years before Jack dumps us,' she said. 'By that time, Miles will have some children.'

Cosmo and Julie discovered that their flat was too small for the baby and all the new paraphernalia we bombarded them with. At the end of their lease, Cosmo made discreet inquiries about the availability of the top floor. We were delighted. It would be great for Fran to have Jack on demand. We were afraid to encourage them; at the same time we didn't say no. It would certainly have made for a dramatic situation: the grandfather and his mistress in the basement; the wife in her quarters; the new family on the top floor.

GG went right off Granny Franny. How she felt about me she made clear one day when she was having trouble with her Dutch cap. Foolishly, I offered some practical advice. 'If you know so much about it, why don't you wear it?' she said.

There was simply no way to avoid the winds of change. GG had enjoyed being a part of the extended family, but, when I mentioned the possibility of Julie and Cosmo moving into our former love nest, she thought I was carrying the concept too far. Jack had replaced her as the focal point in our life. At an exhibition at the Virago bookshop – its theme being women's adverse comments on men, particularly husbands – GG remarked, 'I wish I had a husband to leave.' Fran quickly replied, 'Why don't you try mine?'

It was GG who was now on the defensive and a Girl Guide knows what to do in an emergency – GG started to look elsewhere for amusement. 'You're going to be a hard act to follow,' she admitted, somewhat reluctantly. A few weeks later we were dining at Langan's. I was feeling miserable. I looked at her over the rim of a big brandy glass.

'It's over, isn't it?' I said.

'Yes. I didn't know how to tell you.' She began to cry. I took her hand in mine. The next morning she called in sick. I wished I could have done the same. For something that had started with a casual drink two years ago, it was spectacular – the pain came from imagining that it would never happen again.

The London Book Fair was hardly the place to look for success. I said hello to a dozen ghosts from the past before I found Martin and Judy Shepard's Permanent Press. It had never occurred to me to have Sterling Lord send them *Rebel*, but by now my expectations had lowered. I left a copy of the book with them. 'Just for laughs,' I told Martin.

At dinner the next night, Martin said he had upset his fellow publishers. 'It's all your fault,' he said.

Judy explained: 'Martin started reading your manuscript and laughed so much and so loud our neighbours came around to find out what was going on. We'd like to do your book, Jay. We would consider it a great honour.'

Martin added how exciting it would be to promote the book. 'With those stories of encounters with the talented and famous, you could get on Johnny Carson. I'll send you a contract the minute I get home.' It was the kind of line which could kick-start the dream machine.

Liz Calder, who had moved from Cape to start Bloomsbury Press, asked to have a look. She called later to tell me she loved my book and wanted to do it following its publication in the States. Fran said there was fire in my eyes when I told her the news. The dream machine went into overdrive.

The *News of the World* left a message asking me to call them. It turned out they wanted to interview me on a feature about married men who had affairs. Without a moment's hesitation, I thanked them for the compliment, but suggested several other people who might be more amenable. 'I'm retired,' I told the caller. 'Great,' he enthused. 'Hints from a retired Casanova would be even better.'

G. Legman called me when he heard I was going to be published on two continents. 'Give me the name of a good lawyer,' he yelled. 'I'm going to sue your ass off.' My laugh annoyed him. I asked him if he was going to say terrible things about me in *his* memoirs.

'The worst thing I can say about you, Landesman, is that you were a playboy.'

I told him I'd settle for that. 'What's wrong with having some fun?'

INDEX

Gems, Judy, 55
Genet, Jean, 91
Ginsberg, Allen, 62
Global Village, London, 117–18
Gollner, Richard, 187
Gopal, Sam, 53
Gordon, Asheton, 149
Gordon, Dexter, 153
Graham, Billy, 46
Graham, Charles, 142–3
Graham, Richard, 161, 163
Granger, Farley, 61
Grant, Don, 161
Green, Robin, 118
Greer, Germaine, 69, 91–2
Gus, Pappa, 192–3

Haden-Guest, Anthony, 92
Hamilton, George, 39
Haynes, Jim, Arts Lab, 60, 91, 92–3,
  119
Hell's Angels, 93, 94
Hendrix, Jimi, 69
Herbert, Victor, 113
Hobson, Harold, 37
Holland, Julian, 47, 135
Hollander, John, 68
Holliday, Jason, 89–90
Holmes, John Clellon, 34–5, 56,
  58–62, 66, 213–14
  on JL, 62–4
Holt, Will, 4, 21
Horovitz, Michael, 124
Hymas, John, 134–5

Ingrams, Richard, 13, 218
International Times, 51, 53–4, 55
The Ipcress File, 24, 29
'Irwin', 56, 58

James, Clive, 144
Jenkinson, Philip, 37
Jodorowsky, Alexandro, 112
Johnson, Joyce, 175
Jones, Brian, 61

Jones, Paul, 39, 86, 129

Kasher, Charles, 24, 29, 45
Kearney, Patrick J., 168
Keeler, Christine, 34–5, 56, 105
Keeler, Ruby, 37
Kenny, Mary, 201
Kerouac, Jack, 62, 66, 173, 214
Kesey, Ken, 93–6
King, David, 49
King, Pete, 153
Kismet (club), 33–5
Kochansky, Hanya, 23, 29, 31, 33,
  105, 111, 113, 123, 204–5, 206
Kral, Dana, 89
Kral, Roy, 89
Kretzmer, Herbert, 51
Kustow, Michael, 125–6

Laing, R. D., 28–9, 86, 149
Lake, Alan, 33
Landesman, Cosmo (son), 12, 16,
  21, 22, 24–5, 37, 77–8, 79, 90, 97,
  103–4, 106, 110, 118, 129, 175,
  217, 218, 219
  in publishing, 166–8
  and Julie, 176–8, 181, 183–5, 191,
    196, 201–2, 205, 207, 211, 215–
    16
  on his parents, 47–8, 186, 195,
    205
Landesman, Cutie (mother), 19,
  96–7, 104, 105, 210
  death, 131
Landesman, Fran and Jay
  aspects of love, 64–5, 129–30,
    165, 178–9, 194–5, 198–203
  at family guidance centre, 90–1
  unconventionalism, 155–9
  break-up threatened, 210–11
  grandparents, 211–12, 215, 217,
    218–19
Landesman, Fran 'Peaches', 13, 18,
  33, 57, 61, 102, 103, 105–6, 109,
  113, 129, 145, 149, 152, 182

225